Feminism and Citizenship

Politics and Culture

A Theory, Culture & Society series

Politics and Culture analyses the complex relationships between civil society, identities and contemporary states. Individual books will draw on the major theoretical paradigms in politics, international relations, history and philosophy within which citizenship, rights and social justice can be understood. The series will focus attention on the implications of globalization, the information revolution and postmodernism for the study of politics and society. It will relate these advanced theoretical issues to conventional approaches to welfare, participation and democracy.

SERIES EDITOR: Bryan S. Turner, *Deakin University*

Also in this series

Citizenship and Social Theory
edited by Bryan S. Turner

Citizenship and Social Rights
The Interdependence of Self and Society
Fred Twine

The Condition of Citizenship
edited by Bart van Steenbergen

Nation Formation
Towards a Theory of Abstract Community
Paul James

Virtual Politics
Identity and Community in Cyberspace
edited by David Holmes

Gender and Nation
Nira Yuval-Davies

Feminism and Citizenship

Rian Voet

SAGE Publications
London • Thousand Oaks • New Delhi

© Rian Voet 1998

First published 1998

SAGE Publications Ltd
6 Bonhill Street
London EC2A 4PU

SAGE Publications Inc
2455 Teller Road
Thousand Oaks, California 91320

SAGE Publications India Pvt Ltd
32, M-Block Market
Greater Kailash - I
New Delhi 110 048

British Library Cataloguing in Publication data

A catalogue record for this book is
available from the British Library

ISBN 0 7619 5859 2
ISBN 0 7619 5860 6 (pbk)

Library of Congress catalog record available

Typeset by Type Study, Scarborough

Printed in Great Britain by Redwood Books, Trowbridge,
Wiltshire

For my son Joep Arno Takararo Silvio

Contents

Acknowledgements

Some of the chapters in this book have been presented in their original form at several conferences – the European Consortium for Political Research in Colchester (1991) and Limerick (1992), the Suffrage and Beyond conference in Wellington (1993), the New Zealand Political Studies Association Conference in Christchurch (1993), the Women in a Changing Europe conference in Aalborg (1992) – and at seminars of several academic groups in Amsterdam, Leyden, York and Auckland. I would like to thank all participants, friends and colleagues for their valuable comments. The annual meetings of the European Network for Theory and Research on Women, Citizenship and Welfare State, furthermore, showed me how hard work and international friendship on the topic of citizenship can be combined. Some people deserve special mention for their useful criticism on earlier parts of this book: Carol Bacchi, Mark Bovens, Vicky Franzinetti, Herman van Gunsteren, Bill Jordan, Susan Mendus, Anne Phillips, Helen Rodgers, Selma Sevenhuijsen and Ursula Vogel.

A grant from the Stimuleringsgroep Emancipatieonderzoek enabled me to set up literature research for half a year on the topic of 'feminism and citizenship'. I would also like to thank the Departments of Political Studies at Leyden University and at the University of Auckland for their financial and institutional support, which made it possible to continue this research. The Department of Political Studies at Leyden University allowed me a year free from teaching requirements while I conducted research at the University of York in England. An Erasmus grant gave additional financial support.

Some chapters are based on articles published elsewhere although they are heavily revised for the purpose of this book. I would like to thank the publishers for permission to make use of the following materials: 'Groepsidentiteiten en identiteitspolitiek', *Tijdschrift voor Vrouwenstudies*, 15, no. 1 (1994), 139–148 (used for Chapter 7); 'Political Representation and Quotas: Hanna Pitkin's Concept(s) of Representation in the Context of Feminist Politics', *Acta Politica* 28, no. 4 (1992), 389–404 (used for Chapter 8).

Mike Crawshaw, Heather Devere, Debbie Dunsford and Ruth Symes corrected earlier versions of this text. The final text could not have been completed without the thorough revisions by Chan Dixon. Her useful comments showed me that language difficulties and intellectual difficulties are all too often inextricably linked and that intellectual and administrative support are hard to separate. I would also like to thank my editors, Karen Phillips, Kiren Shoman and Bryan Turner, for their kind support.

Finally, and most importantly, I thank wholeheartedly Jo Vijgen. This book is yours as much as mine.

Introduction

Since the second world war social liberalism has been the dominant theory of citizenship in western liberal democracies. This theory tells us that equal and full citizenship for all adults born within the territory of the state already exists. It tells us that with the disappearance of feudalism and slavery, and the inclusion of all adults in suffrage, political inequality has also been eliminated. After all, as far as public life is concerned, all members of western societies have an equal status and possess equal rights.

Social liberalism does not fit easily with the idea that women still have a secondary status in public life. Women hold few top positions in politics, the economy, the university, the military, the Church, the judiciary and the media. Moreover, women generally play a smaller part than men as workers or producers in economic life, they have lower incomes, participate less in political parties and unions, and seem in general to be less respected in public life than men. In other words, women seem to be second-rate citizens.

If these issues ring true, then we need to alter or modify our theory of citizenship. During the so-called 'second wave' feminists criticized social-liberal ideas, although not explicitly directing their criticism at the idea of citizenship. What they did do, however, was to criticize social liberals on sub-themes that are crucial in any citizenship theory: they criticized social liberals for their ideas on freedom, rights, social equality, political subjectivity, political representation and political judgement. More recently, some feminists have begun to criticize social-liberal and other citizenship theories explicitly on the issue of citizenship. They have argued that the content of citizenship theories should change by addressing women's positions and needs.

This book attempts to strengthen this argument, but not by focusing on male classical and modern citizenship theorists. Many good feminist articles and books have already done this (e.g. Coole 1988; Kennedy and Mendus 1988) and I do not feel it necessary to add another contribution to this area. Besides, it seems obvious: if citizenship theorists want their theories to be relevant to citizens, they must take the needs of one half of the citizens, that is women, into account. Instead then, this book attempts to contribute to the citizenship debate by taking feminism itself seriously and critically assessing feminist publications from the perspective of citizenship.

The main question informing this book is: to what degree did second wave feminism in western liberal democracies offer satisfactory criticisms of, and alternatives to, the social-liberal concept of citizenship? The book has three aims. In line with recent publications, I will argue that feminists on the whole have not taken the issue of citizenship seriously enough and should pay more explicit attention to it. Secondly, however, I will interpret the western feminist publications of the 1970s and 1980s as if they were implicit publications on citizenship. This will be done by examining the feminist responses to the six sub-themes of citizenship: liberty, rights, social equality, political subjectivity, political representation and political judgement. In these responses I distinguish three main feminist positions: humanist, woman-centred and deconstructionist. I will suggest that if we combine the answers of the respective feminist positions to the six sub-themes of citizenship three rudimentary feminist attitudes towards citizenship can be discerned. Finally, I will evaluate the social-liberal and feminist positions on citizenship and provide an alternative.

The book takes issue with both the social-liberal and the familiar feminist approaches to these sub-themes of citizenship. I will argue that neither the social-liberal nor the familiar feminist approaches provide tools for thorough reflection on and improvement of the current difficulties of female citizens in liberal democracies. I will argue that – even though a citizenship theory is unable to affect political practice directly – improvements can be made by adopting a theory which has the ideals of 'sex-equal and active citizenship', and which interprets women's condition in the light of this ideal.

To illustrate these three major feminist positions, I will refer to books and articles by feminist theorists. The reader has to remember that these positions are constructions that do not correspond exactly to existing groups or organizations. The positions do, however, indicate the main forms of feminist thought on citizenship in the second wave era. Individual feminists may jump from one position to another, but here I find it useful and necessary to systematize the positions in order to be able to evaluate them. That is, my arguments in this book are thematically informed, rather than being based on an in-depth overview of feminist literature. Accordingly, I may at times necessarily simplify the arguments of some feminists to illustrate the thematic positions within feminist thought. To those who feel they have been wrongly or too strictly categorized, I apologize, and stress again that it is the positions themselves which form the focus of my debate.

The reader should not expect an empirical study of the social and political position of women (cf. Einhorn 1993). Rather, this book will offer a political-theoretical reflection on women's position, interpreting this position and feminist theories of it in the framework of citizenship. It provides students and scholars with a philosophical argument for woman-friendly citizenship, with reference to important feminist texts in this area.

The structure of the book is as follows. Part I provides background information about feminism and social liberalism. Part II consists of six explorations of the sub-themes of citizenship. I will examine the problems for female citizens concerning these sub-themes and evaluate the responses of social-liberal and feminist perspectives to them. In Part III I draw the evaluations from Part II together and offer my alternative.

It may be helpful for some readers if I include here some introductory remarks about each chapter. Chapter 1 sketches the lack of debate until recently between feminist theorists and citizenship theorists; it will define citizenship, provide an overview of different citizenship theories, justify my restriction to social-liberal citizenship theories in this book and provide a sketch of the recent debate on feminism and citizenship. Chapter 2 defines feminism in general, looks back at some important moments in the history of feminism and citizenship, and outlines humanist, woman-centred and deconstructionist feminism. It will also briefly indicate their general positions towards citizenship. The last chapter of Part I describes this dominant theory of citizenship in general, shows its variations by discussing T.H. Marshall, John Rawls, Bruce Ackerman, Michael Walzer and Will Kymlicka, and examines social-liberal views on difference.

The chapters in Part II are devoted to the sub-themes of citizenship, and all chapters have basically the same structure. I will introduce the topic and remind the reader of the social-liberal position on each sub-theme concerned. I will then describe what the humanist, woman-centred, and deconstructionist feminist responses are, before providing my own analysis. Chapter 4 discusses the issue of women's *Liberty*. Chapter 5 on *Rights* discusses whether women should have equal or special rights. Chapter 6 discusses whether or not *Social Equality* for women is a prerequisite for equal citizenship, examines the relation between the social and political aspects of citizenship, and differentiates social equality in terms of material equality and social participation. Chapter 7 on *Political Subjectivity* covers the question of the capacity in which women should act in the political arena. Should they present themselves as general citizens or as women? This discussion leads to Chapter 8 on *Political Representation*, in which I will examine justifications for including more women in decision-making bodies and focus on the argument that a representative political body should mirror the composition of society. In this chapter I also discuss political participation and refer to recent feminist publications which have emphasized the value of participation more than earlier feminist publications. Chapter 9 on *Political Judgement* asks what kind of judgement should be required of female citizens and discusses whether or not different kinds of political judgement should be suggested for political actors and spectators.

Part III weaves together the threads covered in Parts I and II. Chapter 10 re-evaluates the three feminist positions and returns to my central question of the extent to which second wave feminism offered satisfactory critiques of and alternatives to social-liberal notions of citizenship. Finally, drawing upon my discussion in Part II, Chapter 11 presents my alternative: *Active and Sex-equal Citizenship*.

PART I

BACKGROUND

1

Debates on Feminism and Citizenship

This chapter sets out to sketch the lack of debate between feminist theorists and citizenship theorists in previous decades, and to put forward arguments in favour of connecting the themes of feminism and citizenship. I will be discussing what may be expected from political theory in general and from citizenship theory in particular. I will then provide an overview of different citizenship theories and potential levels of analysis of gender and citizenship, before presenting a brief outline of the recent feminist theoretical debate that does deal explicitly with citizenship.

*   *   *

Until recently, feminism was not a topic considered by citizenship theorists, nor was citizenship a topic considered by feminist theorists. This conclusion can be reached through an examination of two almost distinct discussions: one on the issue of feminism and the other on the issue of citizenship. The people who discussed these two issues seldom met, and neither group incorporated the thoughts of the other group into that of their own.

The so-called second wave feminist movement that emerged at the end of the 1960s addressed the problem of women's formal and material status. While it talked about women's oppression and the need for liberty and equality, and asserted the need for structural and attitudinal change, feminism did not express these concerns explicitly in terms of citizenship (Bryson 1992).

Neither did feminist theorists explicitly use the term 'citizenship' in the two decades that followed. Some feminist theorists such as Caroline Ramazanoglu (1989), Elizabeth Spelman (1988) and Denise Riley (1988) began to attack the idea of a universal theory of women's oppression, emphasizing the differences among women and pointing out the difficulties in presenting a feminist politics in terms of 'the demands of us women'. Instead of grand theories of women's oppression, historical studies of the

construction of femininity in a limited context and period began to dominate the field of women's studies.

Why did feminist activists and theorists on the whole not use the term
'citizenship' in this period? One reason is probably that the term 'citizenship' was not fashionable at the time that second wave feminism originated.
The preferred vocabularies were rather those of democracy, oppression and
self-development. Another reason may have been that feminists of the
'second wave' considered citizenship to be formal membership of a state
and the legal rights following from that membership. They felt that this was
not the level where the 'roots of women's oppression' were to be found.
Feminists felt they ought to search for factors at a more structural or deeper
level, such as in the centuries-old assumptions about masculinity and femininity. In their opinion, changing the cultural expectation that a woman
should be passive and caring required more urgent addressing than
women's 'citizenship position'.

This idea was shared by both the feminists of the grand theory of women's
oppression and by the feminists of the specific construction of femininity.
For the former, citizenship was too formal a cause to be a determinant in
material life. For the latter, citizenship was too universal a narrative to be
appropriate for specific groups of women. Many feminists assumed that
citizenship was concerned with power, political relations, the state, the law,
and issues of political rights and obligations, but not with relations between
the sexes.

The mirror image of this neglect of citizenship by feminists has been the
neglect of feminism and women by citizenship theorists. If one checks
libraries and on-line systems for the term 'citizenship', it becomes clear that
citizenship has been connected with class (Barbalet 1988), ethnicity (Kymlicka 1995), nationality (Spinner 1995) and the European Union (Habermas
1992), but seldom with gender. There are some recent anthologies which
include one or two chapters on citizenship and gender (Andrews 1991; van
Steenbergen 1994; Vogel and Moran 1991), but very few books (Jordan
1989; Roche 1992) integrate gender in a more substantial way with citizenship theory.

Citizenship has become a buzz-word in the social sciences and in social
movements during the last decade (Turner and Hamilton 1994). A wide
variety of issues have been described within this vocabulary: the need for a
welfare state, the costs of the welfare state and the subsequent duties of citizens, the loss of social control and the subsequent need for more citizen
action. Other issues discussed within the parameters of the citizenship
debate are the fragmentation of the nation state and simultaneous globalization of dependency relations, and whether this results in a 'multiple citizenship', the need for a written constitution, new forms of democracy and new
definitions of rights or obligations.

Why did citizenship theorists pay so little attention to the needs of
women? Why did they only rarely try to phrase feminist issues within the
vocabulary of citizenship? One simple reason may be that feminist theories

did not have enough status in the academic world. Nevertheless, I think there is also another reason: many citizenship theorists defined citizenship as being about civil, political and social rights and, following from this definition, women and citizenship in contemporary western democracies was not seen to be a dramatic problem. Believing that men and women had both obtained equal rights under the law, citizenship theorists felt that there was no need to discuss women citizens as a special group. There might still be some inequalities between the sexes, but they have mainly been considered issues of (in)justice and not of citizenship (e.g. Marquand 1989).

For many citizenship theorists, feminism does not appear to have anything to do with citizenship. Feminism, in their view, is about the private, the personal and the particular, whereas citizenship is more about the public, the common and the general. For them, feminism focuses only on issues of sexuality, personal relations, children, the family, and relationships between the sexes. These issues may be important, but in the opinion of many citizenship theorists they have nothing to do with citizenship.

Issues of gender and issues of citizenship were not always disconnected; within the whole tradition of classical political theory, the duties and activities of citizenship have strongly depended upon manliness. Aristotle and Machiavelli were most explicit about this, but one can also recognize this theme in the works of most other classical political theorists. Feminists have written extensively about this (e.g. Elshtain 1981; Shanley and Pateman 1991). In modern political theory, however, citizenship appears to have no connection with gender at all, as feminist theorists have argued (Jones 1990; Pateman 1989: 1–16). Modern political theory suggests that feminist issues therefore ought not to be addressed in terms of citizenship. According to Carole Pateman (1989: 10), '[w]omen's "contribution" is not seen as part of, or as relevant to, their citizenship, but as a necessary part of the private tasks proper to their sex'. She suggests that the problem for women is to be included as citizens and, at the same time, recognized as women.

According to most modern citizenship theorists, it is not necessary that women are recognized as women in modern citizenship because citizenship is gender-neutral. For different reasons, most feminist theorists writing in the period from 1968 to 1989 agreed that feminist issues could not, or could only barely, be phrased in the vocabulary of citizenship. I will discuss their positions in Chapter 2.

Recently, however, a change in this pattern has occurred. Since 1989 several articles and books have explicitly addressed the theme of 'feminism and citizenship'. The emergence of this literature is noteworthy. Obviously, many more feminists have recognized the gap that was apparent between feminist theory and citizenship theory, and have felt the need to fill it. I have benefited from this material and will outline it briefly in the last section of this chapter and also in Chapter 8, as it also differs from earlier feminist literature in that it focuses more on political participation.

Why the vocabularies of citizenship and feminism should be connected

Even before the emergence of the new literature, there were many more common projects between feminists and citizenship theorists than was often assumed by these groups, but they were developed separately. For instance, both feminist theorists and citizenship theorists wrote about the state, the welfare system, social policy, law and democracy. Often they even posed the same questions in these projects; questions such as 'How do we combine the common good with respect for group differences?', 'How should we perceive universality and plurality?', 'How can we meet the preconditions for political equality?' and 'How can we devise a commendable democratic welfare state?'

Many also appear to have had the same ideals and the same hopes. Are not citizenship and feminism both connected with the concepts of freedom, political equality, justice and democracy? Are they not different but related routes leading to the same goals? In this respect it is interesting to note that when the term 'feminism' first originated, it was connected with women's citizenship. As the historian Karen Offen (1988: 126) has pointed out, the first self-proclaimed 'feminist' was the French woman Hubertine Auclert who, from at least 1882 on, used this term in her periodical, *La Citoyenne* (The Woman Citizen), to describe herself and her associates.

It is unfortunate that the connections between feminism and citizenship have remained relatively weak, because strong connections could enrich both fields. For both sides there is much to gain from dialogue: new approaches, new themes to explore within an alternative framework, and criticism of one's own work. For instance, dialogue would alert citizenship theorists to the fact that reflection upon equal or universal citizenship can only be convincing if it includes reflection upon the female half of humankind. It would also alert feminist theorists to the need to spell out the political-institutional consequences of their philosophical arguments and urge them to engage explicitly with the debate on citizenship.

Political philosophy and female citizens

Let me pause here for a moment to reflect upon the relationship between political philosophy and the needs of female citizens. Much of what has been said so far assumes that political philosophy in general and citizenship theory in particular should meet the needs of citizens and thus also the needs of female citizens. But is political philosophy able to do so? What is and what should be the relationship between political philosophy and political practice? I restrict my comments here to normative political philosophy. This type of philosophy ought to do what the name indicates – provide norms or help others to develop norms. I assume that the intention of normative political philosophy is its development into a vital public policy. This implies a philosophy that is meaningful for citizen actions and conducive to political policies. After all, it is precisely within the framework of contemporary issues that political philosophy ought to be meaningful.

Usually, political philosophy does not affect political practice in a direct way. It influences practice indirectly by supporting ideas or programmes. This support may be prospective, in that it may outline future policies or actions, but it is more likely to be retrospective in offering a legitimization or critique of existing policies and actions. Actual programmes or policies are often developed without the foundation of a political philosophy. Even when they have such a foundation, in political practice ideas are often diluted by compromises, conflicting interests and practical difficulties. Nonetheless, an important relationship between political philosophy and political practice remains. Philosophy facilitates critical reflection upon political practice and without such reflection any active opposition to existing practice will only be derived from self-interest and power.

If normative political philosophy cannot ignore the difficulties of citizens, this applies even more to citizenship philosophy. After all, citizenship philosophy does not engage with only one aspect of public life, but with public life as a whole. Therefore, it has to inquire into contemporary predicaments of and obstacles to public life. To be fair, one has to add that citizenship philosophy cannot possibly engage with every difficulty and need of every individual citizen. For example, if someone has psychological problems with becoming a pensioner, this may be an important individual problem but as such it is not related to citizenship and not relevant to citizenship theory. Needs of citizens as citizens are only those needs that relate to public life or its preconditions. The issue is, however, more complex than it at first seems. This is because various citizenship theories exist and they all differ in their views concerning the meaning of public life and the nature of its preconditions. Citizenship theories even differ about the meaning of the term 'citizenship' (Turner and Hamilton 1994). Various needs of female or male citizens are considered to be relevant or otherwise, depending on the meaning of citizenship embodied in each perspective.

Citizenship

In daily life, the term 'citizenship' is usually restricted to talk about crossing state borders or describing membership of a state. In this study, a broader meaning will be used. Citizenship can, in principle, be both the relationships between a state and an individual citizen and the political relationships between citizens themselves. Citizenship might just refer to rights, but it can also refer to the duties, actions, virtues and opinions that follow from the above-mentioned relationships (Barbalet 1988; Heater 1990).

One can distinguish four main modern ideas of citizenship: a communitarian, a civic-republican, a neo-liberal and a social-liberal one (van Gunsteren 1994; Miller 1994). In this book I will focus on the social-liberal concept of citizenship, but let me first say something about the other three traditions.

In the communitarian tradition, for which the political theorists Michael Sandel (1982), Alasdair MacIntyre (1985) and Charles Taylor (1989) are the modern spokesmen, citizenship implies social participation and service to the common good. It strongly emphasizes the underlying community, culture and ethics that citizens share. Communitarians argue that in order to maintain a community certain citizenship activities (or praxes) are morally expected. In their opinion, a tradition is kept alive by 'enacting' citizenship: looking after one's co-citizens, repeating the behaviour that has become a tradition in the community and acting upon shared beliefs and values.

The civic-republican tradition considers citizenship to be political participation. It goes back to Aristotle and Machiavelli. Modern civic-republican theorists include Hannah Arendt (1958), Richard Sennett (1977) and Benjamin Barber (1984). In the civic-republican tradition the term 'citizenship' does not refer to an underlying ethic or substantial community but rather to the idea of citizen participation in decision-making, the value of public life and public debate, and to the idea of realizing ourselves as political beings.

The libertarian or neo-liberal conception of citizenship (cf. Miller 1994) sees citizenship predominantly as a legal status. Neo-liberalism is indeed comparatively new, but it has links with classical liberalism. Its spokesmen – Friedrich Hayek (1944) and Robert Nozick (1975) – attempt to make the political world as limited as possible, in order to give the individual the maximum amount of freedom. They are particularly opposed to the welfare state and in favour of the free market. Neo-liberals think of citizens primarily as rational consumers of public goods and believe self-interest to be the basic motive upon which citizens act. In this respect, we can question whether neo-liberalism really has a concept of citizenship.

Having briefly outlined these traditions, I will focus on social-liberal citizenship, as this has been the dominant concept of citizenship in most western liberal democracies since the second world war. It is also the concept of citizenship to which feminists have mainly responded.

One can find examples of social-liberal theories of citizenship in the work of John Rawls (1971) and T.H. Marshall (1967), which I will describe in Chapter 3. In the social-liberal tradition a narrow, formal and legal interpretation is attached to citizenship. The term implies entitlement to legal rights (such as the right to free speech, to vote, or to receive some kind of sickness benefit). It also implies legal obligations (such as the obligation to pay taxes, the obligation to serve in an army, the obligation to apply for jobs and – if a suitable job is offered – the obligation to accept it rather than to live at the expense of the state).

According to the social-liberal perspective, citizenship should be universal and equal: it should encompass all adults within the territory of a state and it should be equal in the sense that it guarantees equal civil, political and social rights in return for equal duties. Individuals should have as much liberty as possible to exercise their rights and to develop their personalities. Therefore, individuals ought to have as little interference as possible from the state and from their co-citizens. Nevertheless, the idea of social citizenship rights – for instance, the right to unemployment benefit and to a pension – has made the state less minimal than social liberals desire. They may attempt to keep state intervention to a minimum by not asking anything in return for welfare benefits, but once they prescribe the obligation to apply for jobs civil servants have to check whether citizens meet this obligation.

Social-liberal citizenship has a limited code of morality which, for the most part, is to be found in the laws of a state. The limited code is the morality of justice and fairness. It is the idea that everyone should be treated equally in the public sphere: the sphere of justice. In the private sphere – the sphere of the family – we may enact our personal ideas of the good life or our strong ideas of morality. By contrast, in the public sphere, the basic rules are to be tolerant, not to harm each other, not to impose claims upon each other that are too strong and to intervene as little as possible in each other's lives.

Women as second-class citizens

Social liberalism has often been criticized by feminists (Evans, J. 1986; Jaggar 1983a: 27–50, 173–206, 355–358), perhaps on good grounds, for while it has dominated and set ideals for justice and fairness in the western world, women still appear to be second-class, or perhaps more accurately, 'second-sex' citizens. In this section I will present some evidence of this using (unless indicated otherwise) the member states of the European Union as examples of liberal democracies in general.

Women remain relatively strongly underrepresented in the higher levels of decision-making in the member states of the European Union, as evidenced by 1994 statistics (*Women and Men in the European Union* 1995). In elected assemblies of political decision-making and in governments at local, sub-regional and national level 16 per cent were women (p. 193). In the European Parliament women represent 26 per cent (p. 196). Out of every 100 female officials of the European Commission, some 60 are secretaries and just nine are administrators, whereas 46 per cent of male civil servants are administrators (p. 199).

In public administration in the 12 member states in the early 1990s we find 23 per cent of women at the lowest of the senior levels, 10 per cent at management level and 6 per cent at the top (p. 193). Combining public and private sectors, the figure is somewhat higher – almost 30 per cent of people working as legislators, senior officials and managers in 1992 were women (p. 142). In the trade unions only 17 per cent of people on the national executive committees in 1993 were women (p. 200). Furthermore, in 1994 in western Europe only 12 per cent of the senior management positions in broadcasting and 18 per cent in the press were held by women (United Nations 1995: 169–170).

In other respects also the social status of women in the European Union appears to be very low. Taking 1992 as a base, women included in the paid full-time labour force were 1.5 to 2.6 times more likely to be low paid than men and the proportion would be even higher if part-time workers were included (Rubery and Fagan 1995: I). Of the population aged 20–59, 37 per cent of women were unemployed and 56 per cent in work, whereas 12 per cent of men were unemployed and 81 per cent in work (*Women and Men in the European Union* 1995: 123). Of those in the paid labour force 29 per cent of women worked part time, whereas only 4 per cent of men did (p. 150). Finally, recent national studies in six developed countries reveal that 17–28 per cent of adult women have been physically assaulted by an intimate partner and that 27–34 per cent of women reported sexual abuse during childhood or adolescence (United Nations 1995: 160).

These facts about the status of women as second-class citizens relate to the feminist arguments that the dominant social-liberal concept of citizenship is deficient. Are the feminist critiques of social liberalism justified and can one therefore detect in these critiques the beginnings of an alternative and more positive concept of citizenship? Or, have these critiques been unjustified from the start and is there nothing wrong with the social-liberal concept of citizenship? Is there perhaps something else wrong in the social-liberal concept not identified by feminists, and should an alternative concept be developed in a direction other than those indicated in existing feminist critiques? These are the questions which I will be addressing in my discussion throughout this book.

Different levels of analysis of gender and citizenship

Feminist views on citizenship can be discerned in a whole range of books and articles. In order to obtain an overview of the literature, it may be useful to distinguish the various levels of implicit feminist analysis of gender and citizenship.

The first level of analysis is that seen in publications on women and the nation, and women's special position in immigration and emigration law (e.g. Bhabba et al. 1985; Sapiro 1984; Yuval-Davis 1991, 1992). I will not discuss this literature, as my focus is on difficulties with women and citizenship once they are already officially included as members of a state. Of course the two topics are related – people who are considered to be of lower status will have difficulties in both entering a state and in obtaining full citizenship rights – but if the topic of women and migration were to be incorporated here the scope of this book would become too broad.

The second level is that seen in publications on women's position in the welfare state, women and social policy, and women in care arrangements (e.g. O'Connor 1993; Pascall 1986). This literature will only be alluded to when it discusses the ways in which citizenship should be reorganized or reconceptualized, and not if it only points out women's position.

The third level is that of feminists discussing democratic practices and democratic theories (e.g. Pateman 1989: Ch. 9; Phillips 1991a, 1993). I consider this literature to be important for the scope of this book if it deals explicitly with the distinction between formal political equality and actual substantial political equality. Literature that lists facts and figures on women's participation will be alluded to only briefly.

The fourth level is that of feminists revising the mainstream history of political thought with a view to analysing gender assumptions: what did Plato, Marx and others think about women and men (Clark and Lange 1979; Coole 1988; Eisenstein 1981; Elshtain 1981; Kennedy and Mendus 1988; Lloyd 1989; Okin 1979; Pateman 1988; Pateman and Gross 1986; Pitkin 1984; Saxonhouse 1985)? Although this is an important field, my focus is on modern twentieth-century political theory and debate. Besides, this book is not concerned with what male political theorists think about gender, but with what feminist political theorists think about citizenship.

This brings me to the fifth level: that of feminists directly in discussion with modern citizenship theorists and political theorists (e.g. Bock and James 1992; Sullivan and Whitehouse 1996). Although such material is crucial to this book, and although several feminist publications have recently emerged that address citizenship explicitly, not enough has been published at this level. I cannot, therefore, strictly confine my analysis to explicit feminist responses to citizenship. Yet as this material provides such an important background for the theme of this book and for my own position I will pay special attention to it, particularly in the last section of this chapter.

Given the limited range of explicit feminist publications on citizenship, I also include a sixth level: that of implicit or concealed responses to citizenship theories from a feminist perspective. Here, I examine feminist reflections on sub-themes of citizenship: liberty, rights, social equality, political subjectivity, political representation and political judgement. This examination not only includes feminist evaluations of social-liberal ideas on these sub-themes, but also wider feminist reflections on these themes that bear no direct relation to social-liberal thought.

There are two remaining levels at which feminists talk about women and citizenship. One is that of feminist utopian literature, in which feminists search for the good life just as is done within mainstream political theory (e.g. Gilman 1979). The other level is the search to inspire public life by looking at women in history (Gundersen 1987; Kerber 1980, 1992; Lake 1994; Molloy 1992; Pedersen 1990; Rendall 1994; Stanley 1973). For instance, some biographies of women in the eighteenth century may provide us with fascinating possibilities of female political participation in the present. However, whilst both sorts of literature can offer much inspiration, I will not use them in this book, as my focus is on contemporary feminist proposals that are supposed to offer promising programmes and policies in the context of present-day western democracies.

Recent discussions on women and citizenship

Recently a change has occurred in that some feminist theorists have started to discuss citizenship explicitly, combining it with the issues of women, gender and feminism. Here I present a very brief overview of the debate so far (cf. Lister 1990, 1995a).

The discussion was put on the agenda by Jean Bethke Elshtain when she noted in *Public Man, Private Woman* (1981: 202) that feminists have ignored notions of citizenship. She offered an alternative 'vision of citizen' that is inclusive, non-violent and starts with the dignity of human beings. She affirmed (p. 349) that the 'activation of a female participatory capability must begin with her immediate concerns' and argued that these would be a translation to the public sphere of the concerns of the private sphere, and in particular those connected to the protection of children and other vulnerable people. She elaborated on this issue in a number of publications (1986, 1987, 1990), developing a maternal republican conception of citizenship in which republican mothers are truly respected and in which local political communities play an important role.

This emphasis on the importance of motherhood in a woman-friendly conception of citizenship provoked a response. In 1985 the prestigious journal *Political Theory* published in the section 'Citizenship and Maternal Thinking' not only a contribution by Elshtain, but also a critical appraisal of her by Mary Dietz. In her article 'Citizenship with a Feminist Face: The Problem with Maternal Thinking' Dietz argued that the mother–child relationship is a particularly inappropriate model for democratic citizenship. According to her (1985: 30), maternal virtues refer to particularity, exclusiveness, inequality, love and intimacy, whereas democratic citizenship requires collectivity, inclusiveness, generality and distance (cf. Diquinzio 1995). In Dietz's article 'Context is All: Feminism and Theories of Citizenship' (1987) she elaborated on her own notion of citizenship, which is a more confined republicanism in which women appear as participatory citizens in general and not as mothers.

Carole Pateman has been a writer whose theoretical reflections on citizenship have inspired many other feminist theorists (her unpublished paper 'Women and Democratic Citizenship' [1985] is often referred to). Pateman (1989) criticized the fact that liberal theorists (Chs 3 and 4) and participatory democratic theorists (Ch. 9) used a gender-neutral language which gave the impression that women were free and equal democratic citizens, whereas in Pateman's opinion they were not. According to her (1989: 14):

> women have demanded for two centuries that their distinctive qualities and tasks should become part of citizenship – that is, that they should be citizens as women

– their demand cannot be met when it is precisely these marks of womanhood that place women in opposition to, or, at best, in a paradoxical and contradictory relation to, citizenship. . . . All that is clear is that if women are to be citizens as *women*, as autonomous, equal, yet sexually different beings from men, democratic theory and practice has to undergo a radical transformation.

She qualifies this in her article 'Equality, Difference, Subordination: The Politics of Motherhood and Women's Citizenship' (1992), where she argues that women's difference has not always been perceived as a threat to politics and citizenship, but at times has been seen as providing extra value to society.

After these first contributions the general debate on women and citizenship went in different directions. One line of debate was the examination of whether or not citizenship was indeed gendered, meaning more specifically that it assumed a male citizen and left little space for incorporating female citizens. Here the articles of Ursula Vogel (1991) and Sylvia Walby (1994) need to be mentioned, and also some publications by Ruth Lister (1989, 1991, 1993, 1995a) and Sarah Benton (1988, 1991). The consensus in the feminist literature is that notions of citizenship in practice and theory are actually based on the male citizen, even though their outlook may be gender-neutral. In this regard Lister (1995a) also talks about the 'ungendered nature of citizenship'.

Another line in the debate follows logically from the first, namely whether or not citizenship should be gendered and, if so, what this should mean. Feminist theorists differ greatly about this issue. Mary Dietz (1985) and Chantal Mouffe (1993) plead most strongly for a gender-neutral (almost gender-blind) citizenship; whereas Jean Bethke Elshtain (1981), Carole Pateman (1992), Kathleen Jones (1990) and Iris Marion Young (1989) strongly propose a citizenship that incorporates 'women as women' even though they differ on what this might mean. A third and closely linked position is that which argues that the only way in which citizenship can become gender-neutral is by incorporating women 'as women' in citizenship theories and practices (Lister 1989; Phillips 1991b). Gender neutrality would be obtained not by gender blindness but by gendering citizenship for both sexes.

This links to another line of the debate, namely whether or not universal or equal citizenship can be combined with plurality (Voet 1992a). Here the issue reaches a higher level of abstraction and also relates to groups other than women. Iris Marion Young states (1989: 251) on this issue:

Far from implying one another, the universality of citizenship, in the sense of the inclusion and participation of everyone, stands in tension with the two other meanings of universality embedded in modern political ideas: universality as generality and universality as equal treatment.

Young's argument is that feminists should aspire to the ideal of universal citizenship as the inclusion and participation of everyone in discussion and decision-making, but that this implies a 'differentiated citizenship' in the sense of emphasizing women's difference, special rights and group representation. Anne Phillips (1993: Ch. 3) and Chantal Mouffe (1993) stress the importance of universality to achieve solidarity and a view of the common good.

One also has to bear in mind that (apart from historical studies) the debate on women and citizenship takes place in two different disciplines: political theory and social policy. Apart from the above-mentioned lines of the debate these two 'branches' also have their own specific approaches and questions (Voet 1992b). The political theory branch focuses on citizenship as participation. It is concerned with issues of democracy, republicanism, liberalism, the ethic of care, and compatibility of the importance of citizenship with the feminist notion of 'the personal is political'. The social policy branch focuses on citizenship as a status or as legal rights. It is more concerned with the welfare state, the valuation of care work, women's participation in the labour market and a comparison across countries on these issues. However, these approaches are not mutually exclusive – which may explain the dominance of T.H. Marshall in the feminist debate – and some theorists combine them (Lister 1995a; Siim 1994).

*   *   *

In this chapter I have argued that the contemporary feminist debate and citizenship debate have been seldom or never explicitly connected, and that they should be connected in order to meet the needs of female citizens. I have also indicated that more recently some feminist theorists have dealt explicitly with citizenship. Chapter 2 will broaden our insight into the relationship between feminism and citizenship by showing how these issues have been connected in the past, and by suggesting a way in which second wave feminist publications on women's condition can be seen as providing elements of alternative feminist citizenship theories.

2

Feminism

In this book I examine only those feminist ideas that are explicitly or implicitly concerned with citizenship. There are basically three feminist positions on citizenship, which derive from the equality–difference debate that has dominated feminism in recent decades. Though seemingly recent, this debate has influenced feminist thought on citizenship for a much longer period, as can be illustrated by looking at important historical events. For these purposes, I will focus on the French Revolution and on the evolution of women's suffrage organizations into women's citizenship organizations in Britain, before moving to the recent equality–difference debate. I will explain how I have developed my categorization of the three main types of contemporary feminist thought on citizenship and briefly show what these types are, as well as looking at variations of them. First, however, I will reflect upon the definition of feminism in general.

*   *   *

Feminism can be described as all those ideas and movements that have as their fundamental aim the realization of women's liberation or a profound improvement in women's condition (Mitchell and Oakley 1986; Offen 1988). I choose such a broad definition because I do not consider it useful to obscure normative disputes by saying that some authors are not really feminist.

One may ask, however, whether one can talk about feminist reflections on citizenship which occurred before the term 'feminism' came into existence. As Karen Offen (1988) notes, the term 'feminism' was first used by Hubertine Auclert in 1882 in the journal *La Citoyenne* (The Woman Citizen). In contrast to Offen I think that this should not prevent us from using the term to refer to ideas before 1882, even though it is strictly anachronistic. It would be short-sighted to ignore the large body of political thought and action sometimes referred to as 'proto-feminism', 'pre-feminism' or 'feminism *avant la lettre*'. If people fit my above definition, they will be called feminists even if they did or do not call themselves such.

Feminism is often expressed as having two waves. The first wave is the period of suffrage struggles: 1870–1930 in most western-liberal democracies. The second wave is the period of the 'feminist cultural revolution' after 1968. As soon as we take feminist ideas of citizenship as our focus, it becomes obvious that a third and earlier period needs to be mentioned: the period at the end of the eighteenth century in which universal citizenship vocabularies were first applied to women.

In looking at the first period – the end of the eighteenth century – I will concentrate on France, where the vocabulary of equal citizenship first emerged in the context of the Enlightenment and the French Revolution. One finds that during this era, feminists mainly used equality arguments to promote women's citizenship. For the second period I will focus on inter-war Britain, as it provides an interesting case of feminists using both difference and equality arguments in their formulation of citizenship for women. These were not the only contexts in which feminist ideas of citizenship were formulated, but they serve as illustrations of the most important moments in the history of feminism and citizenship: the democratic revolution and the post-suffrage period.

As mentioned, my focus then moves to the feminist publications emerging around 1970, which show surprise and anger that the 'problem' of women and citizenship had still not been resolved.

The first period: the end of the eighteenth century

With only a few exceptions, women were excluded from the legal status of citizenship until some time in the twentieth century (Heater 1990). This was not an accident, but a policy explicitly supported by both politicians and political theorists. The arguments that political theorists provided for this varied slightly. In the civic-republican thought of Aristotle and others, women were considered as essentially apolitical or even anti-political beings who belonged to the private sphere of the family household. Political virtues and qualities were explicitly connected to maleness (Saxonhouse 1985). Within many Christian and patriarchal theories women's citizenship was regarded as superfluous. Women's interests were already represented by their fathers or husbands. Besides, placing women on the same footing as men would be contrary to the natural order ordained by God (Schochet 1975). Running through civic-republican, Christian and patriarchal theories is the argument that women, because of their nature, are incapable of rational thought, which disqualifies them from being potential citizens (Lloyd 1989).

At the end of the eighteenth century 'natural rights' theories were still very popular. These theories held that all 'men' had the same nature, usually that of being able to think rationally, and thus also had the same natural rights. Although these natural rights theories had been used in earlier centuries for conservative purposes, for instance to define common obligations for all people to the monarch, at the end of the eighteenth century they became used for progressive purposes, such as offering citizenship rights (Tuck 1979). Within these theories a distinction was made between men and women. Although women had their own qualities, they were naturally inferior to men and should therefore be excluded from citizenship rights.

This was even argued by theorists that were considered, then and now, to be radical democrats (Vogel 1991, 1994).

The most important of such theorists is Jean-Jacques Rousseau. It is well known that in *The Social Contract* (1762) Rousseau drew up arguments for democracy that were used in the French Revolution. In Rousseau's book, all citizens were assumed to be equal by nature and were symbolically invited to draw up a social contract in which they would outline how the state should be run. What is less well known is that he only allowed men to participate in the social contract. He gave women the important task, as mothers, of educating their sons in the virtues of citizenship, but simultaneously excluded them from the status of citizenship. His ideal boy Emile has to serve the state; his ideal girl Sophie has to serve Emile (Akkerman 1992). In this, Rousseau followed the civic-republican tradition.

A new 'anti-feminist' vocabulary was derived from Rousseau's immensely powerful and popular ideas. In this vocabulary women were considered as valuable to the state in their capacity as mothers as men were in their capacity as citizens. This gender difference was the basis of a strong republic because the republic needed women's motherhood just as much as men's activities. As was the case with political theory before this time, here again women's gender difference was constructed as the foundation of their exclusion from citizenship rights.

This time, however, the anti-feminist vocabulary invoked feminist reactions. These reactions were of two different kinds. The first was that of feminists who argued that even though some differences exist between men and women, these differences should be irrelevant to citizenship and should therefore not restrain women's rights (Landes 1984a; Rendall 1985). In 1790, a member of the legislative assembly in France, Marquis de Condorcet, set the tone for this type of feminist response in his essay, *Sur l'Admission des femmes au droit de cité* (Plea for the Citizenship of Women). In particular, his argument that all people were naturally equal and had the same natural rights was to be used repeatedly to demand equal citizenship rights for both sexes. Condorcet simply asked why, if women met the existing requirements, they were excluded from citizenship. He argued (quoted in Bell and Offen 1983: 99):

> For this exclusion not to be an act of tyranny, it would be necessary either to prove that the natural rights of women are not absolutely identical with those of men, or else to show that women are incapable of exercising them.

Etta Palm d'Aelders was a Dutch woman who lived in France from 1774 onward and who headed a female delegation to the revolutionary assembly in France in 1792. She was a skilful orator on women's causes in French revolutionary clubs between 1791 and 1793. Like Condorcet, Palm used natural law arguments but she went much further (Vega 1989). In her appeal to the revolutionary legislators in 1791 (in Bell and Offen 1983: 103) she proclaimed equal citizenship not only in terms of equal rights and protection, but also in terms of equal power:

August legislators, would you weigh down with chains the hands that helped you to raise the altar of the fatherland with so much ardor? Would you enslave those who contributed so zealously to make you free? Would you brand a Clelia, a Venturia, a Cornelia? No, no, conjugal authority would only be the result of a social past. It is wisdom in legislation, it is in the general interest to establish a balance between despotism and licence; but the powers of the husband and the wife should be equal and individual. The laws cannot establish any distinction between these two authorities; they must offer equal protection and must establish a lasting equilibrium between married persons.

Some months after Etta Palm's appeal, Olympe de Gouges proclaimed the *Déclaration des droits de la femme et de la citoyenne* (Rights of Woman and Woman Citizen), a critique of the revolutionary *Déclaration des droits de l'homme et de citoyen* (Rights of Man and Citizen, 1789). Olympe de Gouges used the vocabulary of natural rights to demand not only equal rights and protection for both sexes, but also equal obligations, equal participation and an equal share in wealth. She stated (quoted in Bell and Offen 1983: 105) that the natural rights to liberty and justice should be guaranteed not just within the public sphere but also within the private sphere:

Liberty and Justice consist of rendering to persons those things that belong to them; thus, the exercise of woman's natural rights is limited only by the perpetual tyranny with which man opposes her; these limits must be changed according to the laws of nature and reason.

So in this period the cause for women's citizenship was usually defended by an appeal to equality. Nonetheless, this is not the whole story. Between feminists who argued for women's citizenship with an appeal to equality and anti-feminists who argued against women's citizenship with an appeal to difference, there stood some feminists who argued for women's citizenship with a mixture of equality and difference arguments.

To these feminists women's gender difference was not considered irrelevant to citizenship, but a potential source of citizenship. It was argued that women should be included in citizenship, among other reasons because their gender difference would lead to a better society or politics. The best example of this type of reaction is found not in a French, but in an English writer: Mary Wollstonecraft who published *Vindication of the Rights of Woman* (1792) three years after the beginning of the French Revolution. In this book she first pointed out her agreement with Rousseau that motherhood forms an important support to citizenship, because it is mothers who educate their children in the values of citizenship. Wollstonecraft, however, disagreed strongly with Rousseau's assumption that republican mothers do not need a citizenship status of their own. The civic-republican discourse of citizenship must be extended to women, and women must be accepted as political equals.

This position need not imply that women cannot be different from men in other respects. Wollstonecraft certainly saw different citizenship activities and duties for men and women. According to her, political equality as citizens does indeed require equal rights and virtues, but does not require exactly the same duties and activities of all citizens. On the contrary, she suggested that the republic is strengthened if citizens are allowed to serve it in various ways.

Carole Pateman (1992) interprets Wollstonecraft's idea of equality and difference as being her dilemma. I do not consider it to be a dilemma. Both equality and difference were used by Wollstonecraft to plead for women's citizenship. This debate took on more significance during the next period of discussion of citizenship.

The second period: from suffrage to citizenship 1918–40

The second important period in feminist thought on women and citizenship was just after women's suffrage was gained in Britain in 1918 (for women over 28 years old). I focus here on the ideas of Eleanor Rathbone, who used a mixture of equality and difference arguments to plead for women's citizenship.

During the period from 1918 to 1940 the dominant concept of citizenship was the (classical) liberal one. Citizenship was a respectable status which was desired by everyone, as it offered an individual equal political and civic rights with all other citizens. It was a guarantee against political and legal discrimination, a weapon against violence, an entry card to educational and other public institutions. Being a citizen gave one a right to state protection. It made sure that in the eyes of the law and politics each citizen counted equally, regardless of their personal background – and, as feminists demanded, regardless of their gender.

Often during the women's suffrage struggle the terms 'suffrage' and 'citizenship' were used as if they had the same meaning (Boyd 1918; Hardie 1906; Metcalfe 1917; Shore 1874). In the inter-war period, however, feminists separated the meanings of the two terms, as Arnold Whittick shows in *Woman into Citizen* (1979). After women obtained the vote, it soon became clear that the vote did not automatically bring the 'equal citizenship' that many feminists had hoped for. In particular, feminists found that, aside from having the vote, more needed to happen so that women's voices might change society and politics (Abbott, G. 1920).

When, in Britain, the Representation of the People Act was accepted in the House of Commons (1917) and the House of Lords (1918), women did not dissolve their suffrage organizations (Alberti 1989; Heitland 1919; NWCA 1933; Whittick 1979). The transformation of suffrage organizations into women citizens' organizations indicates that, for these feminists, citizenship meant something beyond suffrage, and that they still considered it necessary to establish organizations for citizenship along gender lines.

In the National Union of Societies for Equal Citizenship, the most explicit idea concerning the relationship between women and citizenship came from its president from 1919 to 1929, Eleanor Rathbone. It is obvious that her position on this relationship was one of ambivalence. At times she disconnected the capacity of women as women from the capacity of women as citizens. For instance, in her speech entitled 'Changes in Public Life' (1936: 73, 56), Rathbone said:

> We are citizens as well as women. . . . What is the nature of the work that still lies before the British women's movement? Over and above the contribution to public life they will make as citizens concerned with problems affecting both sexes, what is the special contribution which should be looked for from women as women?

In the same text, however, she pointed out (p. 76) the effect of women in political life in terms of a new kind of citizenship:

> There will be a changed attitude on the part of society towards human happiness and suffering, especially towards the happiness and suffering of its less powerful and articulate members, a more scientific study of the reactions of political and economic machinery upon well-being, poverty, disease and ugliness, a more sustained and determined fight against cruelty in all its forms and especially against the cruelty of war.

Then, in a presidential address in 1920, Rathbone (1929: 3–4) suggested that men and women have different natures, which, if given the chance to 'grow', may be the basis of different types of citizenship:

> We want the contribution of women to national life to be a very distinctive contribution and to make a very great difference. But if it is to do that, it must bubble freshly out of the mother earth of women's personalities and must be impregnated with the salt of their own experience. . . . Let us be aware lest it be said of women in future years that they have thrown away the first and greatest opportunity that has been given to them to justify at once their womanhood and citizenship.

As a Member of Parliament she proposed a bill to give women family allowances (Rathbone 1940). In her speech during the final stage of the Family Allowance Bill (Rathbone 1945), Rathbone gave an image of women's citizenship that consists of bearing and rearing future citizens and producers:

> In the early days, I used to describe meetings of employers and employed, landowners and renters, sitting around the table competing for a share in the national income with a woman coming from behind and holding out her hand, saying: 'I am the mother; the future citizens and workers depend on me: where is my share?' This Bill gives the mother through her children her share, although it is only a very little share so far.

Whereas Eleanor Rathbone presented an image of 'mothers as citizens', Mrs Ogilvie Gordon, president of the National Women Citizens Association, gave an image of 'female neighbours as citizens' (NWCA 1936). Women's services in wartime were for her an example of how women can use their specific capabilities in a political way. They could also be a great vitalizing force in all the reconstructive work. Women had shown self-sacrifice and altruism in the home for centuries and their entry into public life would introduce a kindlier feeling to that public life. In her view (NWCA 1936: 6–7):

> [t]rue citizenship does not mean fighting on battlefields, nor is it the greatness of

an Empire won on its battlefields, by its army or by its navy, but by the standard of comfort in the cottage home of the people. . . . In many of our best homes co-operation and love are the guiding motives, and if we can pass those motives into our civic life, what a tremendous improvement will result. . . . Citizenship consists in keeping your eye on your neighbour. Next to our duty to our God is our duty to our neighbour. It is a most sacred duty to see that the best is done for the members of our community.

Gordon perceived citizenship participation in the local council as efficient and sympathetic housekeeping on a larger scale. Women needed to be educated in what their business as citizens should be (cf. Crawhall and Laughton 1928; Hollister 1918; Macadam 1919a, 1919b; Neville-Rolfe 1961).

Rathbone and Gordon are representative of the kinds of arguments on women and citizenship which were prevalent during the immediate post-suffrage period. After the 1940s, literature on women and citizenship seemed to disappear for a while, with a few exceptions during the second world war (vae Amstel-van Loeben Sels 1945; Burton 1942).

The third period: 1970s and after

The third key period in the reflection on women and citizenship is the so-called second wave of feminism. However, during this period feminists seldom dealt explicitly with notions of citizenship. Feminists were disappointed with what the vote had brought women. Despite formal equality, they felt that women were still oppressed and disrespected. That they rarely used the term 'citizenship' can be explained easily by the fact that they associated citizenship with women's formal status and because the term 'citizenship' was not fashionable. For them, it was not women's formal citizenship status that was problematic, but women's gender roles, their position in the labour market, their economic dependency on men, sexual violence against women and so on. The radical feminist Shulamith Firestone writes for instance in her classic book *The Dialectic of Sex* (1970: 34):

> By 1970 the rebellious daughters of this wasted generation no longer, for all practical purposes, even knew there had been a feminist movement. There remained only the unpleasant residue of the aborted revolution, an amazing set of contradictions in their roles: on the one hand, they had most of the legal freedoms, the literal assurance that they were considered full political citizens of society – and yet they had no power. They had educational opportunities – and yet were unable, and not expected, to employ them. They had the freedoms of clothing and sex mores that they had demanded – and yet they were still sexually exploited.

Compare the Dutch feminist Joke Kool-Smit in 1967 (1984: 16. My translation):

> Apart from the formal aspect – suffrage – feminists wanted three things: that woman should become a free human being, that she should be able to realize her potential and that she should become a full member of society. In none of these

three areas has the ideal of feminists been reached, in none of these three areas
have women got as far as should have been possible theoretically speaking. I
speak now about women as a group. Of course there have always been exceptions. . . . As far as the majority of women is concerned one can say that emancipation has halted at the passive stage: the opportunities have come within reach,
but that is all there is: they are just like housewives of fifty years ago and do not
have any further aspirations.

It is interesting to note that these feminists perceived the 'first wave' feminists from the beginning of the twentieth century as primarily seeking formal
equality, although in fact that early movement had been much broader. As
Juliette Mitchell wrote in her bestseller *Woman's Estate* (1971: 120):

> The lesson of these reflections is that the liberation of women can only be
> achieved if all four structures in which they have been integrated are transformed
> – Production, Reproduction, Sexuality and Subordination. . . . In the early twen-
> tieth century . . . [t]he vote – a political right – was eventually won. None the less,
> though a simple completion of the formal legal equality of bourgeois society, it
> left the socio-economic situation of women virtually unchanged. The wider legacy
> of the suffrage was practically nil.

In the 1970s, the feminist slogan 'the personal is political' was used against
this formality and against a rigid split between public and private lives.
There were two major meanings to the slogan. The first was that the situation of women (and men) can be seen as a collective and structural one.
This was seen as the outcome of a political process of oppression and a
psychological process of internalized oppression. Or as Carol Hanish, who
coined this slogan, suggested in her article 'The Personal is Political' (1970),
there are no strictly personal problems and therefore all so-called personal
problems should be open to political debate and the 'private sphere' should
be open to state intervention. The second meaning to the slogan was that
the difference which women in the private sphere stood for should be used
to change public and political life (Aerts 1986; de Vries 1987). The 'personal' was considered as a source that could enrich politics.

The most important term that was employed to analyse women's condition is probably 'patriarchy', used in the sense of 'males dominate females'
(Millett 1970: 32–81). Feminists claimed this status system was still operat-
ing. As Kate Millett explains in *Sexual Politics* (1970: 32–33):

> Groups who rule by birthright are fast disappearing, yet there remains one ancient
> and universal scheme for the domination of one birth group by another – the
> scheme that prevails in the area of sex. . . . [T]he situation between the sexes now,
> and throughout history, is a case of that phenomenon Max Weber defined as
> *Herrschaft*, a relationship of dominance and subordinance.

Soon after the first feminist publications around 1970 the so-called
equality–difference debate arose within feminism (Hermsen and van
Lenning 1991). This debate centred on the question of whether women
should try to become as respected as men by aiming at equality or by aiming
at respect for women's difference. Almost every feminist was involved in the
debate, even postmodern feminists who claimed that one needed to avoid

the choice between equality and difference completely. I will not discuss this debate at length here, because it will be covered in Chapters 4 to 10.

Suffice it to say that although feminists did not use the term 'citizenship' in the equality–difference debate, one can maintain that it was nevertheless under discussion, based on my description of citizenship. Feminists were talking about actual and ideal relations between state and individual citizens; about actual and ideal political relationships among citizens; about rights, public duties, public behaviour, public virtues and about the difficulties in distinguishing public from private life.

One can distinguish three major lines of feminist thinking about citizenship in the equality–difference debate. Nevertheless, it is important to note that such distinctions are always arbitrary. With this in mind, we first need to look at some background to the processes behind dividing feminism into different categories.

Categorizations of feminism

Because feminists do not all have the same opinion or philosophy, several categorizations of feminism have arisen. Theorists reflecting on feminism from the beginning of the twentieth century have suggested dividing feminism into categories like: 'working-class versus bourgeois feminism', 'old versus new feminism' and 'liberal versus socialist feminism'. Contemporary feminism watchers, however, go even further than this. Karen Offen (1988) differentiates between 'individual' versus 'familial' feminism. Alison Jaggar (1983a, 1983b) establishes four categories: 'liberal feminism, traditional Marxism, socialist feminism and radical feminism'. Jean Bethke Elshtain (1981) retains three common categories: 'radical, liberal and Marxist feminism' but adds 'psychoanalytical feminism'. Ursula Vogel (1986) keeps it simpler by distinguishing 'rationalist feminism' from 'romanticist feminism'. A textbook by Maggie Humm (1992), with the appropriate name *Feminisms*, makes it as complex as possible. Of all the distinctions, the following are the most notable: 'first wave feminism', 'second wave feminism', 'Asian, black and women of colour feminism', 'lesbian feminism', 'liberal feminism', 'difference feminism' and 'psychoanalytical feminism'. To illustrate further the variety of feminisms, these feminism watchers do not take into account all the differentiations within 'postmodern feminism' (Braidotti 1991) nor do they talk about 'Christian feminism', 'civic-republican feminism', 'ethic of care feminism' and so forth.

It is not necessary here to understand what these labels signify. There are two things, however, which we must bear in mind: one can identify with almost any type of feminism one likes; and categorization is a political game. Everyone who classifies obscures or highlights, simplifies or shows complexity, divides people into factions, and separates the ones with whom she wants to identify from the ones she dislikes. Despite these constraints, classifications are also useful: they focus one's mind on the allegedly important things and they reduce the complexities of people's thought. Indeed, it is very hard to think systematically without the tool of categorization.

The most common categorizations used by political feminists of the second wave were those of liberal feminists, socialist feminists and radical feminists, although not many of them liked to describe themselves as liberal feminists. Liberal feminists favoured a feminist programme of equal rights and equal treatment; socialist feminists thought the abolition of capitalism necessary for genuine feminism; and radical feminists gave priority to denouncing patriarchal or male norms.

Although this categorization resulted in separate feminist political formations along these lines, the actual opinions of feminists in liberal, socialist and radical groups overlapped much more than one would presume from merely observing the labels. In particular, liberal and socialist feminists share more than they differ on, if citizenship is the main perspective. Both endorse the dominant conception of social-liberal citizenship, even though socialist feminists are more egalitarian than liberal feminists. For this reason, I do not find the separation of liberal and socialist categories to be of use in the context of the citizenship debate. Nor do I want to retain the category of radical feminism, because various types of feminism may be radical in different ways.

I am not comfortable with the currently popular division between 'equality feminism' and 'difference feminism' either. The term 'difference feminism' suggests that its adherents favour difference and oppose equality. It would be more precise to say that they do not aspire to equality in the sense of sameness but in the sense of equal value, equal respect or equity. Further, postmodern or deconstructionist feminism explicitly tries to escape the dichotomy of equality and difference (Bock and James 1992; Scott 1988). With all these theoretical complexities in mind, I have chosen to categorize feminist thought in the recent equality–difference debate into 'humanist feminism', 'woman-centred feminism' and 'deconstructionist feminism'. It is to the explanation of these terms that I now turn.

Humanist and woman-centred feminism

I start from Iris Marion Young's (1990a: 73–91) classification of feminism into humanist feminism and gynocentric (or woman-centred) feminism. This is because a central part of modern feminist thought on citizenship and politics is divided along the main lines of humanist equality and woman-identified equity. My third category, deconstructionist feminism, will be addressed in the latter part of this chapter.

In 'Humanism, Gynocentrism, and Feminist Politics' (1990a: 74) Young describes humanist feminism as a 'revolt against femininity'. It sees gender difference as accidental to humanity. According to humanist feminists, women should simply be offered the same opportunities as men. Implicitly or explicitly, they see 'male' life-styles and types of behaviour as an example for women.

On the other hand gynocentric or woman-centred feminism suggests, according to Young (1990a: 79), that women's oppression consists not of being prevented from participation in full humanity but of the denial and devaluation of specifically feminine values and activities by an overly instrumentalist and authoritarian masculine culture. Women's bodies and traditionally feminine activities are seen as sources of positive values for society and politics. Whereas humanist feminism is moderate and merely incorporates women into the existing ideal, woman-centred feminism claims to have the potential and the will to change the world dramatically.

Humanist feminism could in my view be further divided into liberal and egalitarian feminism. An example of a liberal feminist is Janet Radcliffe Richards (1982). She believes that the only reason why women are not as powerful and active as citizens as men is that women have not made enough effort. If women want to, they will succeed. The only relationship between feminism and citizenship is that feminists should actively encourage women to get into public life and important social positions. The egalitarian feminist position can be illustrated by Susan Moller Okin (1989). For Okin, social liberalism should fulfil its promises of equality and liberty and therefore ought to extend to women and the private sphere. Moreover, equality should mean not only formal equality but also material equality, which implies reducing the social inequalities between men and women.

In my view, woman-centred feminism is not one homogeneous block either. It consists of women's forum feminists, such as Iris Young herself (1990b), who want to add a women-based identity politics to the current system of liberal democracy, although they do not specify what it is that women will contribute. It also includes feminists such as Jean Bethke Elshtain (1981), who promote women's morality as a form of superior ethics that ought to be incorporated in politics and that functions as a foundation for better politics and citizenship. 'Women's morality' is usually considered (Tronto 1993: 1–10) to be an altruistic form of contextual moral judgement and is linked with femininity or motherhood.

In the 'real' world, one will not find people who call themselves humanist feminists or woman-centred feminists. The terms 'humanist feminism' and 'woman-centred feminism' are better considered as systematic constructions for common ways of thinking among feminists. Nevertheless, humanist feminism and woman-centred feminism are two reasonably well established and familiar lines of argument (although the second is much more popular at the moment than the first); indeed they are so familiar that, even if we try alternative approaches, we are likely to fall back into these categories. However, some qualifications to these classifications have to be made. Often feminists try to argue both things at the same time. Moreover, the classification should be seen as more of a continuum than a dichotomy, even though there is a tension between these two main positions.

A third category: deconstructionist feminism

Deconstructionist feminists attempt to think beyond a dichotomy of equality versus difference. They believe that such a dichotomy is a product of the ideas of the Enlightenment and should be overcome. Like other postmodernists, they attempt to distance us from and make us sceptical about ideas from the Enlightenment concerning truth, knowledge, power, history, self and language. As Jane Flax argues in *Thinking Fragments* (1990a: 32–35), postmodernists proclaim three deaths: the death of 'man', of history and of metaphysics. Men or people do not possess an essential nature on which we can base a political philosophy. Neither can we believe in a natural progress in history. Finally, postmodernists believe that there is no absolute truth that goes beyond our subjectivity and power. As a result of these 'deaths', everything is arbitrary: a product of power, tradition and coincidence.

Apart from the deconstructive aspect, postmodern projects also have a 'constructive' aspect, according to Jane Flax (1990b: 180): all of them have heterogeneity, multiplicity and difference as their central values. The constructive aspect appears to follow from the deconstructive aspect in the sense that, by decoupling the binary logic of Enlightenment thinking – man/woman; public/private; rational/irrational; culture/nature – a multiplicity of possibilities will appear.

Deconstructionist feminists have strongly resisted dividing feminism into equality feminism and difference feminism, because this would obscure the complexity of the actual feminist debate, create false opposition and obscure alternative options. Postmodern ideas also directly challenge the content of feminism. Deconstructionist feminists are sceptical about the idea of a general oppression of all women and about the idea of a liberation route for all women. They doubt whether there is a general nature of 'woman' that can serve as a foundation for feminism.

Current feminist positions on citizenship

The categorization of humanist feminism/woman-centred feminism/deconstructionist feminism needs to be specified somewhat further in relation to the scope of this book. Here I can only indicate briefly the feminist positions on citizenship that derive directly from the equality–difference debate.

Humanist feminism insists on a consistent individualism and humanism. It argues that to use the family as a basic unit is to obscure inequalities between husbands and wives, or to turn these inequalities into personal rather than political difficulties. Humanist feminism claims equal rights and duties for all mature individuals wherever they are in the domain of the state and whatever they do. A good example of this humanist-feminist position can be found in April Carter's book, *The Politics of Women's Rights*. Here Carter concludes (1988: 196):

Equal rights for women, who make up over half the population, are a prerequisite for achieving justice. But protecting women's rights is organically linked to promoting the rights of the poor and disadvantaged and to ending discrimination based on the arbitrary grounds of race. This is not only because the poor are most often women, and black women suffer from a dual discrimination, but primarily because women's rights will only be secured in a context of respect for the rights of all and of policies designed to ensure a just society.

In the last chapter I mentioned the paradox of being excluded as women or included as citizens. The humanist-feminist response to this can be summed up as: 'Let us be included as citizens and forget that we are women.'

Woman-centred feminists are not opposed to all meanings of political equality. They prefer some sort of equity or acceptance (Littleton 1987 quoted in Young 1990b: 176–177) over and above an equal-treatment equality, an equality of results and a transcendence of group differences. Equity for them is something like equality of 'voice and access' and this implies equal civil, political and social rights for all adults, unless it is shown that particular groups need special rights and provisions.

Woman-centred feminists do not aim to make citizenship gender-neutral. According to them, the development of a gender-neutral citizenship would be a pointless exercise, doomed to failure. Instead, they argue that we need to rethink citizenship from the viewpoint of the female citizen.

For instance, Carole Pateman responds to the paradox of being included as citizens and excluded as women by saying that we should not eliminate 'men' and 'women' from our reflections on citizenship in favour of gender neutrality. Rather, she argues (1992: 28) that if both sexes are to be full citizens 'the meaning of sexual difference has to cease to be the difference between freedom and subordination'.

The woman-centred feminist response to the paradox of being included as citizens and excluded as women can therefore be summarized as: 'Let us try to become included as woman citizens and, in doing this, change the concept of citizenship.'

Deconstructionist feminism aims at more plurality in politics and society. It is sceptical about the idea of equal and universal citizenship, based on the natural rights tradition which proclaims equal rights for all individuals (Yeatman 1994a: 77). People with different needs cannot be helped by the same formula and the most vulnerable of them will be even further marginalized. On the other hand, they argue, a differentiated citizenship is also dangerous. The existence of different categories of citizens may stigmatize some groups and isolate them even more strongly than before. We need to think of more creative solutions.

Thus the deconstructionist feminist response to the paradox of being excluded as women and included as citizens is that such a paradox is easily overcome: 'We can easily avoid a notion of equality that excludes difference, and vice versa.'

*   *   *

This chapter has shown that the equality–difference debate has informed feminist positions on citizenship throughout history. In the current period three main lines of feminist thinking derive from it. Humanist feminism aims at more equality. It suggests that women should be more nearly equal to male citizens and that this equality should also apply in the private sphere of the family. Woman-centred feminism aims at a revaluation of gender difference. It supports a rethinking of citizenship from the position of the female citizen and a more positive evaluation of women's acting and thinking. Deconstructionist feminism states that we should go beyond this equality–difference dichotomy. It aims at pluralism in general instead of gender pluralism only.

All these main types of feminism assume that the dominant theory of citizenship – social liberalism – opposes difference (whether this is seen as positive or negative). Before I examine in detail their criticisms of and alternatives to social liberalism, I will judge in the next chapter whether or not they have been correct in their assumption that social liberalism inhibits difference.

3

Social-liberal Citizenship

All three types of feminists have perceived social liberalism in terms of an equality philosophy for men and the public realm, and as being opposed to difference (cf. Frazer and Lacey 1993). In this chapter I will examine whether this feminist image of liberalism is correct. Social liberalism is a specific modern form of liberalism. Since the second world war it has dominated western liberal democracies, not only at the level of theory but also at the level of political practice, even though it has not always been followed consistently. In order to understand it we need to explore its roots in classical liberalism.

I will first outline the characteristics of classical liberalism and then indicate the ways in which social liberalism differs from the classical form. I will elaborate upon this picture by giving an account of the different and conflicting strands of political theorizing that make up the category of social liberalism. In doing this, I will present two dominant versions of social liberalism – those of T.H. Marshall and John Rawls; and three atypical variations of social liberalism – those of Bruce Ackerman, Michael Walzer and Will Kymlicka. Following this overview I present a more qualified account of the social-liberal view of citizenship before discussing the way in which social liberalism deals with difference. Finally, I will evaluate the feminist image of social liberalism as an equality philosophy that opposes difference.

Classical liberalism

Classical liberalism is an ideology found in western countries from the seventeenth century to halfway through the twentieth century. It contains the following elements. The first is the idea that all men differ from all animals in that they can think, and in this respect all men are equal (Laski 1936; Sabine 1964: 669–755). The natural equality of 'men', as Carole Pateman argues in *The Sexual Contract* (1988), must not be understood in a metaphorical sense but in a literal sense, since classical liberals regarded women as incapable of rational thought and therefore as inferior to men (cf. Pateman and Brennan 1979).

The second element within classical liberalism is the notion that the natural equality of men leads to men's equal natural rights. For instance, John Locke argued in his two *Treatises of Government* (1690) that men had a natural right to life, liberty and property. According to liberals, these or other natural rights lead logically to the political system in which these rights are best guaranteed. Paradoxically this might mean that a citizen temporarily loses these natural rights because he has given his mandate to the state to protect them. Only if the state fails to do so will the citizen regain his natural rights.

The third element is individualism, central to classical liberalism. The starting point of classical liberalism has always been the individual, or perhaps more correctly the individual man. This individualism has had its effects in different areas. In ethics (Frankena 1973) at least two different forms have been given to it. In utilitarian liberalism individualism has taken the form of Jeremy Bentham's idea of 'the greatest happiness of the greatest number'. In Kantian liberalism individualism has led to the thought that people should not be treated as means but as ends in themselves. In the area of politics, individualism has predominantly led to the system of 'one man, one vote', although other models have also been explored (MacPherson 1977).

Another obvious element is the ideal of liberty or the autonomy of the individual. State intervention is only legitimized in order to promote the liberty of citizens. Classical liberalism also makes a strong distinction between the public sphere in which state intervention is allowed, and the private sphere of the family which is free from state intervention. As John Stuart Mill argues in *On Liberty* (1859), people's liberty has to be constrained more in the public sphere since in this sphere the chances are higher that other people will be harmed.

Finally, the most important element of classical liberalism in the context of this book is the ideal of a rather passive form of citizenship. Classical liberalism was radical in its idea that the political relations in a state should not be between a monarch and his or her obedient subjects, but should take the form of a monarch being bound by a kind of social contract with the citizens. Citizenship is a privileged status which entitles an individual to respect and to some rights. The ordinary citizen is not required to engage in any kind of political participation apart from voting. All other tasks are transferred to political representatives. Classical liberalism therefore puts a strong trust in parliamentarianism and in representative democracy.

The core of classical-liberal citizenship is thus formed by the equal civil and political rights that every citizen possesses. There is, however, one significant restriction: not everyone, even amongst men, is granted the status of equal citizenship. Those who do not possess a certain amount of property are financially dependent upon other people and are not considered capable of autonomous thought and action (MacPherson 1962). In other words, they do not yet possess the necessary capacities for being a citizen and should therefore not be granted this status.

Social liberalism

The modern version of liberalism that emerged after the second world war, social liberalism, has recognized the threat of economic dependency to the autonomy of citizens but has found a different solution to the problem in the form of the welfare state (Girvetz 1963). This should protect people against poverty so that they will not be financially dependent upon others. Social liberals assume that through the existence of the welfare state everyone can be an autonomous citizen.

The heart of social-liberal citizenship comprises not only civic and political rights but also social rights (or rights to welfare benefits). It strongly supports the idea of equal and universal citizenship. Not only has it incorporated the lower classes into this ideal but also the female sex. By doing this, social liberals proclaim an ideal of classless and gender-neutral citizenship: they assume that they have made liberalism genuinely individualistic.

The other elements of classical liberalism, though, have remained the main ones of social liberalism: the passive notion of citizenship, the perception of rights as the core of citizenship, individualism, the ideal of liberty and individual autonomy, the public–private divide and the belief in the natural equality of men. Nonetheless, something more needs to be said about these in order to understand their slightly altered form in the modern context.

It can be argued that the social-liberal idea of citizenship has become even more passive. Within classical liberalism citizens were still expected to pass some autonomous judgement; now within social liberalism it is more or less assumed that judgement is a matter for experts. This might be due to the number of citizens that now exist, the scope of the state and the complexities of problems in modern life, all reasons to let public affairs be matters for political representatives and not for ordinary citizens. There is however another critical voice which argues that the welfare state furthers this notion of passive citizenship by excusing people from taking responsibility for taking care of their own affairs (cf. MacIntyre 1985; Mead 1986; Roche 1992).

Social liberalism has also found itself the focus of criticism in other ways in recent years, and as such needs to be considered not as a static theory but one evolving in response to challenges. For example, social liberalism is still individualistic, but is increasingly under pressure to look more closely at group perspectives. Social liberalism still holds a public–private distinction, but allows control of private life by civil servants of the welfare state. Furthermore, social liberalism still aims for a maximum amount of liberty for citizens, but has developed a stronger form of public morality than before (Rosenblum 1989). The natural equality of 'men' has been changed to the natural equality of individuals, but apart from adding women to citizens and using a gender-neutral language, this has not really changed the content of the liberal ideology and of the theories that follow from it, and this is under challenge from feminists.

Social liberalism, then, has moulded the institutions of public life in the west, even to the degree that we talk of western liberal democracies as a matter of course. Talking about social liberalism is therefore talking about modern western life. Yet because of all the critiques of it, social liberalism is now in a state of transition to accommodate some of these criticisms.

Five examples of social-liberal theorists

In order to understand social liberalism 'in transition' we cannot be satisfied with a simple one-dimensional picture; we need to observe the variety of views among its adherents. Thomas Humphrey Marshall, John Rawls, Bruce Ackerman, Michael Walzer and Will Kymlicka are all influential social-liberal political theorists, each representing a unique variation of the social-liberal concept of citizenship. They show that social liberalism can be combined with a theory of duties (Marshall), with Kantianism and contract theory (Rawls), with discourse theory and proceduralism (Ackerman), with civic republicanism (Walzer) and with group thinking (Kymlicka).

Not all of them, however, have the same status. Marshall and Rawls can be seen as presenting the dominant version of social liberalism: Marshall does this in an historical way, Rawls in a deontological way (starting from principles and deducing the implications). This main version of social liberalism strongly emphasizes equality for all citizens. Ackerman, Walzer and Kymlicka, on the other hand, represent the atypical forms of social liberalism in that they want to accommodate differences far more strongly than does the main version of social liberalism.

Thomas Humphrey Marshall

In his essay, 'Citizenship and Social Class' (1967) T.H. Marshall presents a sociological-historical perspective on citizenship. For Marshall, citizenship is not only a status bestowed on those who are full members of the (national) community; it is also an institution that has developed historically in western countries. By taking this historical approach, Marshall discloses (1967: 78) three different kinds of citizenship rights for all citizens. *Civil* citizenship, according to Marshall, has been granted to most people since the eighteenth century and is composed of the rights necessary for individual freedom. In the nineteenth century most people were given *political* citizenship, which is the right to political participation. Finally, Marshall argues, *social* citizenship will be established for most people in western democracies during the twentieth century and concerns welfare benefits and provisions.

Marshall's story is thus first a story of general progress. He argues that for a long time citizenship and capitalism have been 'at war' and that social citizenship, like the Trojan horse, will eventually undermine capitalism. Marshall argues that the possession of civil and political rights alone will not liberate people from the overwhelming power of private property and from the profit principle within capitalism. For real liberation, people also need social citizenship.

His story is, in the second place, also a normative story. It details not only an historical trend towards universal citizenship, but also one determined by morality, caused by the difference between existing unequal citizenship and ideal equal citizenship. Marshall contends (p. 92):

> The urge forward along the path thus plotted is an urge towards a fuller measure of equality, an enrichment of the stuff of which the status is made and an increase in the number of those on whom the status is bestowed.

In Marshall's ideal world, the equal rights of citizenship will generate a direct sense of community membership for previously excluded groups.

Universal equal citizenship will not, however, emerge automatically. Some private and social preconditions must be fulfilled. In particular, class consciousness, mobilization and struggle are necessary to gain citizenship rights. He also argues that such rights need to be guaranteed institutionally. Citizenship rights therefore demand political struggle if they are to be acknowledged in a formal and legal sense, and an active state to be secured in a material sense.

This distinction between formal and actual citizenship status also implies his qualified approach towards the idea of equality. Marshall emphasizes that actual citizenship status may be different for different groups, even though in his ideal world there is equal treatment of and equal results for citizens where their civil and political rights and citizenship obligations are concerned. In this ideal form of citizenship, the universal possession of all citizenship rights will modify social and private inequalities. Universal citizenship may in his view (pp. 127–128) only include those inequalities that are dynamic or that provide an incentive for change and betterment.

One may however doubt whether even his ideal view of citizenship is as universal as he claims. On the one hand, the concept of an ideal equal and universal citizenship must also be understood as a gender-neutral citizenship, in the sense that Marshall does not explicitly exclude women from the possibility of reaching it. On the other hand, Marshall only seems to talk about male citizens. Not only does Marshall continuously use the pronoun 'he', but he also explicitly refers to men and fathers only. For instance (p. 113):

> What matters is that there is a general enrichment of the concrete substance of civilized life, a general reduction of risk and insecurity, an equalization between the more and the less fortunate at all levels – between the healthy and the sick, the employed and the unemployed, the old and the active, the bachelor and the father of a large family.

Although from Marshall's perspective citizenship is mainly a matter of rights, in order to become a full member of the community of citizens participation is also required. Not only does he argue that acquiring new individual rights necessitates collective use of old rights, but he also provides a long list of the obligations that citizens have. Now and then, a hint of Isaiah Berlin's (1969) idea of positive freedom, not freedom *from* but freedom *to* in the sense of participation, appears in Marshall's lectures. The participation Marshall demands of citizens, though, is social and not political. It refers to work and service to promote the welfare of the community. Political participation is only a possible, temporary tool to extend citizenship rights, not a valuable activity in itself. Also, political judgement takes place only within the institutions immediately concerned with political rights, namely parliament and local councils.

John Rawls

John Rawls discusses citizenship by asking what justice in the public world would presuppose. He addresses this question in *A Theory of Justice* (1971: 12, 19, 136–142) through the hypothetical model of the 'veil of ignorance'.[1] In this procedure, we are invited to imagine ourselves without any particular characteristics and are asked: on what kind of hypothetical contract would we like to found our society, if we did not know what kind of position we would have in this new society? Rawls concludes (p. 302) that this thought experiment would result in two principles of justice, which would constitute the hypothetical contract. These are:

1 Each person is to have an equal right to the most extensive total system of equal basic liberties compatible with a similar system of liberty for all.
2 Social and economic inequalities are to be arranged so that they are both:
    (a) to the greatest benefit of the least advantaged, consistent with the just saving principle, and
    (b) attached to offices and positions open to all under conditions of fair equality and opportunity.

These principles of justice should, according to Rawls, apply to social and political institutions only. From his perspective, citizenship is the kind of status that will result for individual citizens if institutions apply these principles in the ideal public world. Social inequalities will be modified when institutions implement his two principles of justice. Yet Rawls does not explain how justice in the private world can be realized. It is no coincidence that Rawls neglects the private sphere. On the contrary, this is necessary, according to him, in order to give people as much freedom as possible. For Rawls, no view of the good life should be imposed on people in their private realm.

Rawls's theory is a universal theory of citizenship. 'In a well-ordered society,' he contends (p. 545), 'self-respect is secured by the public affirmation of the status of equal citizenship for all.' He deliberately makes minimal assumptions of what citizenship is, so they can be applied to everyone in the public realm. No natural characteristics and no comprehensive doctrines about moral life are required from citizens. Rawls takes the 'ordinary individual' as a starting point for his argument. In his view, this means someone who is financially responsible for family dependants (a head of a household), is ambitious, cares about the future generation and dwells, for an important part of time, in the public sphere (Okin 1989).

Equality, in Rawls's description, generally signifies equal rights and equality of opportunity, but it also suggests a fair distribution of goods, jobs and services. Fairness would imply that the distribution must be to the greatest benefit of the least advantaged and have regard to the well-being of the future generation. In socio-economic policy, therefore, equality can be translated as the aspiration to more equality of result.

It is also important to understand the significance of the term 'free' in Rawls's conception of the citizen. It indicates that citizens 'claim the right to view their persons as independent from and as not identified with any particular conception of the good' (1985: 241) and as 'capable of taking responsibility for their ends' (pp. 243–244). Freedom is mainly negative freedom, in Berlin's (1969: 121–125) sense of being protected from intervention, and this applies particularly to the private sphere.

Rawls considers participation not as an obligation but as a right. According to him (1971: 227, 221):

> [T]he principle of participation applies to institutions. It does not define an ideal of citizenship; nor does it lay down a duty requiring all to take an active part in political affairs. . . . the principle of (equal) participation . . . requires that all citizens are to have an equal right to take part in, and to determine the outcome of, the constitutional process that establishes the laws with which they are to comply.

Political judgement, in a Rawlsian perspective, first requires reasoning behind the veil of ignorance: trying to detach oneself from one's characteristics to discover what the word 'justice' would signify. Additionally, political judgement employs the two principles of justice in public practice (Rawls 1985). It requires (1971: 536) the neglect of 'comprehensive doctrines' because 'the contract conception of justice supports the self-esteem of citizens generally more firmly than other political principles' (cf. Rawls 1987, 1989). In another respect, however, his view does support a particular kind of political judgement. A common component of citizenship that is based on his conception advances an approach of 'reasonableness and a sense of fairness, a spirit of compromise and a readiness to meet others halfway' (Rawls 1987: 21).

Bruce Ackerman

In *Social Justice in a Liberal State* (1980) Bruce Ackerman offers a different variation of social liberalism by focusing not on the substance of the debate, but on the procedures by which agreements are formulated. What Ackerman wants to retain from the liberal tradition is 'an insistence that the forms of social life be rooted in the self-conscious value affirmations of autonomous individuals' (p. 196). Yet the core of his argument does not focus on individual will, but on dialogue.

Ackerman values public debate much more than private dialogue, quite simply because of the consequences which arise from public debate over the distribution of goods and the rules under which we live with each other. This does not imply that questions regarding the good life are excluded from public debate. Ackerman asks us to imagine ourselves, with our different concrete identities, in a space shuttle going to a new planet. The debate on justice will focus on how we are going to divide the resources to be found on that new planet, taking our different identities into account. This implies an initial imagined equality in resources (as everyone arrives at the planet with no resources) and a difference in identities as the starting point of the debate. Furthermore, it implies equal rights and duties, as well as different identities and different conceptions of the good life. Ackerman realizes that private conceptions of the good life might influence the way in which we want our new society to be ruled. He does not try to exclude these ideas. He only demands that we give reasons as to why we think that our private conceptions are better than those of others.

Ackerman prefers a minimal amount of argumentation rules as a procedure to achieve universal citizenship (cf. Habermas 1990). He mentions (1980, 1989) three necessary conversation constraints to resolve disagreements. The first one is that we always have to offer good reasons for why we think that some conceptions of the good are better than others. The second is that the only possible use of force in the debate is that used by the commander (the authority in the state). The third restraint arises at the moment of fundamental disagreement. Ackerman argues (1989: 16) that in this case it is better not to discuss it any further at all, in order to save the agreement on other (minor) points. In his view, this is the only way to make policy and maintain stability in a society. Plurality is restrained, but only in a minimal way and only if it appears to be a problem in practice.

Although everyone has equal rights and restraints in public debate, this does not necessarily result in equal rights and duties in the society to be built. Justice does not imply equal treatment. Rather it implies trying to do as much justice to differences as one can. This may result in giving relatively more resources to people in disadvantaged situations. It is plausible to plead for reverse discrimination for disabled people, because they will need more resources to realize their view of the good life, according to Ackerman. Unlike Marshall and Rawls, Ackerman applies social equality to individuals, not to families.

The freedom that Ackerman promotes is negative freedom: the freedom to realize one's vision of the good life without interference by other citizens or the state. Nonetheless, there is also a notion of positive freedom revealed in participation in the public debate. Ackerman says in his article 'Why Dialogue?' (1989: 6) that 'although a morally reflective person *can* permissibly cut herself off from real-world dialogue, a responsible citizen *cannot* with similar propriety cut herself off from political dialogue'. He sees a public debate about the way to coexist not only as an instrument to some higher end, but as being inherently essential to citizenship. Dialogue itself is crucial in the practice of citizenship. Citizens will gain consciousness through the process of debating and negotiating the ways in which goods will be distributed, and through deciding upon the rules. Citizens create their own society by talking to each other about their different interests and identities. In Ackerman's view, participating means debating – acts other than acts of speech do not seem to exist.

According to Ackerman, then, political judgement implies that people debate the question of how to build a society in which one can do as much justice as possible to differences. Particular identities, interests and characteristics are taken into account. Political judgement is not abstract but as concrete as possible, and is directed towards the distribution of goods and the content of the constitution.

Michael Walzer

Michael Walzer also desires a more active citizenship than ordinary social-liberal citizenship, in which a citizen is a passive recipient of certain benefits from the state. According to Walzer in his essay 'Three Kinds of Citizenship' (1970: 215), in practice we are not sufficiently passive and alienated from the public world to reflect this image of the citizen. Nor are we all sufficiently active to be political animals. Political activity in the modern nation state simply requires such hard work that most citizens cannot bring themselves to do it.

Society, according to Walzer in *Spheres of Justice* (1983), is divided into many social spheres. Within each sphere personal abilities may have a tremendous influence on citizens' status. Nevertheless, although people have different capabilities, the end result over all spheres should be that the status of citizens will be approximately the same.

Walzer combines pluralism and equality by discarding 'simple equality' and choosing 'complex equality' instead. Simple equality, according to Walzer, has been too long the ideal of the left. The aim of simple equality is to have goods, services, jobs and political participation exactly distributed among the different groups within society. Apart from the fact that fulfilling this aim would lead towards totalitarianism, Walzer says that it would not be desirable because people do not want to participate always and everywhere. Moreover, it would not be good for art, education and so forth to have incompetent people in leadership roles. In complex equality, some people rule in one 'sphere' and others rule in another 'sphere', with the result that no group rules in several spheres at the same time. Complex equality precludes the values of one elite from being influential in several spheres. In this regard, Walzer suggests (p. 241) that gender inequalities within the family will gradually disappear when 'the structures of kinship are no longer reiterated in other distributive spheres'.

Walzer's theory of citizenship is universalist at the basic level of a nation state. According to Walzer, no country can have half-citizens and full citizens. Walzer's biggest fear is a division among citizens: 'If a community is so radically divided that a single citizenship is impossible, then its territory must be divided, too' (p. 62). Only by assuming a certain homogeneity among citizens can Walzer take 'particularities' into account. No wonder he often speaks about the national association of citizens as a certain 'club' with its own identity and with equal rights for all members.

Freedom for Walzer is neither a negative freedom that protects citizens, nor a positive freedom that consists of political participation and a concern for the common good, but a freedom that is connected to the terms 'plurality', 'heterogeneity' and to different power settings in a multitude of spheres. In Walzer's mind, politics is not a separate sphere like art, economics or education. It has an overall influence on all other spheres. We cannot therefore simply find a competent elite and build fences between politics and all other spheres.

No wonder Walzer struggles with himself more on this point than on any other theme in his book. On the one hand, he disagrees with the classical political theorist Plato, who gives a picture of the state as a ship that has to be ruled by a competent captain. Here, Walzer's republican heart says that politics is not solely the realm of a competent elite but of all citizens. On the other hand, he cannot deny his liberal longing for pluralism and his former insight (1970) that political work is simply too demanding for us all.

Walzer finds the solution to this dilemma by making a sharp distinction between the citizen politician and the citizen voter. He presents a republican argument – in the sense of the values of political participation – where it concerns the citizen politician; and a liberal argument – in the sense of equal rights – where it concerns the citizen voter. Subsequently, political judgement differs for the citizen voter and for the citizen politician. The voter may use his or her own conception of the good life in questions concerning the aims of politics, whereas the politician has to think of the most efficient means to achieve them.

Will Kymlicka

In *Liberalism, Community and Culture* (1989) Will Kymlicka defends group specified rights for ethnic minorities. He approaches this from a liberal perspective with the old liberal appeals to liberty and equality, and argues that most liberals have wrongly assumed a homogeneous society in their theory. He takes this argument further in *Multicultural Citizenship: A Liberal Theory of Minority Rights* (1995).

His argument starts off with the value of freedom. Freedom for Kymlicka implies freedom of choice. In his version of liberalism, it is essential that every individual is able to make her or his own choices over what sort of life to live, and is able to revise these choices. The fact that we can get it wrong is important (1995: 81). Freedom does not only imply free choice but also a context of choice. We do not make choices as atomistic individuals, but as part of a societal culture which is institutionally embodied, tends to be territorially concentrated and based on a shared language (p. 76). This societal culture is constitutive of our identity, self-respect and feeling of belonging, and provides us with an intelligible context of choice (p. 105). Cultural membership provides the 'meaningful options' and the 'boundaries of the imaginable' (p. 89). Our culture also determines how other people perceive us, which affects the way in which we see ourselves. According to Kymlicka, '[i]f a culture is not generally respected, then the dignity and self-respect of its members will also be threatened' (1995: 89).

In Kymlicka's view, most people can best flourish within their own culture, although some can also do this in other cultures. Because people are deeply connected to their own culture and because it provides their meaningful context of choice, we cannot simply take this context away from others. Liberals can only allow the disintegration of culture if it occurs because of a lack of interest or through amendments by the members themselves. As the viability of a culture promotes people's self-identity and thus their autonomy, liberals should support it, according to Kymlicka. He argues (p. 125) that 'in multi-nation states, some people's cultural membership can only be recognized and protected by endorsing group-differentiated rights within the state'.

He qualifies this argument by stating that this might imply protection of the cultures of indigenous people in the sense of self-government rights, but not those of immigrants, because they voluntarily enter a new societal culture. However, polyethnic rights may be justified for migrants, such as subsidies for cultural activities or exemption from certain laws. Furthermore, representation rights can most easily be defended for indigenous people, but also for other groups such as migrants, blacks or women. According to Kymlicka, there is nothing inherently illiberal or undemocratic in group representation, but the exact forms of it have to be defended within a particular context (p. 150).

Equality does not mean equal rights but equal participation in the national culture. He argues that some groups, like women, still feel excluded from participation in the national culture despite possessing the common rights of citizenship. Kymlicka does not plead for a universalistic theory of citizenship but for, in Iris Young's terms, a differentiated citizenship: apart from equal individual rights there are also group-specified rights. He calls citizenship an 'inherently group-differentiated notion' (p. 124) because certain rights are only given to certain groups for the protection of their group membership. No country allows universal citizenship, according to Kymlicka, but some countries integrate citizens in a uniform way and other countries in a group-specified way. He argues nevertheless that many forms of group-differentiated citizenship are consistent with the liberal principles of freedom and equality.

A fully integrative citizenship must take group differences into account, Kymlicka argues. What this means is not difficult to conclude from his book: allowing individuals within these groups (even though Kymlicka restricts himself to ethnic groups) special civic and representation rights, and allowing groups themselves subsidies for cultural activities and (if a civil war threatens) self-government rights.

Given his idea of equality, it is remarkable that Kymlicka has little to say about participation. He does note that there is a growing fear that even liberal democracies may decline without the public spirit of citizens. Yet he assumes the solution to be a matter of identity, integration and participation in the national culture. Lack of public spirit can be resolved by distributing civic or political rights (and special representation rights for minority groups). It does not seem relevant to Kymlicka whether this leads to *more* participation. Kymlicka also seldom discusses political judgement apart from stating his basic idea that we cannot expect an endorsement of 'national' values by all groups and that group difference has to be taken into account.

Similarities

If we look at the similarities among these five variations of social liberalism, bearing in mind that there is a main version of social liberalism and some atypical versions, we can obtain a more qualified picture of social liberalism. Within the main version of social-liberal citizenship citizens are free and should remain free from the state; all adults should have equal rights and be treated equally before the law; one person should have one vote with which he or she can choose a representative; and citizens should be liberated from poverty. There should be justice, but only in the public sphere. Social equality does not imply equality for different members of a family. Finally, political judgement is a matter of finding out what justice is, and such judgement is not a matter for ordinary citizens, but for political theorists or philosophers.

Within the atypical versions of social liberalism more attention is paid to differences other than class differences. Differences in ability, in identity and in ethnicity are addressed. Yet social liberals as a whole are notably silent on the issue of gender differences.

The social-liberal concept of citizenship can not simply be described as an equality philosophy. It also contains an emphasis on freedom, protection against poverty and minimal state intervention. One observes that the citizenship concept is somewhat passive since social liberals comprehend citizenship primarily in terms of rights and formal status. They are hesitant to incorporate desirable duties, types of participation, values and virtues into their concept of citizenship. Social liberals prefer a thin concept, so that citizens will have a maximum degree of personal freedom. These aspects are just as important in the social-liberal concept of citizenship as the ideal of equality.

Social liberals on equality and difference

Feminists have claimed that liberalism is a philosophy of equality for men and the public sphere and that it opposes difference. This feminist criticism is more relevant to classical liberalism than to social liberalism, as social liberalism has tried to overcome some class and gender inequalities, whereas classical liberalism simply excluded women and the lower classes from equality. Furthermore, feminist criticism also appears to be more applicable to the main version of social liberalism (that of Marshall and Rawls), than to the atypical versions of it. Ackerman, Walzer and Kymlicka cannot be accused of presenting a simple equality philosophy, as all of them argue that social liberalism should reflect more upon the group differences of some minorities.

Moreover, in general the social-liberal approach to differences is more complex than feminists contend. Social liberals do not all simply opt for equality over difference. Furthermore, the meanings of 'equality' and 'difference' depend, for social liberals, on the sub-theme of citizenship concerned. For instance, equality does not always simply mean equal treatment because that could mean that we have to treat everyone as a representative or everyone as a voter. This cannot be the case, as social liberals make a strong distinction between the two.

The approach of social liberals to equality and difference is further qualified in another way. There are certain distinctions to be made which run through all sub-themes of citizenship. Several are at stake here: the status of biological differences; the importance of social differences; the public–private spheres; and the theme of individual difference versus group difference.

According to social liberals, biological differences should not affect one's political status. There are only two exceptional biological differences, both relating to one's rational capability (Ackerman 1980: 75, 96). First, being a child implies that one has not yet obtained mature rationality. Therefore, during one's youth, one is a citizen-in-being who is in need of protection. Secondly, someone who is seriously mentally disabled cannot be perceived as an autonomous citizen able to reason and be held accountable for his or her deeds. These individuals, therefore, may also be excluded from particular civil and political rights. According to some social liberals, this is also the case with the 'temporary mentally disabled' such as drug addicts or alcoholics. These people need protection against themselves (Hart 1963: 31–34).

Differences in social position should not affect one's official citizenship status either, social liberals suggest. Everyone, be they capitalist or blue-collar worker, has only one vote and has the same civil rights. However, social liberals differ from classical liberals and neo-liberals in demanding state benefits for those who cannot provide an income for themselves.

Furthermore, social liberals make a distinction between the private sphere (the family), in which one can enact one's differences, and the public sphere, which centres on minimum assumptions of what justice, correct public behaviour, politics and citizenship are (Hampshire 1980). We may differ enormously in private, as long as we can maintain the idea of civil, social and political equality in public.

Finally, it should be noted that difference is mostly reviewed in a positive way if it concerns individual difference, and in a negative way if it concerns group difference (with the exception of Kymlicka). Individual differentiation indicates that we have an autonomous personality, a free will, individuality. By contrast, group difference refers to the prejudices of society towards certain groups, discrimination against others, inequality, constrained growth, and injustice (Dworkin 1987a, 1987b). Most social liberals are positive about difference insofar as it is a difference for which someone is personally responsible and insofar as it does not harm others in the exercise of their rights (Hart 1963). They are negative about those differences that are unchosen and by which one is discriminated against or disadvantaged; these differences should be made irrelevant in public life.

Within the social-liberal concept of citizenship, groups are able to stand up and complain that they are discriminated against because of their group difference. However, social liberals, with the exception of Kymlicka (cf. Kukathas 1992a, 1992b; Kymlicka 1989), seem to have far more difficulties with those groups who claim that their differences should be respected and maintained.

*　　*　　*

In this chapter I have examined whether the feminist image of social liberalism is correct. Feminists have depicted liberalism as a philosophy of equality for men and the public sphere, which opposes difference. I have to conclude that this image is right as far as classical liberalism is concerned, not entirely correct for social liberalism, and more correct for the main version of social liberalism than for the atypical versions of Kymlicka, Ackerman and Walzer. Social liberalism involves much more than the equality philosophy feminists have referred to. Other aspects are just as important in its theory: freedom, the protection against poverty and the passive, formal and legal character of its notion of citizenship. Besides, social-liberal thought on equality and difference is qualified much more than feminists have contended. Social liberals do take account of difference but usually only in the sense of socio-economic differences between classes. Other differences are usually ignored or considered irrelevant to citizenship (again with the important exception of Kymlicka).

This does not imply that all feminist critiques of and alternatives to social liberalism are valueless. It is too early at this stage to say whether the concept of social-liberal citizenship should incorporate more equality, as humanist feminists argue, or more difference, as woman-centred and deconstructionist feminists argue. In order to make such judgements we need to examine in detail the feminist critiques of and alternatives to social-liberal citizenship in the context of the six sub-themes of citizenship: liberty, rights, social equality, political identity, political representation/participation and political judgement.

Note

1 I have used this book rather than his *Political Liberalism* (1993) to incorporate a more Kantian approach and one that contrasts with Walzer's and Kymlicka's social-liberal approaches.

PART II

SUB-THEMES OF CITIZENSHIP

4

Liberty

Since the 1960s, 'liberty' has been a hot topic in western political debate. In the official canon of political philosophy the most important discussion on freedom was one that concerned the question of how freedom was to be combined with equality. Central authors in this discussion were John Rawls (1971) and Robert Nozick (1975). However, the discussion was not connected to women's liberty.

Recently different angles on liberty have entered the official canon of political philosophy. The first is that of postmodernism, which fundamentally doubts the possibility of freedom. Michel Foucault (1970) introduced some notions of this by suggesting that almost everything we say, do or think is a product of existing dominant discourses, though he still allowed for the idea of resistance. Richard Rorty (1989) and Jean François Lyotard (1984), however, were more radical and consistently drew the political conclusions of postmodernism: politics is not a struggle for freedom, but an ironic play with words. As far as this discussion was relevant to women's liberty, it made it even more difficult to proclaim.

The second perspective, which is taken more seriously is that of cultural difference. Will Kymlicka (1989, 1995) opened the door here by proclaiming as a liberal that the liberty of cultural minorities needs to be rethought in political philosophy (cf. Kukathas 1993; Wilson and Yeatman 1995). However, because in this discussion cultural minorities are considered as ethnic minorities only, the discussion has not been linked to women either.

The lack of attention to the issue of women's liberty within the official canon of political philosophy is striking, since liberty appears to be of no value if it is not also relevant to women. A long-standing yet separate feminist debate on women's liberty can be noted, starting from Mary Astell's question in *Some Reflections on Marriage* (1706: 151) 'if all Men are born Free, how is it that all Women are born Slaves?'

The fact that this seems to have hardly influenced the canon is perhaps not so remarkable. Some feminists wrote about male philosophers and related their ideas about women to the latter's concept of freedom. Other feminist theorists wrote books in which they argued that women were oppressed, and examined which feminist theory and politics would offer women liberation: liberal, socialist or radical feminism. Yet, despite the fact that feminism was called the 'women's liberation movement' and despite the fact that feminists claimed to have a better understanding of liberty than, for instance, social liberals, there have been no extensive feminist philosophical treatises about liberty.

Moreover, hidden in the feminist debate are different notions of liberty itself. For instance, in the abortion debate (Dahlerup 1986: Chs 1–4), most feminists have claimed that women should be free to do whatever they want to do, for reasons of bodily integrity and self-determination. By contrast, in the pornography debate, many feminists (Rich 1986; Russo 1987) have argued that the distribution of pornography should be restricted because it is harmful and oppressive for women. So at times liberty for feminists has implied self-determination, and at other times restriction, protection and censorship.

In this chapter I will examine social-liberal and feminist ideas of liberty. In the first part I will describe their ideas on liberty, oppression and liberation. In the second part I will judge which notion of liberty is most useful for female citizens through critical dialogue with each position.

Social liberals on liberty

Social liberals perceive women in western democracies as free because they assume that all citizens in western liberal democracies are free and equal citizens. Formal and legal freedom has been crucial in the struggle against discrimination. Women now have the same formal rights as men and receive the same protection from the state. There are no longer legal barriers for women; they have open access to all educational institutions, professions and political positions. According to social liberals, women are free to do whatever they want, because they are equal citizens by law.

Furthermore, social liberals perceive a woman as a free citizen because of their idea of liberty as negative liberty. This term is defined by Isaiah Berlin in his essay 'Two Conceptions of Liberty' (1969: 134) as the freedom from intervention in personal decision-making, in particular by the state. It aims at limiting state intervention to the public sphere: the sphere outside the family. Women are as much protected against intervention by the state and other citizens as are men, social liberals argue. Women too have the privacy of the family in which they can safeguard themselves against intervention by other citizens. Feminists may argue that women are oppressed, but women are consenting adults and as long as no tangible harm is done, they are to be considered free citizens. Because of this idea of negative liberty, social liberals do not look at inequalities in the participation of the sexes in the public realm or division of power between men and women in the private realm.

Some things should be added to this social-liberal idea of liberty to avoid misunderstanding or exaggeration. Within their idea of negative liberty social liberals include the right to be free from oppression by poverty. Moreover, negative liberty for social liberals is not the same as formal freedom since some material conditions are considered necessary so that all classes have the financial means to exercise their freedom (Dahl 1970: 105–115; Roche 1992). Furthermore, social liberals accept that this requires an active state. The state should guarantee people's citizenship rights, protect them from harmful activities of other citizens, provide welfare benefits, and ensure that policies will work in the interest of the economically disadvantaged (Rawls 1971).

If these conditions for liberty are met, the following social-liberal image of liberty arises. In the public sphere, there will be justice: all people will be treated equally, their liberties will be safeguarded and there is a moderate egalitarianism between people. In the private sphere, people will be able to be really free. Because they do not have to live together with all kinds of different people, they can cultivate their own version of the good life.

Two main exceptions to this social-liberal idea of liberty need to be mentioned: Will Kymlicka and Ronald Dworkin. Kymlicka differs by suggesting that in order to be free as a person, one must also be free to express oneself as a member of a group. He argues (1989, 1995) that to be a free person one should be able to choose one's own preferences in life. Thus the culture of a threatened minority community must be protected in order that a child born into the community will have the life-style option later in life to live in this community and is able to identify with this community and its values. In order to promote freedom, then, according to Kymlicka, a liberal must support group rights to protect a minority community.

Dworkin differs from the main social-liberal picture because he does not support negative freedom. In his essay 'Liberty and Liberalism' (1987a: 259–266) he makes an explicit distinction between liberty as licence and liberty as independence. Liberty as licence, according to Dworkin (p. 262) means 'the degree to which a person is free from social or legal constraint to do what he might wish to do'. Liberty as independence, on the other hand, means 'the status of a person as independent and equal rather than subservient'. We can interpret liberty as licence as the already familiar liberal concept of negative freedom, but liberty as independence offers another liberal concept of freedom.

Liberty for humanist feminists: self-determination and emancipation

Humanist feminists emphasize that women are still oppressed or have a far smaller degree of freedom than men have, as the title of Michèle Barrett's book *Women's Oppression Today* (1980) illustrates. They have acknowledged that formal freedom – as social liberals have pleaded – is crucial.

However, they argue that formal freedom is not enough as it has not led to women's liberty. In their view, there is still a great deal of direct and indirect discrimination against women. According to humanist feminists, in our concept of liberty we must look at both formal and material liberty.

Furthermore, humanist feminists argue that social liberals do not see that women, like men, are also oppressed by gender roles. To be really free to do whatever one wants, one needs to be free from the kind of social conditioning that produces stereotypes of men and women (Chodorow 1978). A good example of the humanist feminist position on liberty can be found in Susan James's article 'The Good-Enough Citizen' (1992), in which James defends the liberal idea of independence for feminist purposes, and suggests that we should interpret this ideal as deriving from the value of self-esteem.

Humanist feminists have also criticized social liberals for applying liberty to families, but not to individuals (Okin 1989). In this respect, they argue, social liberals can only perceive the lack of freedom in poor households. They are not able to see the lack of women's freedom in the private sphere. Humanist feminists argue that if the state does not intervene to uphold the idea of negative freedom *within* families, then it is only protecting men's and not women's negative freedom.

The way in which women ought to be liberated from their oppressed state is ambiguous for humanist feminists. Egalitarian humanist feminists embrace the idea of emancipation more than liberal humanist feminists. The former argue that, as long as women are not doing the same things as men are doing, they are not emancipated. An active state that furthers emancipation is required. According to egalitarian feminists (and particularly socialist feminists), women who do not want to emancipate themselves have a false consciousness (cf. Jaggar 1983a: 44, 149–151).

Liberal humanist feminists have far more difficulties stating this because they try to combine the idea of emancipation with the idea of self-determination. On the one hand liberal feminists think that as long as women remain behind men in their careers, they are not really free and emancipated (Firestone 1970). On the other hand real freedom is doing whatever you want to do, and in this sense women should be able to determine for themselves whether or not they want a career. They thus fall back on a notion of negative liberty as non-intervention. Another example of the use made of negative liberty by humanist feminists can be found in the abortion debate, where they argue that each individual has the right to decide about his/her own body.

Liberty for woman-centred feminists: feminization

The woman-centred feminist position also assumes that women are oppressed or discriminated against in social-liberal states, yet their argument is from a different perspective. Women's problem is not that they are forced into female positions or gender roles, but that these positions and roles are given little value. In other words, women should be free to choose these female roles and positions, which should be judged as being just as important as male roles. At the moment, however, as Anna Yeatman (1984: 175) claims, 'patriarchal' citizenship limits women, as women have to face the enforced acquisition of masculine individuality when they enter civil society.

The emancipation-liberation strategy of humanist feminists is merely an assimilation strategy, according to the woman-centred feminist perspective. For instance, Iris Young (1990b: 158–159) remarks that 'liberation as assimilation' assumes that the truly non-sexist society is one in which sex would be the functional equivalent of eye colour in today's society. Physiological sex differences would have no significance for a person's sense of identity or for the way in which others regard him or her. Being a man or a woman would bear no relevance to one's political rights, duties or political activities, nor to the direction of state policy.

The ideal of 'liberation as assimilation' has, at first glance, three strong points, according to Young (1990b: 163–164): it exposes the arbitrariness of group-based social distinctions that are thought natural and necessary, it presents a clear and unambiguous standard of equality and justice, and it maximizes choice by abolishing the political significance of group differences while retaining diversity in the private sphere.

Nevertheless, Young argues that there are many good reasons to reject the ideal of 'liberation as assimilation'. A society without group differences is neither possible nor desirable. According to her (p. 164), '[t]he achievement of formal equality does not eliminate social differences, and rhetorical commitment to the sameness of persons makes it impossible even to name how those differences presently structure privilege and oppression'. She points out that blindness to difference will disadvantage non-privileged groups, because they deviate from an allegedly neutral standard.

Within woman-centred feminism, liberation as 'feminization' is preferred. The female way of life should have just as high a status as the male way of life. Freedom is closely related to the idea of 'equal respect'. According to woman-centred feminism (e.g. Elshtain 1981), public life and politics would improve if women's activities, opinions and virtues were taken as an example (sometimes in addition to the existing system).

Feminization implies that negative freedom is inadequate, as Catharine MacKinnon points out in *Toward a Feminist Theory of the State* (1989: 164):

> If one group is socially granted the positive freedom to do whatever it wants to another group, to determine that the second group will be and do this rather than that, no amount of negative freedom legally guaranteed to the second group will make it the equal of the first.

Real freedom implies the replacement of patriarchal values by feminine values or other values that women are able to formulate in a power-free debate.

A further differentiation can be established within woman-centred feminism as to what liberation as feminization means. On the one hand, we can distinguish the 'women's forum feminists', for whom feminization means exploring female difference in a separate political group (e.g. Fraser 1990). Iris Marion Young (1990b: 163) speaks in this context of 'liberation as democratic cultural pluralism'. Women are one of the socially and culturally differentiated groups, who mutually respect one another and affirm one another in their differences. Like other women's forum feminists, she argues that there will only be real liberty if women's values, activities, virtues and opinions are respected as much as men's.

Young (1990b: 166) mentions four advantages in this ideal. First, the positive side of affirming group differences in unequal circumstances is that it is liberating and empowering. Secondly, it causes a relativism of the dominant culture. Thirdly, it promotes a notion of group solidarity and, fourthly, it provides standpoints from which a critique of prevailing institutions and norms is possible.

On the other hand, we can distinguish 'women's morality feminists' like Jean Elshtain (1990) and Sarah Ruddick (1980), for whom feminization does not imply separatism, but changing mainstream ideas and practices. Even if 'male' or patriarchal values were only shared by men, this would still limit people's possible freedom. In order to be really free, female values like caring should be accepted by everyone. These feminists want to change the existing paradigm through which we judge liberation. The new paradigm should be based on women's own experiences.

Woman-centred feminists have used the pornography case to question the social-liberal concept of negative liberty. Woman-centred feminists claim that pornography is oppressive to women, because it imposes male sexual standards and puts women in the position of the sexual object and victim. This is not a free-choice argument and thus not an argument for negative liberty, but an argument for intervention. Freedom has to be combined with equal respect. As Christina Spaulding (1988–89: 160) remarks in her article 'Anti-Pornography Laws as a Claim for Equal Respect':

> If equal respect is reformulated to take account of persons in this richer sense, then it will reach beyond the formal equality of equal citizenship, and will comprehend the ways in which systems of subordinations bar full membership in society.

This implies that the content of 'pornography', or rather 'erotica', should change, not just the conditions of its distribution (MacKinnon 1987).

Liberty for deconstructionist feminists: what is liberty anyway?

The deconstructionist-feminist position (Nicholson 1990) questions the Enlightenment beliefs that we are all free by virtue of our human nature and that we can make autonomous judgements. It tends to see liberty as a dangerous illusion. It is an illusion because we are not free from the influence of others in our reflections and judgement. It is dangerous because the Enlightenment ideal of liberty will lead us to demand independence in every area and this is not always the most sensible strategy. It is also dangerous because it overlooks existing dependencies.

Moreover, deconstructionist feminism assumes that it is foolish to develop a general theory of women's oppression (Barrett and Phillips 1992). Such a generalization may stereotype women and place them in a victim role. This will not help women. It is better to look at small opportunities for change, and to be aware of situations in which some women have a relatively better position than others. Therefore, feminists should conduct more studies of women's specific conditions.

According to the deconstructionist-feminist perspective, we should be careful of an either/or choice in liberty in the sense of forcing women to choose between a male or female route of freedom. Instead it pleads for plurality in a much broader sense than gender plurality (Gunew and Yeatman 1993).

Deconstructionist feminists see Berlin's concept of negative liberty as detrimental to women. In her article 'Constructing and Deconstructing Liberty' (1993), Diana Coole argues that this concept suggests a division between a private vacuous haven for subjectivity and a public sphere in which individuals are legitimately subjected to power. According to Coole, within this framework there remains no essential female space or feminine self to be defended: neither exists in the absence of the power that constructs them. It also defines women's liberty in a negative way – women's liberty is that of the 'other'. The female subject achieves unprescribed vacuity.

In the deconstructionist-feminist view, Berlin's idea of positive liberty does not present a viable alternative for feminists either. Positive liberty is, according to Isaiah Berlin (1969: 134), the idea that 'I am my own master'. This does not presuppose the withdrawal of interference, but presupposes rational choice and control of the mind over the passions. In this idea of positive liberty, a personality is split into two: the transcendent, dominant controller, and the empirical bundle of desires and passions to be disciplined and brought to heel. The kind of self-realization which this liberty aims for is not independence, but total self-identification with a specific principle or ideal.

Here Diana Coole can again serve as an example of deconstructionist feminism. She argues that Berlin's idea of positive liberty as self-mastery invokes a quite specific view of what the authentic, free subject would be like: essential, rational, autonomous and self-controlled. According to Coole (1993: 94) this conception of positive freedom also excludes femininity, because femininity is seen as the other side of reason and control.

The only choice open to us, according to deconstructionist feminists, is to be aware of how we are categorized as a result of power relations and to try to stop ourselves submitting to these attacks (cf. Di Stefano 1994; Yeatman 1994a). After all, we still have some capacity for agency even though we cannot speak independently of the language around us. We can play with it, we can use irony and we can use negative words as positive labels (Haraway 1990).

The feminist debate

If we look at the feminist debate on liberty, we see feminists fighting social-liberal assumptions from almost opposite perspectives. What humanist feminists perceive as real emancipation, woman-centred feminists consider restrictive assimilation. What woman-centred feminists see as respect for women, humanist feminists label as 'stereotype', 'discrimination' and 'inequality'.

The feminist debate on liberty is not helped by the emancipation/feminization dichotomy. The choice of being either free as a man or free as a woman has rather sidetracked the feminist debate on liberty. This is not only because more plurality is needed, as deconstructionist feminists indicate, but also because more crucial difficulties in the social-liberal idea of liberty need to be emphasized by feminists.

Deconstructionist feminists provide us with tools to analyse this debate. They cannot, however, provide us with an alternative idea of what liberty ought to be (cf. Soper 1990). They are too sceptical about the ideas of liberty and autonomy. This may have the serious political consequence that women will no longer be able to demand genuine liberty and autonomy. It can, in effect, hinder women's entry to the public sphere and women's inclusion in decision-making bodies.

Feminists cannot afford the luxury of giving up the idea of liberty and autonomy. If feminists did not have 'free female citizens' as their aim, they would lose an important oppositional tool in the citizenship debate. They would lose the opportunity to say that women are second-class citizens because they are not free. After all, is it not precisely freedom that forms the difference between a citizen and a subject? Not all women need to take the power route, but if women are seldom present in decision-making bodies, it implies that women as a group are still not free (or more specifically, in Young's terms, that women are still powerless).

Oppression

Perhaps it is better to start at the other end – not with the ideal of liberty itself, but with oppression and the situation of women. Within western liberal democracies women as a group are still less free than men as a group. In a democratic state that promises all adults equal citizenship this ought to be unacceptable, because it means that women are not equal citizens. Being a woman ought not restrict one's freedom in a western liberal democracy. Yet it still does.

It is wrong to speak in general – as social liberalism does – of citizens as free individuals. This overlooks the specific pressures under which some people find themselves. Defining everyone as a free citizen does not allow us to make distinctions as to their degree of liberty. Having defined everyone as being free in theory makes social liberals blind to oppression in practice. Besides, an individualistic perspective is too restrictive to be helpful in making distinctions concerning liberty. One may have a privileged position as a judge, but still often be discriminated against as a woman. Therefore a group perspective is also needed. Kymlicka (1989, 1995) offers a group perspective, but only one of ethnic communities. Other social liberals sometimes take class perspectives into account. They are blind to differences between sexes, however, so do not perceive differences in the freedom of men and women.

Although in western democracies people are neither completely oppressed nor completely free, it still makes sense to talk about women as a relatively oppressed group. This argument can be effectively made by using Iris Young's categorization of oppression and applying it to women. According to Young (1990b: Ch. 2), it is wrong to speak about oppression as a general category which can be applied to all political minorities. In this sense, the term does not have much analytical value. We should, in her view, differentiate between exploitation, powerlessness, marginalization, violence and cultural imperialism.

Following on from and extending upon the views of Marx, Young says (1990b: 53) 'the injustice of exploitation consists in social processes that bring about a transfer of energies from one group to another to produce unequal distributions, and in the way in which social institutions enable a few to accumulate while they constrain many more'. Women are exploited as a group since they work more hours than men and more often care for and labour for the benefit of others.

Marginalization, according to Young (p. 53), is the process of expelling a whole category of people from useful participation in socio-economic life, and thus potentially subjecting them to severe material deprivation and even extermination. People on the margin are those whom the system of labour cannot, or will not, use. Women more than men are dependent on the benefits and authorities of social security systems – as unemployed people or as part-time workers. Women are also isolated in the private sphere much more than men.

Powerlessness is defined by Young (p. 57) as a lack of the authority, status and sense of self that professionals tend to have. Women are nearly absent from decision-making positions and are thus powerless as a group, as she suggests.

Furthermore, according to Young (p. 59) cultural imperialism involves the universalization of a dominant group's experience and culture and its establishment as the norm. Women are, in her view, a culturally dominated group because they are marked out by stereotypes more often than men and, at the same time, are rendered invisible.

Violence, finally, refers to both systematic and random physical violence or harassment against the members of a particular group. Women suffer from this violence more than men, so are in Young's sense an oppressed group.

Formal versus material freedom

What conceptualization of liberty will help us to understand and overcome these difficulties? Social liberals and humanist feminists put great hopes in the concept of *formal*, legal freedom. Formal liberty is terribly important for women in the struggle against legal discrimination and we must note that this liberty has not been realized for women everywhere. However, in western liberal democracies this is not the crucial problem for women. Formal, legal freedom for women is almost completely realized. There is almost nothing to which women do not have access, as social liberals rightly indicate.

Besides, many of women's difficulties occur not in situations in which the formal rules are disregarded, but in 'ruleless' or 'lawless' situations. Women's liberty is often restricted where there is no rule or law that women can invoke in their defence. Sometimes the solution will be to make a rule for these occasions (for instance that rape in marriage is a crime). At other times more regulation will be impossible or undesirable, if we want to avoid totalitarianism (for instance, the banning of all sexual objectification of women). Therefore, feminists must not concentrate on formal freedom.

A concentration on *material* freedom (see Karl Marx *Zur Judenfrage* (*On the Jewish Question*) [1844]) for women is necessary. It is fundamental for certain material conditions to be guaranteed before people can exercise formal liberties. Yet these conditions are much wider than those proposed by social liberals. Social liberals only argue for redistribution of incomes between families. With a view to women's condition, a redistribution of other goods and positions is also necessary, and furthermore, redistribution should not only take place between families, but also between individual members of families. I will return to this issue in the chapter on social equality.

Negative versus positive liberty

Woman-centred feminists have rightly criticized the notion of negative liberty. A notion that suggests that the family is a safe haven cannot be helpful to women. The family has proven not to be a power-free sphere. If the state does not intervene in family life, a woman has no avenue of redress when her male partner uses violence, does not give her any money, tells her what to do or not to do.

The issue of pornography highlights the limitations in the private sphere of the concept of liberty as self-determination, and thus of negative liberty. It appears to rule out any restrictions on the production and consumption of pornography. If humanist feminists want to argue against pornography, they have to use other arguments, for example 'It is harmful' or, 'Not all producers and consumers are consenting adults.'

However, in some respects woman-centred feminists' criticism of negative liberty is misfocused. They criticize the liberal negative conception of freedom only from the viewpoint that it leads to assimilation into a 'male' life-style. They overlook another problem with the concept – the assumption that the private sphere is the sphere of freedom. They do not offer a view of freedom in the public sphere. Yet women's freedom in both spheres is restricted and, from a citizenship perspective, it is liberty in public life that matters. Liberty in private life is of course important, but in this context only as a pre-condition to the realization of public freedom. A citizenship perspective which is helpful for women needs to look at freedom in both spheres.

Woman-centred feminists have argued that positive liberty is necessary, but without exploring the concept very deeply. They have argued that it is important to be free *as women*. Indeed, as even the social liberal Kymlicka indicates, it is crucial to realize oneself not only as an individual but as a member of a group. Respect for women as women is therefore required. It is also true that at times, if one is attacked as a member of a group, one should perhaps defend oneself as a member of a group. Yet the general statement 'free as women' may easily lead to an uncritical attitude towards all opinions and actions of women.

My other objection is that woman-centred feminists have not specified what it is that women will be doing when they are 'free as women' and thus have not amended Berlin's notion of positive liberty. Traditionally, in Berlin's overview positive liberty was identified with sovereignty. Yet, this is not necessarily so. I want to refer here to Hannah Arendt's notion of positive liberty, which differs from that proposed by Berlin. According to Arendt, in her essay 'What is Freedom' (1961: 164):

> Politically, this identification of freedom with sovereignty is perhaps the most pernicious and dangerous consequence of the philosophical equation of freedom and free will.

Instead of positive liberty as sovereignty Arendt suggests positive liberty as participation (Voet 1988a). She perceives positive freedom as realizing ourselves as political animals, invoking an idea of 'positive' liberty that is democratic and participatory. According to Arendt (1961: 153), 'men are free . . . as long as they act, neither before nor after; for to be free and to act are the same'. This freedom has nothing to do with 'to be free from', 'the free will' or 'sovereignty'. As in Benjamin Constant's classic essay 'The Liberty of the Ancients Compared with That of the Modern' (1819), freedom is not the opposite of power, but is power at work in collective action.

Groups which act do not act because of some ideal of the common good that will transcend differences, but because of an ideal of the common life in which group differences and individual differences can and should be disclosed. Thus, freedom is not obtained by hiding away in some sort of walled, private sphere, but by active participation in groups.

Liberty and participation are related for two reasons: one inherent and one instrumental. First, participation in decision-making is in itself an important and highly regarded liberty. As Arendt argues (1958), it is one of the most profound ways in which we realize ourselves as human and, therefore, acting beings. Secondly, participation forms part of a wider structure of liberties, because the extent to which this liberty is accorded and exercised will usually also affect the extent to which liberty is available in other areas of social life.

What is necessary for this 'positive liberty as participation' is a public space where citizens act together visibly for an audience (Arendt 1961: 154), where they can realize themselves as individuals or as members of a group. It is exactly this kind of liberty that is crucial for citizenship, and it is exactly this kind of liberty that women lack. Women as a group are still oppressed, are often marginalized within the private sphere, and, in particular, are seldom present in political activities and in decision-making. In this respect it is worrying that at the very moment when women are starting to liberate themselves, public identity and public space are under ridicule or question and that the existence of liberty and autonomy is itself being questioned.

Oppression and liberty

If it is true, as Iris Young assumes (1990b: Ch. 2), that oppression is not one thing but several (exploitation, marginalization, powerlessness, cultural imperialism and violence), then we also need to differentiate liberation strategies for different kinds of oppression instead of offering only one strategy, such as Young's 'democratic cultural pluralism'. This means for instance that we may see abortion and pornography as different cases. In the case of abortion, women from many countries still suffer the powerlessness that results from other people deciding their fate. In the case of pornography, however, women tend to suffer more from cultural imperialism: masculine or patriarchal norms of sexuality are imposed on them. This may imply different liberation strategies. Both liberation cases, however, need to be accompanied by Arendt's concept of positive liberty: feminist action and participation are required, not only to get laws enacted, but also to influence and generate public morality and culture.

It seems logical that the task of realizing women's material freedom should be a task for three partners: the state, men and women. It should be a task for the state because furthering women's inclusion as equal citizens will directly benefit the democratic state, given the incorporation of new talents and skills. It should be a task for men because, although they benefit from women's second-class status and lesser freedom, the task should arise out of solidarity with a group of co-citizens who are restricted in their freedom. In a democratic state, the political relationships between groups of citizens ought to be characterized by equal respect, not disrespect, neglect or even oppression.

Finally, it should be a task for women themselves. After all, perhaps what August Bebel said is true: why should men try to end women's dependence in the family and society, when this dependency directly benefits them? According to Bebel (1910: 72):

> It gratifies their vanity, feeds their pride, and suits their interests to play the part of master and lord, and in this role, they are like rulers and well nigh inaccessible to reason. This makes it all the more imperative on women to exert themselves in bringing about new conditions, which will enable them to free themselves from this degrading position. Women have as little to hope from men as the workmen from the middle classes.

Although Bebel himself, through this argument, shows that some men may further women's liberation, women need to take responsibility for liberation themselves. Only by taking part can women influence the direction in which it is going and avoid liberating themselves on male terms only. If women want to find out what other terms are possible, they will have to participate in the process of defining, discussing and negotiating them.

*   *   *

In this chapter I have suggested that feminists have criticized social liberals too much on the emancipation-feminization line of argument. Through this, the most important difficulties with the social-liberal view of liberty have been largely overlooked: the fact that social liberalism already defines everyone as free citizens and therefore cannot make distinctions, the fact that it has a predominantly individualistic perspective on liberty from which it is unable to see differences in freedom between groups (such as men and women), and the fact that it confines itself to a formal and negative view of liberty with attention to material conditions only in the sense of more class equality. Such a view of liberty cannot encourage women to participate as citizens in the public sphere.

Only a positive notion of liberty as participation can do so. Liberty is not something every citizen simply receives from the state, but something that has to be sustained continuously by enacting it. It needs and is based upon formal liberty, but also upon material conditions and respect for women. After all, it is not usually in formal liberty that there are inequalities between the sexes, but in material, substantive freedom. This is crucial for citizenship, if the term 'equal citizenship' is to refer to the freedom to act for all citizens.

This notion of liberty also questions the place and interpretation of rights that social liberals have offered within their idea of citizenship. In particular, I will argue that a notion of liberty as participation questions the centrality of rights within citizenship.

5

Rights

Rights are often seen as fundamental to citizenship. In every citizenship vocabulary the status of citizenship gives citizens access to important rights. These are not all the rights one can possibly think of, because there remains a key distinction between human rights and citizenship rights. Human rights may be defined in international resolutions, but citizenship rights are those rights that a particular state guarantees its citizens by law. Citizenship rights are thus concrete, specific, legal and can be claimed in court cases. It is in the context of this meaning that I want to discuss rights in this chapter.

In citizenship theory and political theory during the last decades citizenship rights have usually been discussed in terms of individual rights. It is only very recently that discussion in academic circles has centred on the need for group rights. Mostly this is done with regard to 'cultural' minorities, which in practice implies ethnic minorities. For instance, the argument put forward by the social liberal Will Kymlicka (1989, 1995) is that indigenous groups and migrant groups may need special 'collective rights' to protect their cultures. Group rights however are usually considered as contrary to the idea of equal citizenship rights for all citizens. In particular, they are considered as being opposed to social-liberal citizenship. Stuart Hall and David Held (1989: 17) argue that the question of 'difference is, in some ways, the joker in the citizenship pack'.

Here I want to connect the issue of citizenship rights not to rights for ethnic groups but to rights for women. Feminists have criticized social liberalism for not providing enough rights for women. Feminism is, in the *Oxford Encyclopedic English Dictionary*, described as 'the advocacy for women's rights on the ground of the equality of the sexes'. Yet a great deal, if not most, of the feminist debate has centred on the question of what is meant by the term 'women's rights': equal or special rights for women. I want to interpret this discussion from a citizenship perspective. If being a citizen gives one all the citizenship rights one needs – as for instance social liberals assume – why should women need women's rights? Does this mean that women do not possess all the citizenship rights or do women for some reason need extra, collective rights? Or is the social-liberal idea about the relation between citizenship and rights flawed?

In this chapter I will first examine existing social-liberal and feminist ideas about the relation between citizenship, rights and women. Then I will give my own account of this relation, suggesting that the social-liberal position on rights needs to be criticized from a completely different angle than feminists have done so far.

Social liberalism

Social liberalism uses the concept of individual rights, as derived from the natural right tradition, as its main tool to signify the relations between the citizen and the state, and amongst citizens themselves. Individual rights have been used to 'implement' the liberal value of autonomy. In our liberal era, it has become impossible to imagine citizenship without the centrality of rights.

The main social-liberal position on rights emphasizes equal rights and equal treatment for all citizens. For instance, T.H. Marshall (1967) argues that being a citizen gives an individual rights equal to all other citizens. He distinguishes three kinds of citizenship rights: civil, political and social. Civil rights pertain to liberty of the person, freedom of speech, thought, faith, the right to own property and to conclude valid contracts and the right to justice. Political rights are the right to vote and to be elected. Social rights guarantee economic welfare and security. John Rawls (1971) also assumes in his theory of justice that each citizen should have an equal right to the most extensive total system of equal basic liberties compatible with a similar system of liberty for all. Jürgen Habermas (1990) and Bruce Ackerman (1980, 1989) begin their communicative versions of social liberalism by giving every citizen the same communication rights.

Recently however a different view has emerged within social liberalism. Some theorists have argued that collective group rights can be defended from a liberal position. For instance, in *Taking Rights Seriously* (1987a: 232–239) Ronald Dworkin approves the moderate use of quotas as long as it leads to a community that is better off and as long as it is not based on racial or gender prejudices (cf. Dworkin 1985: 298).

Will Kymlicka has gone one step further in arguing that, in addition to individual rights, special rights for ethnic groups may be necessary, not to establish equality, but to allow for difference. Collective rights may be necessary to maintain a societal culture, a context of choice in which these groups can opt for cultural difference. Social-cultural membership is constitutive of the freedom, self-respect and identity of individuals. In his opinion, collective rights will not be a threat to freedom and equality, but will lead to even more freedom and equality: a more nearly equal division of respect and of participation.

Kymlicka notes (1995: 45) that the term 'collective rights' is ambiguous. Sometimes collective rights are in the hands of the collective itself (for instance self-government rights or group-representation rights), sometimes in the hands of individuals from that collective (for instance exemption from laws), and at other times collective rights refer to special provisions or practices that can be installed 'where numbers warrant' (for instance the right to go to schools that teach in a different language). Kymlicka only wants to use collective rights to promote a societal culture for ethnic minority groups; he does not talk about group rights for other purposes, as in the case of women's rights.

What is still common in all these social-liberal positions is the imagined relationship between rights and citizenship. The possession of rights is considered the essential characteristic of citizenship. Citizens receive rights, but whether or not they exercise them is their business. According to social liberals, we should not include moral guidelines for citizen behaviour within the concept of citizenship. This would be interference with the liberty of the citizen.

Humanist feminists: equal rights and equal treatment for all citizens

I will use the term 'collective rights' in the rest of this chapter only in the sense of rights that can be used by individuals belonging to the group of women and not for instance as self-government rights. Humanist feminists are not in favour of these special collective rights for women. They want to extend the main social-liberal equal rights philosophy to women. Nonetheless, they criticize social liberals in some respects. For instance, they criticize social liberals for their view that all citizens already possess equal rights; they also criticize the social liberal Marshall for his historically inaccurate picture of the accumulation of those rights.

Let me start with the last point. One feminist argument holds that Marshall ignores the fact that women received civil, political and social citizenship rights much later than men did (McIntosh 1984: 236; Vogel 1988: 138, 1991: 66; Walby 1994: 380). Margaret Stacey and Marion Price (1981: 48) argue that '[w]omen were in the end accorded political citizenship before they were granted full civil citizenship'. An even more radical argument against Marshall is that he did not see that the exclusion of married women from equal citizenship was not a coincidence, but the condition for men's inclusion in citizenship (Fraser and Gordon 1994: 97; Vogel 1991: 78).

According to many humanist feminists, these so-called universal citizenship rights have still not been fully realized for women (Lister 1989: 11; 1991, 1995a: 30–31; Pascall 1986: 9; Vogel 1994: 86). Women's political rights are now equal to men's, but major problems still exist with regard to women's civil and social rights. Civil rights are often not guaranteed within the private sphere of the family (Benton 1988, 1991; Fraser and Gordon 1994; Lister 1989, 1991; Walby 1994: 388). This fact has more negative consequences for women than for men, because women need rights within private hetero-relationships more than men do. Social citizenship rights, such as the right to unemployment benefits, pensions and social security, are often discriminatory (Fraser and Gordon 1994; Lister 1992; Pascall 1993). For example, in order to receive these rights, a citizen is often required to have a curriculum vitae of paid jobs, while in other cases these rights are restricted if, for instance, one has a wage-earning partner.

Humanist feminists accept the social-liberal premise that we are all equal human beings and should all have equal rights (Carter 1988). Nevertheless, they think that social liberals have been inconsistent. Furthermore, the citizenship rights they have come up with are rights which are advantageous to men; social liberals have not tried to imagine what rights would be needed for female citizens.

One of the humanist feminist aims, therefore, is to apply all citizenship rights to women. This means applying social rights – welfare benefits – to women, but it also means applying civil rights – such as the right to safety – to women. Another aim is to apply social-liberal citizenship rights to the private and social spheres (Holmes 1984; Lister 1991; Orloff 1993). It is even considered necessary by humanist feminists to extend the list of citizenship rights by developing rights that would be advantageous to both women and men in similar situations, such as the right to parental leave and the right to affordable childcare (Lister 1993: 13, 1994: 44; Vogel 1994: 87).

Nevertheless, the crucial issue remains whether or not the humanist-feminist position can be combined with demanding special, collective rights for women, and if so in what sense? Humanist feminists may demand temporary special treatment for women to (re)install equal opportunities. Affirmative action programmes in companies and universities may serve as an example of this. These are considered necessary to overcome the old boys' network which works to exclude women. The humanist-feminist assumption is that once equality has been installed by artificial measures, females and males will be employed in equal numbers. When this is the case, affirmative action programmes can be abolished.

Humanist feminists, however, are very careful with 'special, collective rights', because they are afraid that special rights may return us to a situation of discrimination and oppression. Despite the good intentions with which special rights may be provided for one group, it is a threat to the idea of equality under the law and equal citizenship. If not enough effort is made to show that special rights for a particular group are only a temporary instrument to create genuinely equal citizenship in practice, people will feel that equal citizenship no longer exists. After all, not every citizen can claim special rights. Thus, if humanist feminists argue for temporary special rights for women, they do so to establish equality, not to protect (gender) difference.

Woman-centred feminism: special collective rights and care

Woman-centred feminists are sceptical about the strategy of equal individual rights (Rhode 1986). Usually they suggest that collective rights for women would be a better alternative, although some of them argue that it would be preferable to disregard the language of rights completely and have a language of needs instead. I want to discuss the argument for collective rights first. What are the reasons of woman-centred feminists for rejecting the strategy of equal individual rights and for suggesting that we need (at least some) collective rights for women?

The first reason that woman-centred feminists offer in their critique of individual equal rights is that because these rights are individual (with a man as the model for the universal, disembodied human being), they are not appropriate to women's special needs. This argument is usually presented in the context of women's 'body rights', as in Elizabeth Wolgast's book *Equality and the Rights of Women* (1980). For instance, individual equal rights hardly provide special protection for pregnant female workers because there are no other people with whom pregnant women can be compared (cf. Wolgast 1987).

Woman-centred feminists also argue that the equal division of rights, and especially political rights, which liberalism assumes, offers political minorities limited capacity to defend themselves against the political majority, because they can be easily outvoted (Young 1989). Even though women may numerically be a majority, politically they are a minority.

Liberal equal rights are only formal and, therefore, relatively empty, according to woman-centred feminists (Young 1990b: 25). These rights do not prevent an imbalance in their exercise between the sexes. They leave the public–private split intact so that many people cannot overcome problems in the private sphere and cannot use their rights and freedom in the public sphere. This argument draws attention to the social conditions required in order to achieve an equal use of rights.

Furthermore, woman-centred feminists like Iris Young (1989: 267–273, 1990b: 164–165) claim that in a situation of inequality, equal rights and equal treatment will only perpetuate inequality. After all, this situation favours those who are in a privileged position. If equal results are one's aim, then one should go beyond equal rights and equal treatment.

Finally, liberal equal rights are problematic, according to woman-centred feminists, because they presuppose a reciprocal relationship with equal duties. In fact, this raises a complexity of different arguments. One is that equal rights require equal duties and that this is not desirable, because certain conditions are not yet met and because women should not be expected to become like men. Often the case of military conscription (Carter 1996; Jones 1984) or the duty to get a job are used in this type of argument. Another is that equal rights would suppose equal duties, but that liberalism does not impose the latter (Cass 1990, 1994). Consider for instance the right to parental leave for the father, where there is not the duty to share 'care work'. A final argument is that women have several duties but do not have compensating rights and therefore reciprocity is not assured. For instance, it is argued that women have been ascribed care duties in the household without the right to payment.

What do woman-centred feminists propose as an alternative to the equal rights strategy? One strategy of woman-centred feminists – particularly of woman's morality feminists – is to move away from the language of rights and justice and use the language of needs and care instead (Noddings 1984; Sevenhuijsen 1996; Tronto 1993). According to them, the discourse of rights is closely connected to the discourse of interests. Both discourses suggest that society consists of rational, economic units seeking to maximize their utility. Woman-centred feminists view people as being motivated by more than interests alone. This alternative perspective would imply turning away from an individualistic view towards a relational one. The focus would be on relationships of dependency in which the dependent and vulnerable need comparatively more protection or care than others. The language used here (Diamond and Hartsock 1981; Hanen and Nielsen 1987) is that of extra provisions and extra care, more than that of extra rights.

Another strategy is to demand special collective rights for women, usually as an addition to and in order to correct equal rights for all citizens (Littleton 1987; Wolgast 1980, 1987). Woman-centred feminists do not emphasize special rights for women as a temporary measure to compensate for injustice in the past or to (re)install equal opportunities. Rather, they see special collective rights for women, such as maternity rights, special group representation and quotas, as a way to obtain public recognition for the female element in society and as a safeguard against assimilation. They defend such rights not with an appeal to equality, but with an appeal to the protection of gender difference. For instance, Iris Young (1989) demands group-representation rights and veto rights for women on policy proposals that are considered crucial to women and where every other means to counteract or to implement them has failed.

Deconstructionists: deconstructing equal versus special rights

Deconstructionist feminists criticize the equal rights strategy of social liberals and humanist feminists because this may overlook the different needs of particular people (McClure 1992a). However, they are also very reluctant to opt exclusively for special collective rights for women, because they are afraid that this will put women in a separate category of deviants and will give the illusion that women are all the same.

Deconstructionism dismantles the idea that equal individual rights and special group rights are mutually exclusive. For instance, in *Same Difference. Feminism and Sexual Difference* (1990) the Australian feminist Carol Bacchi uses the case of 'protective' legislation in factories to illustrate this. She states (p. 133) that 'the problem has never been "difference" but "difference which matters", in the sense that it is the cause of disadvantage. Pregnancy becomes a "difference which matters" when groups in power make it matter by leaving it as women's responsibility'. The equal versus special treatment dichotomy should lead feminists to ask 'Special in what respect?', 'Different from whom?' and 'Why is this difference perceived as problematic?' Bacchi urges feminists to deconstruct the dichotomy as one of the many sameness versus difference alternatives. According to Bacchi (p. 262):

> [t]he 'sameness' alternative is insufficiently critical of the status quo. The 'difference' option *is* critical of the status quo, but seems to conjecture that women can exist in some sort of separate world. Seeing women as the 'same' as men prevents us *challenging* the model against which women are being compared; seeing women as 'different' prevents us *changing* it.

Deconstructionism also debunks the opposition between the rights discourse and the care discourse. In contrast to the conventional opinion that the rights discourse is founded on principles and the care discourse implies contextual argument, deconstructionism shows that, to a certain degree, both have principles and a need for contextualization (cf. Sevenhuijsen 1992).

An example of a deconstructionist approach to rights can be found in the strategy of 'relational rights', a scheme proposed by the American legal theorist Martha Minow in *Making All the Difference* (1990). Like Bacchi, Minow warns against a dichotomy between same rights and special rights. She argues that these two sorts of rights have been juxtaposed because equal rights go back to the natural law tradition, in which the individual is perceived as being independent from others, and because special rights are embedded in a communitarian vocabulary in which interdependence and the special characteristics of a group are emphasized. She demonstrates the difficulties that these different vocabularies lead to. In the following passage (p. 144), Minow focuses on the rights of mentally retarded persons:

> How may advocates demand that law treat mentally retarded persons the same as others for purposes of freedom from constraints and abuse, but differently from others for the purpose of securing the attention, resources, and care that others do not need? Legal innovation may produce the worst of both worlds: a prescription of 'same' rights to be free from institutionalization but with no special rights in the community, or of 'different' rights to special care without the fundamental rights to freedom from injury due to abuse or negligence by others.

According to Minow (pp. 218–219), claims for women's rights are likely to fall into the same dichotomy as claims for equal or special treatment.

She develops a new concept of rights (p. 225), namely 'rights in relationship' (or, as I will call them, 'relational rights'), where rights may be claimed by everyone within the same situation (cf. Cornell 1992 who proposes the idea of 'equivalent rights'; Wolgast 1980: 48). According to Minow, the special rights approach has both the problem of an arbitrary distinction between 'normal' and 'deviant' people, and the problem of locating difference solely in one person. Difference, in her opinion (1990: 111), is meaningful only as a comparison:

> A comparison draws a relationship: a short person is different only in relation to a taller one. As a relational notion, difference is reciprocal: I am no different from you than you are from me. But the statement distributes power. The name of difference is produced by those with the power to name and the power to treat themselves as the norm.

Minow proposes an alternative (pp. 295, 383), namely the social relations approach, which emphasizes basic connections between people and the injuries which result from social isolation and exclusion. She understands differences as a function of comparisons between people and tries to imagine the perspective of 'the other' and to share deliberations with that 'other'. In one of her footnotes (p. 390, note 51) she gives an interesting example of such a deliberation:

> 'Sesame Street', which asks children to answer, 'which one of these things is not like the other?' has recently changed its reply. If, for example, the question points to a chair, a table, a book, and a bed, the television program no longer gives only one answer but instead identifies different answers based on a choice of conceptual schemes. Perhaps the book is the anomaly, since the other items are articles of furniture. Perhaps the bed is the oddball, if the category selected looks at what belongs in a study. The program thus shows that the choice of categories is a choice of purposes; differences are not intrinsic but relative to chosen ends.

Minow argues here that we do not need to choose between equal rights and special rights. Instead, rights are granted according to which are the most suitable in a particular situation. For example, a disabled person needs extra rights in order to be guaranteed physical access to a building. These rights may be considered universal in the sense that they apply to everyone who is or will be disabled. Yet, they are special in the sense that they only apply to people who find themselves in this particular situation.

Individual rights

In my opinion, humanist feminists rightly assume that formal individual rights are important. They are also right in their caution against special collective rights for women, in that these might lead again to discrimination and inequality. It has taken centuries of struggle to obtain formal equal rights for individuals. If one does not want to return to the dark ages of feudalism and slavery, one should be very careful when attacking the concept of individual rights.

However, humanist feminists assume too easily that rights are the central and ultimate part of citizenship. They are central insofar as they concern passive citizenship, but they only form the preconditions for active citizenship. When feminists attempt to increase women's involvement in public affairs, they should not spend too much time on the question of equal versus special rights, but should concentrate on the issue of the equal exercise of rights. It is at the level of participation that we see the major distinctions between male citizens and female citizens, not at the level of rights. Women in western society have got enough rights; the point is that they need to (be able to) use them (Voet 1994a). Both feminists and citizenship theorists should pay attention to participation (or the conditions for equal use of rights) rather than to formal rights. As long as women do not exercise their rights to the same degree as men do, equal citizenship does not exist.

Saying that on the whole women in western society have got enough rights, does not imply that any feminist action in courts is of no value. I think that feminist pressure in courts is important, not only for its direct consequences for women, but also because it is a type of citizenship action hardly distinguishable from political participation. But what feminists are trying to obtain here does not usually concern new rights for women, in the sense of rights that individual citizens can claim. Usually, they are trying to achieve new interpretations of existing rights and in particular demanding an authorization or condemnation of particular kinds of policies, regulations and treatments. For instance, they try to get an endorsement via jurisprudence that a particular kind of affirmative action policy is permitted. In other words, this is not strictly a matter of rights, but a judgement about the fairness of particular policies given the effects of them on some people. Thus, women in western society have enough rights on the whole, but simultaneously need more woman-friendly policies, regulations and interpretations of existing rights.

Special collective rights versus equal rights

Woman-centred feminists do not see that special collective rights for women will not provide the panacea to all the disadvantages which they believe equal rights have. Alternative, and perhaps better solutions may exist for the five problems they have with equal rights.

In order to protect 'women's particularities', it does not seem necessary to invoke a notion of special collective rights, as woman-centred feminists claim. Other equal rights may have the same effect and do not label women as 'abnormal'. For instance, one can add the right to protection in cases of pregnancy or rights to body protection in working situations. One can also reinterpret existing social, civil and political rights so that the right to bodily integrity implies a protection against rape in marriage and other kinds of sexual harassment (Brünott 1991). It is not necessary that all citizens make use of these rights, as the example of tenant rights or tenant protection shows.

The woman-centred argument that equal rights do not sufficiently protect a political minority against a majority is, in my opinion, a valid one. However, it does not follow that women as a political minority need special collective rights. Protection may lead to women being seen as weak, non-political beings, as losers instead of as potential rulers. It may be better to think about setting up a system of checks and balances to counteract the power of the political majority. Collective special rights for women could be part of these checks and balances in the sense of rights for political minorities, but feminists have to be very careful with this measure, precisely because it is meant for a political minority. If women do not intend to remain a political minority – and I hope they will not – then they should think about other measures.

Next we come to the argument that liberal individual rights are only formal and do not prevent the unequal use of these rights. This is not really an argument against individual rights as such, but an argument against the emphasis on rights, including collective rights. I share this view but formal rights remain important as an instrument against abuse of power.

This leads us to the woman-centred feminist argument that, in a situation of inequality, equal treatment and equal rights may easily perpetuate inequality. However, this does not have to be the case. Political minorities may effectively use their rights and convince others of their arguments. It is not true that people have fixed interests and that political minorities and majorities will always remain the same.

The last argument points to the problematic relationship between the concept of rights and duties. Yet again, this problematic also exists in the case of collective rights. So far, my argument has been that woman-centred feminists do not see that collective rights are not the panacea to all the difficulties they have with the liberal concept of equal individual rights. It might be that the notion of collective rights is often mentioned as a solution, because it seems an answer to each difficulty. Nonetheless, for each of these difficulties, other, and sometimes better alternatives appear to be available.

The disadvantages of special collective rights

Woman-centred feminists also close their eyes to the fact that, in principle, special collective rights have many disadvantages of their own. To start with, there is the risk of 'stigmatization'. Giving women special rights because they are women and therefore disadvantaged can stigmatize women in their traditional roles by using only one stereotype. This approach tends to suggest that women are victims and that the differences they stand for are negative. Several cases have been reported of women who refuse the special treatment offered to them, because they do not want to be perceived as 'underdogs'.

The Dutch legal theorist Riki Holtmaat (1988a, 1988b) adds to these arguments the view that special rights reinforce the idea that women are deviants from the norm (normal rights). 'Special rights' leave the 'normality' of male-oriented law unchallenged. Besides, she says, special rights may lead to a backlash against women. If employers are forced to give women special rights in the workplace, then they may simply choose to employ male workers.

Following from this are doubts about a potential extension of special treatment to other groups and about the scope of special treatment. Iris Young (1989) proposes special group representation for each disadvantaged group. She mentions not only women but also 13 other disadvantaged groups. However, this might lead to an endless fragmentation of the group of 'women' and to a complex relationship between the rights of all these groups. In how many respects can one be oppressed? Will one group take priority over others or will they all have the same status? What should be done with people who belong to more than one group?

The scope of special rights causes problems too. Young (1989) proposes giving these groups veto rights on issues that are fundamentally linked with their interests and on which they cannot exercise their influence in any other way. But it is hard to decide on which specific issues women should have a veto right. Should it simply be on abortion or on issues relating to female biology, or on every issue in which women claim to have a special interest?

There is also the danger that special treatment may result in discrimination and injustice, against which there does not seem to be any safeguard. Good intentions certainly do not provide enough protection against this. Finally, feminists cannot really use Kymlicka's arguments in favour of the protection of a community or culture. Women hardly form a community: they do not live together geographically; they do not claim rights to a particular piece of land (Krosenbrink-Gelisen 1991); they are strongly integrated in other 'cultures' and therefore differ strongly amongst themselves.

Relational rights

Women may not need protection (in the form of special collective rights for women) in all cases, but only in those for which being a woman is relevant. A combination of equal rights and special collective rights for women would then be more logical. Sometimes, special rights or special facilities may be desirable. For instance, special training courses for women in the higher levels of bureaucracy, quotas or other affirmative action programmes may be useful in order to promote the employment of more women in decision-making bodies. In these cases it is preferable not to use the argument of women as a special community guaranteeing a certain kind of difference, but to restrict oneself to arguments of injustice in the past or present and attempts to install equal opportunities and equal result. It is easy here to fall back on liberalism, because it allows temporary special treatment in cases of disadvantage beyond one's responsibility.

However, to avoid the above-mentioned disadvantages of the special rights strategy completely, it may be better and also possible to obtain rights through the deconstructionist-feminist strategy of 'relational rights'. Relational rights is another term for offering special rights to all people in a particular situation of vulnerability, for instance special protection for tenants or workers. An example that is especially relevant to women is the example of the Belgian laws which state that a maximum of two-thirds of all people on candidate lists (adopted in 1994) and on advisory bodies to parliament (adopted in 1996) can consist of one gender. These laws are advantageous to women, who are a political minority in these political bodies, but the law could also be applied to men if they were in the same situation.

Underlying the relational rights idea is in fact the same strategy as that expressed by Aristotle's maxim: justice means treating like cases alike and unlike cases differently. Here too, we have to decide what the most relevant features of a certain case are: what is it that makes a case like or unlike another case? When are people in a vulnerable situation and thus in need of special rights? When does a difference mean vulnerability or disadvantage? Why is a particular similarity or difference relevant to the issue of justice?

Contextual argument does not mean, however, that we have to start from scratch in each case. After all, as Minow shows in her work, case law may form an excellent basis for a judgement that allows for change. In fact, the existing practice of law is already working with the formula of 'treating like cases alike and different cases differently'. It is only mainstream social-liberal philosophy that suggests that we should always treat all citizens equally.

Using the concept of relational rights would not only imply going back to Aristotle's slogan and therefore basing judgement on the relevant features of a particular situation – but it might also imply the participation in court of groups which have to come up with arguments for judgement. It might thus imply 'class action' by women, active involvement of feminist lawyers, the development of a 'feminist law' discipline in universities and in journals, and feminist legal organizations. For instance, Vrouw en Recht (Women and Law) in the Netherlands invokes trial cases, offers legal assistance to women in them and publishes the resulting jurisprudence in the feminist legal journal *Nemesis*.

The emphasis of deconstructionist feminists on power rather than on rights also seems very useful to me. However, their focus remains too much within the equal rights/special rights continuum, rather than addressing the issue of the exercise of rights. Discussing power does not automatically increase women's involvement in public affairs, especially when the exercise of rights and participation are not considered necessary.

The use of rights

Nor is it necessary to argue that women form a special community or culture that needs to be protected in order to claim relational rights for women. This line of argument is sometimes used by feminists as a response to the increasing popularity of the concept of cultural rights. However, that women form a special community or culture is a problematic argument, as we have seen. Besides, so many things can be argued for within the rhetoric of compensation for past wrongs and temporary affirmative action to reinstall equal opportunities, that it is not strictly necessary to come up with alternative justifications for special treatment.

Rights are empty if a state does not guarantee them or realize them (Arendt 1979: 290–302). The value of the 1979 United Nations Convention on the Elimination of All Forms of Discrimination against Women, its Declaration on the Elimination of Violence against Women (1993), its Vienna Declaration on Human Rights (1993) and its Beijing Declaration (1995), which specifies the implications of the idea that women's rights are also human rights, depends, therefore, on the ways in which such rights will be guaranteed and enforced (cf. Brünott 1991; Langley 1991).

By taking rights as the topic for this chapter and by seeing citizenship rights as crucial to one's citizenship status, I may have given the illusion that rights are the central factor in the problem of women and citizenship. Currently, however, there is nothing problematic in women's formal rights. Furthermore, there are enough opportunities within the current legal system and the existing rhetoric of rights for women to claim special provisions, without having to claim special rights as a separate community.

We should make a distinction between formal citizenship rights, effective (or by practical measures guaranteed) citizenship rights and the exercise of citizenship rights. Equal citizenship rights may exist formally, but that does not guarantee that they can be realized in practice, nor does it say anything about the degree to which these rights are exercised by both sexes. Nonetheless, this is no reason to be opposed to equal formal rights. As Anne Phillips suggests (1993: Chs 2 and 3) equal rights have not guaranteed women equal access to power, equal jobs or equal pay, but it is still worth fighting against discrimination.

Despite the attention of feminist theorists to rights today, the difficulties of women and citizenship do not lie in the area of rights, but in participation. In contrast to third world countries (Schuler 1990), within contemporary western liberal democracies women have enough equal rights, and enough possibilities exist to claim some special rights. Now they need to use them. Of course, women cannot participate in politics and society without rights. As Ruth Lister points out (1995b: 7–8): 'Citizenship as participation represents an expression of human agency in the political arena broadly defined; citizenship as rights enables people to act as agents.'

*   *   *

Social liberals have usually been attacked by feminists for the wrong reason. Woman-centred and deconstructionist feminists have attacked social liberalism for not allowing special rights for special groups. As I have shown, this is an exaggeration.

First of all, social-liberal practice is much more advanced than social-liberal theory. Mainstream social-liberal theory does not account for legal practice in social-liberal countries. Mainstream social-liberal theory suggests that every individual should always receive equal individual rights. In court practice however, and even in positive law, special laws are made for special groups by following Aristotle's maxim of 'treating like cases alike and different cases differently'. In this respect, we might say that social-liberal practice has already incorporated 'relational rights' and that it is only theory that falls behind by not finding a justification for it.

Besides, a minority strand within social liberalism aims to incorporate demands for special group rights into its citizenship theory. However, this only occurs in the context of a background appeal to equality, for instance to compensate for injustice in the past and present or to reinstall equal opportunities. Dworkin's argumentation can also be used to plead for special rights that promote an equal result. Kymlicka offers other arguments, but they are not easily used by groups that do not form an ethnic community. Thus, already within some strands of social liberalism, equal rights and special collective rights are not seen as mutually exclusive.

It would be preferable if feminists attacked social liberals on a far more important point: the social-liberal suggestion that rights are the centre of citizenship and that possessing the same rights as others is enough to make someone a full citizen. In contrast to Marshall's and Rawls's theory, equal citizenship is not realized simply by providing individual rights to all citizens. Women are second-class citizens despite equal individual rights. The social-liberal view makes it impossible to question the enormously unequal social and political participation of female and male citizens.

To question this unequal division from a citizenship perspective, participation must be looked at as an indicator of full citizenship. This also means that we need to reverse the social-liberal relationship between rights and citizenship. Instead of seeing citizenship as the means to realize rights, we should see rights as one of the means to realize equal citizenship. This implies that feminism ought to be more than a movement for women's rights; it ought to be a movement for women's participation.

This puts emphasis on the use of rights. One need not automatically receive all provisions from the state, but must attempt to achieve some of these through citizenship action. Such action may take place in the courtroom by individual women, feminist lawyers or by feminist collectives invoking trial cases in order to get a judgement of the fairness of policies or regulations. This use of rights has both an instrumental and an inherent value. It may promote sex equality by obtaining better regulation, treatment, policies or interpretation of rights, thus gaining a better legal citizenship status for women. Participation in court itself already means showing the capabilities of participating female citizens and is therefore also a way of enacting citizenship.

With regard to rights themselves, if we see rights as a means to realize equal citizenship, then this will be best achieved through a combination of individual, collective and relational rights for women. Yet feminists should be careful of using the strategy of collective rights for women, because it is not a panacea for all the difficulties with equal individual rights, and because women's collective rights can stereotype and stigmatize women too much. It may be better to combine individual equal citizenship rights with relational rights, whereby people in vulnerable situations are offered extra protection without reference to biological groups.

The next chapter on another sub-theme of citizenship – social equality – will take this issue further. It will focus on one of the often-mentioned preconditions for the equal use of rights, namely material equality, and on one of the ways to make use of rights, namely social participation.

6

Social Equality

One of the most controversial issues in the citizenship debate is the issue of whether social equality really belongs to citizenship and, if so, in what sense. Is it a condition for equal citizenship or a part of citizenship itself? There are two dominant positions in this debate: the social-liberal position, which presupposes that social equality (mostly in the sense of material equality) is a necessary part of citizenship if citizens are to be both free and equal; and the classical-liberal (and classical-republican) position, which suggests that social affairs have nothing to do with (equal) citizenship.

This debate has an impact on our evaluation of women as equal or second-class citizens, as is pointed out in Barbara Nelson's article, 'Women's Poverty and Women's Citizenship: Some Political Consequences of Economic Marginality' (1984), and by many other feminists (Abbott and Bompas 1943; Borchost and Siim 1987; Fraser 1989; Lister 1990, 1994; O'Connor 1993; Parker 1993; Pascall 1993; Riley 1992). It often seems difficult to question the existing social inequality of women and men from a citizenship perspective. After all, women and men are already equal citizens in most western liberal democracies. How is it possible then to speak of the second-class citizenship of women?

We might say that those people who speak of equal citizenship and those who speak of second-class citizenship have as their base different citizenship philosophies with different evaluations of the importance of social equality. Furthermore, there are two different meanings of social equality – material equality and social participation defined as paid labour – and again political philosophies differ on the respective importance of those for citizenship.

Two meanings of social equality

There is often a suggestion that there are only two possible sides to take in the debate on social equality. On the one hand, an egalitarian position is possible, in which one argues for equal material welfare and the importance of equal social participation. On the other hand, a pluralist position can be taken, in which one argues for different levels of welfare for citizens and different kinds of social participation.

In her article 'The Paradoxes of Pluralism' Louise Marcil-Lacoste (1992) argues that there are many more possible sides. According to her, it is a misconception to say that pluralism necessarily leads to inegalitarianism. Neither unity and equality nor plurality and inequality are automatically combined. Marcil-Lacoste argues that the only way such a mistake can be made is by considering equality, equity or justice as synonymous with identity.

We find similar arguments put forward by Elizabeth Meehan and Selma Sevenhuijsen in their introduction to *Equality, Politics and Gender* (1991). They warn that equality should not be considered as sameness. Like Marcil-Lacoste they point out the consequences of this for feminism. A feminist pleading for equality between women and men might automatically conclude that the sexes will have to act and think in the same way (usually women following men). By contrast, Meehan and Sevenhuijsen prefer to plead for equality not as sameness, but as equal value, equal respect or equity between the sexes. The feminist theorist Ute Gerhard puts this thought in mathematical language in her book *Gleichheit ohne Angleichung* (Equality without Sameness 1990: 13 – my translation):

> Equality is neither an absolute principle nor a strict measure, but rather a relative concept. . . . The formula for sameness is $a = a$, whereas equality can be expressed as $a = b$.

Without saying that equity is a better aim for feminists than equality, I admit that it is important to note that there are more possibilities and that we should distinguish them in the debate on social equality. The first meaning of social equality, material welfare, can indeed be best discussed in terms of sameness. The second meaning, social participation, is more complex. Social participation, defined here as paid labour, can be discussed in terms of same or different *amounts* of social participation, but also different *kinds* of social participation, *levels* of social participation and *ways* of participating.

Social liberalism

Classical liberals and neo-liberals have tended to argue against perceiving 'the social question' in terms of citizenship. The reason they have given for this is their concern with independent judgement. Citizens need not be involved with the social question, because this 'question' is already resolved for them. Citizens only acquire their citizenship by virtue of the fact that they have property. After all, according to classical liberals and neo-liberals, property makes people autonomous and responsible. Once the issue of who is able to be a citizen is resolved, formal equality of citizens should guarantee that social inequalities between them are no longer politically relevant.

In his essay 'On the Common Saying: This May be True in Theory, but It Does Not Apply in Practice', Immanuel Kant formulates the basic liberal thought that lies behind this:

The only qualification required by a citizen (apart, of course, from being an adult male) [sic] is that he must be his *own master* (*sui iuris*), and must have some *property*, (which can include any skill, trade, fine art or science) to support himself. In cases where he must earn his living from others, he must earn it only by *selling* what is his. . . , and not by allowing others to make use of him; for he must in the true sense of the word *serve* no-one but the commonwealth. (1990: 78, italic in original)

One can, of course, draw opposite conclusions from this perspective: that social equality is no concern of the state; and that the state should encourage people to overcome poverty and become genuinely equal citizens. The first conclusion is that of classical liberals and neo-liberals. The second and opposite conclusion is drawn by social liberals.

Social liberals do talk about social equality. For instance, they acknowledge that in order to be a citizen one cannot live in poverty. Citizens are granted social rights (rights to welfare benefits) by them in order to escape poverty. Social liberals like John Rawls (1971) also recognize that the design of a fair and just public system must not only guarantee equal rights but must also be formed to benefit the socially weakest. The construction of a fair and just public system is centred on the redistribution of money, not on social participation or labour.

Another example is the social liberal T.H. Marshall. In his opinion (1967: 78), every adult should have an equal right to 'a modicum of economic welfare and security and the right to share to the full in the social heritage and to live the life of a civilized being according to the standards prevailing in society'. The institutions most closely connected to social citizenship are, according to him, the education system and social services. The state should act to meet the conditions under which citizens can be approximately socially equal. In any case, the differences between rich and poor citizens should be diminished (Rawls 1971). Only in this way can the excluded classes be incorporated in the national identity and the war between capitalism and citizenship be resolved.

For social liberals, therefore, social equality is such a fundamental condition for equal citizenship that it is the duty of the state to ensure that everyone is at least able to live the life of a civilized being. Furthermore, income differences should not be so large that they result in a second-class citizenship for the economically weakest. Solving 'the social question' is a crucial task for the democratic state if equal citizenship is to be achieved.

However, social liberals seldom or never talk about the other meaning of social equality: social participation. If they do, they differ vastly on such issues as paid labour for everyone or a basic income. Social activity itself does not appear to have a direct relationship with citizenship, only an indirect one: it leads to an unequal income distribution between citizens, which affects their power. According to social-liberal philosophy, men and women are equal citizens, because they have equal civil, political and social rights. Since it defines citizenship as rights, participation is not important, nor is inequality in participation.

Humanist feminism: same jobs, same wages

The humanist-feminist position is that women need to emulate men to become full citizens (Ellis 1991; Hernes 1984, 1987, 1988). Through participation in the public sphere, women will earn money, learn to deal with responsibility and will thus also earn respect. Humanist feminists urge women to obtain paid jobs in the public sphere and follow the same career tracks that men have followed.

One of the first examples of this school of thought is Josephine F. Milburn, who published *Women as Citizens: A Comparative Review* in 1976. If women are to become full citizens, they must, according to Milburn (p. 38), become fully active participants in society. She interprets this as meaning that women should be active decision-makers and that they therefore must approach education and careers as primary concerns. Of course, society should change too, in order to allow women this employment route. Milburn does not use the term 'employment route' herself. It occurs, in a negative way, in contemporary feminist publications on citizenship which suggest that this route devalues motherhood and obliges women to emulate men. Note that it is usually forgotten that this route was originally meant as a necessary step towards gender equality in decision-making.

Milburn refers to several studies on women's rights and participation in various countries. Equal economic participation should, according to her, lead to equal political participation and influence in decision-making. She suggests that decision-making not only occurs in politics, but in the economy and careers also. Social equality is perceived as equal participation and equal payment in the official economy, and as equal education levels for men and women.

In their views on social equality, it is important to make a distinction between liberal-humanist feminists and egalitarian-humanist feminists. The liberal-feminist position on social equality looks like the classical-liberal one. Women have to work under the same conditions as men (Richards 1982, Wolf 1993). Moreover, there needs to be equality of opportunity, but not necessarily equality of result. If women do not make use of equal opportunities, it is their own fault and there is nothing that the state or other groups and institutions should do about it.

Liberal feminists emphasize the importance of social participation, by which they mean paid labour in the public sphere. Their main instruments are: equal access to all educational institutions and professions, no discrimination, encouragement for women by means of public childcare and an individualized tax system. They disapprove of active redistribution of money by the state. Incomes should be based on merit, and if inequalities can be traced back to different degrees of participation or to the fact that some people do not work in the paid economy, then that is their own fault.

The egalitarian-humanist feminists go further than this (Hernes 1987, 1988). Whilst they also think that women should simply be treated as individual citizens, they demand not only equality of opportunity but also equality of result for the sexes. They therefore emphasize that social equality is to be measured by differences in income levels not only between classes or households, but also between sexes and within households. Egalitarian-humanist feminists aspire not only to equality of social partici-pation, but also to a redistribution of material welfare, so that there will be less material inequality.

Ruth Lister is a good example of an egalitarian-humanist feminist. Full citizenship, in her view, implies equal formal rights and duties and the social and economic conditions under which these rights and duties are exercised. She aims (1990: 67) at 'a form of social citizenship that will embody the prin-ciples of social justice and accountability and reconcile the demands of uni-versalism with those of the different groups that make up our community'. Concerning women, this requires: (1) equality of spare time between the sexes; (2) equal distribution of paid and unpaid work; (3) obliteration of the split between private and public; (4) a balance of rights and obligations to paid employment and care; (5) equal mobility between the sexes; (6) facil-ities to combine paid labour with caring responsibilities; and (7) a social security system that provides women with an independent entitlement through improvement to, and extension of, the national insurance scheme on a non-contributory basis.

Lister's view of social equality implies that women should take the public route, but this will only be possible if men share care work with women and if there is a benefit for care work. She also states in her article 'Women, Economic Dependency and Citizenship' (1990: 458) that the exercise of political citizenship rights is related to social and economic rights:

> Poverty and gender, lack of money and lack of time, thus combine to curtail the exercise of the political rights of citizenship. This underlines the inter-relationship between the political and social elements of citizenship. The exercise of political citizenship rights is, in part, a function of social and economic rights and can, in turn, influence the quality and nature of those rights.

In her later publications Lister becomes slightly more sympathetic towards the care approach. For instance, in 'Dilemmas in Engendering Citizenship' (1995a: 33) she concludes:

> The aim is a 'woman-friendly' conception of citizenship: one which combines the gender-neutrality of an approach which seeks to enable women to participate with men as equals in the public sphere (suitably transformed) with a gender-differentiated recognition and valuing of women's responsibilities in the private sphere.

Woman-centred feminism: different kinds of participation by the sexes

Woman-centred feminists do not think it necessary that women follow the same life path as most men. They take more pride in what women them-selves are doing (Code 1986; Thornton 1986). However, this does not imply that the term 'social equality' has no meaning for them.

The women's forum position has, in principle, little to say about the topic of social equality, as its major theme is political representation. Nonetheless, there are individual women who do incorporate it into their argument. Nancy Fraser, for instance, attempts to combine plurality (different social participation) with egalitarianism (redistribution of material welfare). In *Unruly Practices* Fraser (1989: 128–129; cf. 1994) argues:

> As long as the worker and childrearer roles are constituted as fundamentally incompatible with one another, it will not be possible to universalize either of them to include both genders. Thus some forms of dedifferentiation of unpaid childrearing and other work is required. Similarly, as long as the citizen role is defined to encompass death-dealing soldiering but not life-fostering childrearing, as long as it is tied to male-dominated modes of dialogue, then it, too, will remain incapable of including women fully.

A less egalitarian variation of women's forum feminism is presented by Iris Marion Young (1990b: Ch. 1). She attacks the distributive paradigm of social liberals in that it focuses only on the results and not on the power positions that have caused them. If one does not change the power relations, there will remain economic and social inequalities. Alterations should be made at the beginning of the process, rather than a redistribution at the end. Moreover, she is afraid that people's identities will be endangered if we are all required to do the same things. Social justice is not related to equal distribution of incomes but to equal access to jobs and decision-making positions and to an equality of voice. Once these positions are attained, the task is to do things differently.

The women's morality position within woman-centred feminism pleads for a reappraisal of women's activities and the values that should derive from them. In particular, women's care work should receive as much respect as men's paid labour. Both activities are perceived by women's morality feminists as social participation and therefore as of value for citizenship. In this respect Arnlaug Leira has argued (1989: 208 quoted in Lister 1995a: 17), 'what is lacking is a concept of citizenship which recognizes the importance of care to society'. A feminist who draws radical conclusions from such a perspective is Bettina Cass. She argues (1994: 115 quoted in Lister 1995a: 19; cf. Cass 1990) that men should not be 'accorded full citizenship if they do not fulfill their responsibilities for care-giving work'.

Women's morality feminists are opposed to having to perform paid labour in the public sphere and to affirmative action as an attempt to get more women into the labour market. According to them, this would force women into the employment route of citizenship whereas there are other routes that may be taken, such as motherhood. The egalitarians amongst them favour payment for carers. In this respect Claire Ungerson (1993) articulates doubts about whether the citizenship discourse is appropriate for carers and prefers the language of rights for both citizens and carers.

Other women's morality feminists demand instead that mothering be respected as equal to other forms of social participation, but not necessarily in a material and financial sense. The emphasis is not on mothers being paid or on female care-givers being financially independent from their partners. Jean Bethke Elshtain (1981), Nel Noddings (1984) and Sarah Ruddick (1983b, 1989) are examples of those arguing for mothering to be respected by using its values in political theory and action.

Deconstructionist social equality

A consensus seems to have recently emerged that a feminist citizenship perspective should incorporate elements from an ethics of justice and an ethics of care (Benhabib and Cornell 1987; Sevenhuijsen 1991, 1992). For the issue of social equality this implies that attention needs to be given to both paid labour and caring work. One way of taking this up is provided by deconstructionist feminism.

Deconstructionist feminists try to combine social equality with difference. In this respect they inspire feminists who take other positions. Deconstructionist influences can, for instance, be discovered in Fraser and Young. Deconstructionism is against sameness, suggesting that it is inegalitarian. Yet at the same time, it talks about the welfare state. It is pro-pluralism, and so includes attention to differences amongst women. However, it is not clear whether it advocates the disappearance or the hailing of these differences.

Neither does it say much about the issue of economic inequality among women (an exception is Yeatman 1992). This may be because deconstructionists claim that power is not to be found in one single space, such as in the labour market, but everywhere that disciplining processes occur. Participating in the labour market and having greater material welfare would not automatically make women more powerful.

Deconstructionism can be a method by which pluralism and inegalitarianism may be distinguished. It mentions several possible instruments to combine equality with difference, but it cannot choose between them. Wendy Sarvasy is one of the few deconstructionist feminists who pays attention to the issue of social equality. She argues (1992: 332) that feminists need equality and difference in their concept of citizenship: 'women need a new gender-differentiated and equal conception of citizenship supported by a nonpatriarchal welfare state'. She calls such a perspective a social-democratic view of citizenship. It would democratize social relations and use democratic processes to address social inequalities.

According to Sarvasy, there are at least four ways in which gender difference and gender equality can be combined: (1) shared commitment to the creation of a feminist welfare state; (2) structuring gender-differentiated needs into universal programmes; (3) the drawing out of the emancipatory potential of gender difference within a new context of greater substantive and formal gender equality; (4) using gender difference to redefine formal gender equality. Furthermore more attention should be paid to the issue of differences amongst women. Despite Sarvasy's proclaimed positive judgement of difference, it seems that difference is repeatedly emphasized to obtain a fuller and more satisfactory idea of social equality (cf. Sarvasy 1994).

Deconstructionist feminists list several possibilities of combining social equality with positive plurality without having to opt for one of them. Their aim is simply to show the many options available. They neither choose nor make exclusions themselves. This is why there is no point in outlining the concrete deconstructionist position on social equality.

The existing feminist debate

On the whole, the feminist debate on social equality appears more substantial than the social-liberal one, because it does not discuss material welfare in the sense of income distribution only, but also in terms of other necessary distributions. Furthermore, the feminist debate also deals with social participation. The content of the debate is again, however, strongly phrased in terms of equality and difference.

In my opinion, humanist feminists have rightly judged social equality to be important for the aim of equal citizenship. They see that many other conditions are necessary to reach social equality than equal rights alone. For instance, they have suggested that affirmative action programmes are necessary, that paid and unpaid labour should be redistributed more equally between partners, that education for children should be free from 'sex roles', that young women should be encouraged to take up jobs, that an individualized social security and tax system should be established, that there should be more public childcare available, more flexible work arrangements, safer work environments and more public transport.

Another strong point of humanist feminists is their claim that women must enter the public realm. Yet, it seems that humanist feminists believe too strongly in the inherent value of social participation and overlook its instrumental value. For some, there is nothing beyond social participation (important exceptions are Lister 1995a; Siim 1988, 1994). Too often they assume that equal social participation is the same as equal citizenship. They seem to value material welfare for itself, not as a tool for gaining respect and as a condition for equal citizenship.

Woman-centred feminists rightly state that the social-liberal distributive paradigm leaves existing norms and values as they are. This is not reason enough to reject the distributive paradigm; however, it is reason to go beyond it. They have also warned that, in imitating men, women's actions will perpetuate disrespect for the female element in society and will not automatically change male norms or associations between citizenship, politics and men. Nevertheless, this must not lead feminists to embrace only what women do or think. In particular, the special value of public activities should not be overlooked.

Of course, parenthood and education are important for citizenship, but it is also important that women enter the public sphere to the same degree as men. Participating in public activities does not imply that women have to participate in exactly the same way as men have done. They are able to take new initiatives, and to criticize existing perspectives and current ways of doing things. Before they can do this, however, women must be present in all those places in which norms are created, where decisions are made about how to do things, and about what sorts of products should be supplied.

Deconstructionist feminists are right in saying that power does not work solely from top to bottom and that one can have a part in changing the discourse from wherever one is. In spite of this, it makes a great deal of difference whether one is amongst the participants or the spectators, amongst the elites or the masses. It is difficult to predict what kind of change women would effect if they made up 50 per cent of the social participants at all levels, but it is almost certain that changes would occur.

Deconstructionist feminists are good at reflecting upon the ways in which equality and difference can be combined. However, they lack a normative perspective that might indicate what social equality ought to be. They are skilled in avoiding the choice between humanist feminism or woman-centred feminism, but appear unable to show why a particular form of material welfare and social participation should be a necessary condition for equal citizenship.

Two sub-themes of social equality

The level and distribution of material welfare does indeed influence women's citizenship. It appears relevant to the condition of women's citizenship that women in (semi-)capitalist countries own only a small percentage of all the property, have a much lower income level than men, are much more financially dependent on their partners and the state than are men and have less influence in the economic decision-making world.

Economics has such a significant influence in politics that it is hardly possible to distinguish between economic and political power. A person's economic position affects the possible exercise of that person's citizenship rights. The level of material welfare affects women's citizenship in yet another way: being poor in itself devalues one to a second-class citizen in capitalist society. One is disrespected simply because of a lack of money; one's opinion is not heard, because it is the voice of a 'loser'. Even if participation is more important than status in citizenship, we should not forget this aspect.

In *Zur Judenfrage* (On the Jewish Question) (1844) Karl Marx notes that in order for political emancipation to occur, one must first have social emancipation. One cannot behave as a free citizen in politics if one is still oppressed in society. He refers of course to workers, but there is nothing to stop us using this idea for women. Women in liberal democracies cannot be regarded as equal citizens if they are still oppressed as a group in society. If one regards oppression as exploitation, violence, marginalization, cultural imperialism or powerlessness, one might probably indeed say that women are oppressed as a group within society.

One could go even further than Marx, but within the same line of thought: women cannot be free citizens in politics if they are still oppressed in the private sphere of the family. One has to be free from poverty, from violence and from humiliation to be able to respect oneself and to think autonomously. Economic independence and material welfare will assist women in liberating themselves and in being able to act as citizens. Women in liberal democracies are currently only equal citizens in a formal sense. In a material sense they are still second-class citizens or even subjects who need to be liberated.

Social participation also influences one's citizenship. Both the level and the kind of social participation are important in this regard. Bill Jordan suggests in *The Common Good. Citizenship, Morality and Self-Interest* (1989) that social, public participation – having a part in the rulership of society – affects one's ideas of rights, self-esteem, intellect, feelings, manners and democracy. Through social participation, people learn all kind of skills that are extremely useful in democratic citizenship.

Jordan is inspired by Tocqueville, who can be placed between republicanism and liberalism. In his two volumes of *Democracy in America* (1835, 1840), Tocqueville showed his surprise and admiration for the many social and political associations in which citizens were active. Indeed, according to him, social and political participation are hard to separate. Through many different jobs and activities in the public sphere citizens learn to cooperate, to think, to discuss and to decide. Tocqueville argued that these skills are very useful for political participation, but also that jobs in which these skills are used are already a kind of political participation. Tocqueville suggested that in their labour, people not only learn and use instrumental rationality, but also regenerate their society by the use of new ideas and talents.

Jordan argues that this is now more true than ever. Particularly in the age of the interventionist state, public and private spheres or political and social relations cannot be clearly separated. For Jordan, fundamental distinctions between social participation (in the sense of economic participation and participation in all kinds of cooperation in civil life) and political participation are rendered meaningless.

Following Jordan, we should note that women have a marginal role in social participation. They are less often in the public sphere than men, with the exception of the feminist movement in the 1970s (Allen 1981); women's public activities are less frequent and worse paid in comparison to men's activities. Particularly relevant to citizenship is that female citizens are seldom present in the decision-making activities of society. Society is indeed almost exclusively man-made.

On the other hand, decision-making processes are very slow if *everyone* needs to have a say in them. It is not that important that everyone undertakes exactly the same kind of social participation at the same time, but that there is fluctuation among the decision-makers and that one is prepared (in the widest sense) for such a task. It is this fluctuation – and the training in all kinds of social participation – that is important, rather than having all citizens engaged in the same kind of social participation. After all, we need different kinds of skills, specialities and activities in order to have an active, lively society.

It is true that public activities (meaning activities undertaken together with relative strangers) have an extra value, because they help us to see other citizens' perspectives; they compel people to put their thoughts into words and to discuss them with other people; they teach people to cooperate and to see the links between their private interests and the common good. Social participation within the family does not offer the skills for political participation that public social participation offers. Public social participation, in sum, is pertinent to citizenship, yet it is not necessary to have *all* citizens doing exactly the same thing, as long as a great deal of their social activities are public activities.

What does this imply for the relation between social and political citizenship? For several reasons we cannot dismiss socio-economic affairs and claim that they have nothing whatsoever to do with citizenship. As I have argued, one's social status is likely to affect one's political activity and power. Moreover, if participation in decision-making is important in the conception of citizenship, then it is impossible to draw a clear line between social and political participation.

Other conditions for equal citizenship

However important social equality may be for equal citizenship, feminists should not focus on this issue exclusively. Feminists have extended 'social equality', describing it so that it not only encompasses income levels, job functions, property, education and social participation, but also refers to a division of time (paid/unpaid labour, care time, spare time), a degree of mobility and safety and a degree of responsibility for the care of dependants. Even if we accept such a broad scope of 'social equality', there are still other requirements to be met if equal citizenship is to be realized.

To start off with, as Mary Dietz argues in 'Context is All: Feminism and Theories of Citizenship' (1987: 15), feminists should not exclusively focus on questions of social and economic concern. They should highlight the fact that social and economic concerns can only be pursued through the active involvement of citizens in the public world.

Moreover, some feminists have correctly drawn attention to the fact that it is first necessary to look at particularities before one can construct the idea of a general will or the policy preferences of citizens (Benhabib 1992a: 140). It must therefore be possible to show one's differences in politics: to be a citizen of a specific kind. Acknowledging this will (and must) lead to a wider meaning of the term 'political participation' and to seeing the line between public and private as something that is repeatedly constructed in a particular way.

In addition, feminists have rightly pointed out that it will be necessary to ensure 'equal respect' for women, to create strong images of female citizens and female politicians with the same variety as existing images of male citizens and male politicians. This does not mean that gender will no longer play a role when we talk about citizens and politicians, for there will still be gendered images. It only implies that being a man no longer makes a person automatically more suitable as a citizen or a politician than being a woman.

In order to obtain equal citizenship for both men and women, feminists also need to create another vocabulary of citizenship. The concept and practice of citizenship constructed by men should be corrected by female and by feminist perspectives. This means that the language not only of equality, but of freedom, political participation and political judgement needs to be reconstructed (Jones 1990).

*   *   *

Equal citizenship cannot exist when social and private inequalities between individuals are ignored. As long as men and women are socially unequal, they are not equal citizens. The material welfare of women should be improved and conditions must be realized so that men and women can participate 'equally' in the private and the public realm. I understand 'equally' here in the sense of the same amount of time and in positions at the same levels. It does not necessarily require that women have to participate in the same way as men do.

Before women's full political emancipation can be realized, social emancipation is required, not only of the marginalized class but also of the marginalized sex, not only in the social sphere but also in the family, not only in the sense of material equality but also in the sense of social participation.

We should not give the illusion that social equality will automatically lead to political equality. Equality in resources does not imply equality in decision-making and equality in power. Furthermore, in order to realize political equality of the sexes, other views of political subjectivity and political judgement are also needed. The next two chapters will deal with these issues.

7

Political Subjectivity

The term 'political subjectivity' refers to the way in which people present themselves in politics, their public image or public self. Whether or not this is different from someone's private self is subject to debate. Some republican political philosophers have pleaded for a strong distinction between the two. In *On Revolution* (1963: 112–113) Hannah Arendt connects the term 'public person' with the Latin word *persona*. In its original meaning *persona* referred to the mask that the actors in classical plays wore. The mask concealed the natural face but made sure that one's voice could reach the audience. Arendt uses it as a metaphor for the public role which assists a citizen in the ability to act playfully and freely. It protects us and enriches us by showing the plurality amongst people.

The same argument was made more recently by Richard Sennett in *The Fall of Public Man* (1977). He emphasizes that it is exactly by being able to play a political role – and not being scrutinized in one's personal life – that public freedom and civilization is realized. By implication (pp. 286–292), politicians should not be questioned on their misbehaviour in their private life, because – as Aristotle has stated – the good citizen is not the same as the good man. For each self different qualities are required.

One may say that it is exactly this 'fall of public man' that many feminists have desired. They have wanted it in at least two respects, both of which can be shown in Jean Bethke Elshtain's book *Public Man, Private Woman* (1981). First she attacks the fact that many women remain isolated in the private sphere. Secondly, she questions the kind of public self that is required of the political actor. She criticizes the fact that politicians are supposed to be beyond the level of human needs. In her opinion, women should not act like this. They should draw inspiration from the values of the private sphere and bring them 'as women' into the public sphere. So the public woman Elshtain wants has a lot in common with the private woman. Many feminists have also suggested that one *should* be able to criticize public figures on their personal life – for instance in the case of sexual harassment in the past – because these public figures need to set an example and if they are found guilty of misconduct they have lost their authority.

This chapter will describe and evaluate social-liberal and feminist positions on the issue of how people should present themselves in politics and on whether or not their public self needs to differ from their private self. In order to understand their stances towards political subjectivity, we first need to look at the general view of subjectivity that forms the basis of their political philosophy. Do these political philosophies base themselves on a particular human, male or female 'nature' or do they think that our subjectivity is constructed anyway and that we should allow for a multiplicity of identities, as postmodernism has suggested? And does it matter what kind of subject a political philosophy bases itself upon?

Here I am interested in the question of whether one's stand on the ontological foundation of political theory – who we are – has a direct impact on one's stand on the desirable subjectivity in political practice – the way we should present ourselves politically. In particular, I want to examine whether or not the feminist challenge to the subjects 'man' and 'the individual' in social-liberal political theory should lead towards a female identity politics in which women present and organize themselves as women in political practice.

Liberalism

Classical liberalism apparently takes the autonomous individual as its foundation: because we are all human beings with the capacity to reason, we should have equal rights and equal status as citizens. Thomas Paine is the clearest example of someone who used the idea of being equal human beings to claim the rights of man (1791–92) in the political arena. Classical liberals also seem to suggest that one can present oneself in politics either as a citizen in general or as a man.

Feminists from Mary Wollstonecraft onwards have attacked the inconsistency in the application of this Enlightenment ideal. On the one hand, Enlightenment theorists claimed that we are all equal human beings; on the other hand, they stated that men and women are so dramatically different that this equality does not apply to women. This does not mean to say, however, that these feminists themselves insisted on equality of the sexes in all respects. Mary Wollstonecraft, for instance, in *A Vindication of the Rights of Woman* (1792) claimed equal rights for both sexes, but thought that men and women should have different citizen duties. Classical feminists argued that women should be incorporated in political theories, but differed about whether they should present themselves in politics as women or as citizens in general (Rendall 1985, 1987).

When women obtained the vote, it seemed as if the problem of political subjectivity and gender no longer existed. Both men and women were acknowledged as political subjects and, slowly, political theorists added the phrase 'and women' to what they said about men or, alternatively, they talked about citizens in general, but changed nothing in the content of their analysis. Both on the level of ontology in political philosophy and on the level of political presentation, most modern political theorists have chosen the individual gender-neutral citizen as their base.

For instance, social liberals claim to be gender-neutral and view the equal capacity to reason as the foundation for a gender-neutral politics. According to them, political equality of all adult citizens implies that people's biological and social differences should not matter for their political status. The fact that men and women occupy such different positions in reality is not a contradiction of the political equality of the sexes. After all, political equality is interpreted by social liberals as equal treatment in political procedures and not as equality of outcome.

A good example of the mainstream social-liberal perspective on political subjectivity is offered by John Rawls. His book *Theory of Justice* (1971) has as its foundation a human being who is behind a veil of ignorance and who therefore has to act as if he or she is not aware of his or her personal characteristics. In other words, the subject here is 'Anybody'. Because we do not know the position in which we will end up in the actual world, Rawls argues that we will designate a world that is reasonably good for the worst off – that is for heads of households of the lowest classes with several financial dependants to provide for.

At the level of political presentation, Rawls acknowledges that in practice people will have all kinds of political identities. Yet, precisely because they are so 'particular' it is better to stick to the abstract individual devoid of particular characteristics in order to determine the rights and duties of citizens. However, the social liberals Bruce Ackerman (1980) and Will Kymlicka (1989, 1995) argue that we should imagine the positions of people with different identities and needs before we determine the rights and provisions citizens ought to have. Both theorists also seem to suggest that in political dialogue people should be able to present themselves as the bearers of different identities and interests, for instance those of daughters (Ackerman) or ethnic minorities (Kymlicka), even though they are also citizens in general. (Kymlicka [1995: 174] is the most radical in this respect, proposing differentiated citizenship.)

Humanist feminism: gender neutrality and the general interest

Humanist feminists accept the social-liberal foundation for politics – namely the human individual with equal capacity for reason – even though they argue that in several social-liberal theories this individual is still not gender-neutral enough and still looks more like a man. A good example of a humanist-feminist position can be found in Pauline Johnson's book *Feminism as Radical Humanism* (1994). Johnson argues (p. 10) that radical humanism incorporates two interconnected values: the equal value of all people as members of a generic 'humanity', and the value of someone's uniqueness and individuality. She argues strongly (p. 134) against the currently dominant anti-humanist mode amongst feminists:

> The central claim raised in [this] book is that feminism is a humanism. The anti-humanist's attempt to establish that modern humanism is hostile to the principle of diversity and difference – that it insists on 'measuring women and men according to the same standards and treating them in the same way' – is an assessment

which fails to recognise humanism's universalising claims as the underside of its own commitment to the idea of the unique difference of each personality. Each time a feminist theory raises, once called upon to account for its own motivations, a principled commitment to the idea of the autonomy, the unique and rightful diversity of feminine selves, it speaks in the language of humanist values.

Humanist feminists emphasize in their politics that women are ordinary human beings just as men are. As Jean Grimshaw points out in *Feminist Philosophers* (1986: 118), human nature itself is then seen as something that is the same in men and women. In this respect, Simone de Beauvoir had already stated in *The Second Sex* (1953: 38) that 'one is not born, but rather becomes, a woman'. Modern humanist feminists indicate this same idea with the difference between 'sex' and 'gender'. For instance, Ann Oakley argues in *Sex, Gender and Society* (1972: 189) that 'sex differences may be "natural" but gender differences have their source in culture, not nature'.

Humanist feminists also argue that in public life we should present ourselves as all being part of the same humanity and therefore as all deserving equal respect. We should encourage everyone to develop their talents as human beings. Regardless of people's sex, they should be considered 'equal citizens'. We should all count as one person in politics and in law, as this is the difference between modern democracy and the status system of the past. The political role or subjectivity is, therefore, the same for women and men: the rational individual.

Political equality for humanist feminists means that people's particularities should not matter to their political status (see Phillips 1993: 43). Eye colour should not matter; likewise, sex should not matter. Nevertheless, if people have been discriminated against in the past, then they may claim compensation for this injustice, according to humanist feminists. Sometimes, it will be necessary to identify women as an unjustly treated group, and so sex difference must be recognized. However, they view this as being very unfortunate (Okin 1989; Richards 1982). They argue that we should aim for a situation in which this is no longer necessary. We should aim for a gender-neutral political identification.

For liberal humanist feminists political equality implies equality of opportunity (cf. Jaggar 1983a: 193–197), but for the egalitarians amongst them it also means equality in outcome (Franzway et al. 1988). As long as there is no equality in outcome, egalitarian humanist feminists suspect that there must be some hidden discrimination and injustice.

For humanist feminists, feminist politics is a temporary necessary evil. Once we have real political equality, there will no longer be a basis for feminist politics. Meanwhile, feminist groups must claim that, 'unfortunately', it is still necessary to draw attention to the category of female political subjects, because women cannot genuinely be individuals while they are still discriminated against.

Woman-centred feminism: identity politics

Woman-centred feminists claim that despite the good intentions of social liberals they seek to emancipate women only when these women are willing to conform to male norms. Instead of this sort of assimilation, woman-centred feminists argue for a positive cultural politics: feminization. For instance, Carole Pateman argues in *The Sexual Contract* (1988: 231) that 'women's equal standing must be accepted as an expression of the freedom of women *as women*, and not treated as an indication that women can be just like men'.

Some people argue that woman-centred feminism falls short by offering an essentialist view of female nature (e.g. Alcoff 1988, using the term 'cultural feminism'). However, it need not have (an essentially defined) female nature as its foundation. It may consider female identities as social constructions or the results of decades of gender socialization, or both. Whether it is natural or constructed, woman-centred feminists take 'femininity' as another foundation for politics and citizenship (Held 1993; Noddings 1984).

One point of their criticism is that an androgynous subject is impossible. As Mary Daly has suggested, 'it is something like John Wayne and Brigitte Bardot scotch-taped together – as if two distorted "halves" could make a whole' (in Jaggar 1983a: 87). Another point of criticism is that an androgynous subject is undesirable because it is female subjectivity that provides desirable qualities on which to base a political philosophy.

For instance, Kathleen Jones refers in her essay 'Citizenship in a Woman-Friendly Polity' (1990: 784) to a remark by Genevieve Lloyd (1986: 76): 'Women qua woman – as a symbol of attachment to individual bodies, private interests and natural feeling – represent all that war and citizenship are supposed to contain and transcend.' Jones proposes (1990: 785) to found ideas of citizenship on the image of the female citizen. Then, an alternative woman-friendly discourse of citizenship might emphasize the body in relation to the body politics, recognize that sexual harassment is sometimes used as a political strategy against women, and suggest that the slogan 'the personal is political' leads to new duties, responsibilities, rights, and forms and areas of democracies (cf. Jones 1988, 1993).

Woman-centred feminists also plead for 'woman' as the foundation for feminist political practice. There are two variations here. The first one is that of women's forum feminists (Landes 1984b, 1992; Young 1990b) who leave open what it is that women will contribute to society and politics and merely state that women can more easily discover what their interests and needs are if they organize themselves as women-only groups in politics and society. For instance, Nancy Fraser argues (1990: 119) that in mixed groups male dominance affects deliberation. She therefore pleads for differentiating public spheres, and her 'politics of needs interpretation' (1989: 144–187) facilitates the creation of female and feminist publics.

In a 'politics of needs interpretation', the specific needs of different groups have to be taken into account before a view of justice is arrived at.

Fraser is suspicious of concepts of a general will and of unity. She urges women to gather in women's groups to develop their views, to articulate their voices, to find out what their needs are, to reinterpret these and those of others (Fraser 1990; 1989: 162–164). Only in this way can an equality be found which neither neglects nor immediately transcends particular differences (cf. Benhabib 1992a; Voet 1990).

The second variation is that of women's morality feminists, such as Jean Bethke Elshtain (1983, 1992), who have a substantive idea of what women will add to existing society and politics, usually implying that they will become more caring and less competitive (Feder Kittay and Meyers 1987; Maihofer 1988). Sometimes they suggest that these values derive directly from women's nature, but at other times that they derive from women's practices. In the latter case, it is fortuitous that women usually uphold these values (Ruddick 1980, 1983a, 1983b).

Both types of woman-centred feminism see positive virtues in 'sisterhood' (Ackelsberg 1983; Benton 1988; cf. Phillips 1993: 32–33). Women's political subjectivity is not rational, cool and neutral but connected by friendship with other women (Raymond 1986). Again, this is based either on the idea of substantive commonalities between women (through nature or socialization) or on common oppression.

Moreover, both types of woman-centred feminism argue for a female *identity politics* (Voet 1994b). Even though identities may be seen as only temporary and constituted, they can still function as sound foundations for a female identity politics. Identity politics is best described by Carl Schmitt in *Der Begriff des Politischen* (*The Concept of the Political* 1976) even though he refers to politics in general. The 'other' is seen as so fundamentally different that one's own existence seems to have come under threat. Through this subjectively felt threat, one feels the need to defend oneself and to articulate one's identity. If this does not happen, the danger is that one will be 'overthrown' and alienated from oneself. Identity politics is therefore based on a friend–foe distinction. Within identity politics a 'we' is placed opposite a 'they'. Inevitably the 'we' has a much more positive character than the 'they'. The we-group tries to protect itself against assimilation into the other group and to judge itself by its own standards. Within an identity politics, one also assumes that all the members of the we-group, who are oppressed in the same way, aim to liberate themselves in the same way.

Within an identity politics there is a great deal of outrage about the oppression with which one has to deal as a woman, homosexual or black, yet many members of these groups appear not to be able to live without this oppression. After all, if a repressed identity can be worn as a 'mantle of virtue', there is a danger of 'hunkering down in one's oppression', as is pointed out in Mary Louise Adams's article 'There's No Place Like Home: On the Place of Identity in Feminist Politics' (1989: 31). In any case, oppression gives members of these groups an identity by which others can be made to feel uncomfortable and guilty. This aspect of identity politics has been coined 'the politics of *ressentiment*' (Sennett 1977: 277–279; Tapper 1993; Yeatman 1993: 230, 1994b: 91–93).

The last aspect of identity politics is that there is no distinction between one's private identity and one's public identity. Within a female identity politics, women always perform the same role. Their only aim is to get more public recognition for that role. They emphasize that they want to be themselves in politics and celebrate the value of authenticity.

Deconstructionist feminism: deconstructing identities

In the beginning of the 1980s, assumptions that all women had the same interests, opinions, beliefs and virtues were questioned emphatically (Spelman 1988). Working-class, black and lesbian women angrily claimed their differences and accused the feminist movement as a whole of elitism, racism and heterosexism.

In the same period, deconstructionist feminists began to deconstruct the many meanings of 'femininity', 'women' and 'woman' and to criticize 'essentialism' (Alcoff 1988: 415–422). For instance, Denise Riley argues in *'Am I That Name?': Feminism and the Category of 'women' in History* (1988) that the category of 'women' refers to many different social meanings that have nothing to do with essential biological nature. Instead of taking Woman as the foundation for political theory, deconstructionist feminists acknowledge a multiplicity of identities. One individual consists of many different and even conflicting selves (Haraway 1992).

Deconstructionist feminists also have difficulties with the 'subject' as it assumes autonomy. They think that the political actor is somewhere in between a subject and an agent. There is no governing self. Deconstructionist feminists do not see the public self as being of more value than the private self, but rather deconstruct the distinctions between the two 'selves'. Every self is constructed on the basis of existing discourses; therefore, there is no exclusive 'private' self. Neither is there an inherent positive value in any 'self'.

The more differences discovered amongst women, the less sense it makes for deconstructionist feminists to suggest that women ought to enter politics 'as women'. They have also warned against notions of women's morality and sisterhood. These terms may be used in a tactical game, but are dangerous if one starts to believe in them. Deconstructionist feminists hope that the terms 'citizen' and 'woman' are no longer seen as oppositions. Instead, they want to have a plurality of political subjectivities from which women can choose.

For instance, Judith Butler in *Gender Trouble. Feminism and the Subversion of Identity* (1990a), argues that the choice is not humanist feminism or woman-centred feminism, or whether to use the human individual or the woman as a foundation for politics. Rather, the question for her is whether human or female nature can ever serve as a foundation for politics, as this nature is empty and constructed. Woman can serve as a foundation for feminist politics just as little as man or the individual can for humanist politics (Butler 1991). Butler argues (1990b: 325) further that, in taking the category of women as fundamental to any political claims, feminists were unaware that this would result in political closure.

Instead of founding oneself on one type of political subject, deconstructionist feminists plead for thinking about political subjectivity in the sense of playing a multiplicity of roles. In her article 'Reconstructing the Subject: Feminism, Modernism and Postmodernism' Susan Hekman (1991: 51) argues that political subjectivity or agency is obtained by jumping from one sort of discourse to another, from one sort of conversation game to the next, from one role to another.

Positive political identities for women

What is problematic in the humanist-feminist position is that it overlooks how dangerous it is to transcend gender differences and to talk about citizens in general in political theory and in political practice. In doing this, it pays little attention to the interests and opinions of political minorities. If political women cannot emphasize the specific difficulties women have, politics need not address these problems and gender inequalities will be reinforced.

Further, humanist feminism usually considers women in negative terms. If humanists talk about women, they talk about inequality, discrimination and oppression. In doing this, they represent women as victims. They assume that women ought to be emancipated, but it is difficult to imagine how this may happen if women do not have a positive basis for self-respect.

Moreover, the humanist-feminist position neither sees it as necessary to give citizens a political identity, nor does it demand that they have one. Because one's identity as a political actor does not matter for humanist feminists, they are not concerned that men are more socialized into a political identity than women are. In this way, they evade the issue of the discrepancies in public and political participation between the sexes. Neither do they question the fact that girls are socialized into non-political beings, nor focus on the impact of almost all images of the citizen and the politician being male.

Feminist theorists need to pay attention to the socialization of girls into political subjects, since research shows repeatedly that girls are less politically socialized than boys and that this has an enormous impact on their adult attitudes towards politics (e.g. Kelly and Boutelier 1978; Sapiro 1983). Equally positive images of male and female political actors are crucial to equal citizenship.

If citizenship is to acquire meanings important for feminists, if 'patriarchal' citizenship is to be changed into a 'woman-friendly' citizenship, then women will have to make sure that they are incorporated in political theories and that their needs are addressed. Women should also turn themselves into political actors and participate in the political process.

A female identity politics: 'we' and 'they'

Although I accordingly believe that feminists should encourage positive political identities for women, I am opposed to a female identity politics. My objections here are not based on the idea that identities are constructed and therefore are no true basis for politics. On the contrary, politics exists only through artificiality and construction. My objections are related to the specific form an identity politics takes.

The difficulties that the we–they distinction causes are twofold. First, the strict closure of the they-group precludes members of that group from sympathizing and affiliating with the we-group. Men with good intentions, who would like to call themselves feminists but are constantly treated as enemies, are likely to become reserved about feminism.

Secondly, the we–they distinction will also put a heavy burden on the shoulders of the members of the we-group. After all, they are supposed to constantly defend the group's interests. The woman who, after much lobbying, eventually succeeds in getting on to some committee will be expected by her lobby group, and perhaps even by 'liberal' members of that committee, to behave as a woman and articulate the interests, opinions and virtues of women. Who would like to be chosen 'as a woman' under those conditions? Either one will stereotype oneself and freeze one's identity, or one will be constantly accused of betrayal and of taking the job on false grounds. There is also another negative effect: that minorities within these identity groups will be overlooked and not represented at all.

These exclusion and inclusion difficulties of identity politics will not be solved by endless fragmentation. If the women's movement splits itself up into groups, such as Aboriginal women, lesbian women, Islamic women and so forth, there will be a multitude of different identities, but exclusion and inclusion difficulties will simply occur within these more specific groups. Besides, such a strategy will cause difficulties for the solidarity of the women's movement as a whole.

Partner in misery, partner in change?

Lately, there has been a great deal of resistance to the idea that all women are oppressed in the same way, yet there has been little protest about the idea that all women will liberate themselves in the same way. Within an identity politics one still assumes that, if there has been enough fragmentation, the reduced we-group will be able to engage in a clear and strong liberation struggle. Indeed, all members now have more or less the same backgrounds and interests.

Here, one completely denies the importance of opinions and of judgement. June Jordan, an American poet (in Adams 1989: 28) has put it like
this:

> It occurs to me that much organizational grief could be avoided if people under-
> stood that partnership in misery does not necessarily provide for partnership in
> change: when we get the monsters off our backs all of us may want to run in very
> different directions.

Even though two people might find themselves in exactly the same situation, they could arrive at opposite judgements of that situation. Further,
even if each makes exactly the same negative judgement, they could still
have completely opposite ideas as to how to get out of that situation and
what the aim of the struggle should be.

Politics of *ressentiment*

As Anna Yeatman has argued (1994b), the biggest danger of the politics of
ressentiment, in which groups hunker down in their oppression, is the idea
that power and oppression go hand in hand, with the result that some
oppressed groups would rather stay away from power. It is easier to be inno-
cent and repressed than to be responsible and to be held responsible.

The objection to this is that it leads to indignity for the group concerned,
and that if one does not desire to be in a position of power, one does not
learn to deal with power and to deal with responsibility. Responsible policy-
making can only be learned through a multitude of experiences, not simply
by complaining from a position of powerlessness.

Private person/public person

It is also problematic if there is no distinction between one's private identity and one's public identity. The American feminist political theorist Joan
Landes accurately points out in *Women and the Public Sphere in the Age of
the French Revolution* (1984a: 1):

> How difficult it is to uncouple women from domestic life. How much more diffi-
> cult, once uncoupled, to imagine a world in which women's proper place is the
> public sphere.

Indeed while the term 'public man' has a positive connotation, 'public
woman' is still a derogatory term. Nonetheless, this does not necessarily
imply that women in the public sphere must appear 'as women' and that
there will be no distinction between public and private selves. As Carl
Schmitt (1976) points out, one of the advantages of making a distinction
between a private self and a public self is that a political enemy does not
necessarily have to become a personal enemy. This would civilize relationships and would be quite useful to the feminist movement. One would not

have to lose so many friends over disagreement on a particular issue. This
implies the value of 'civic friendship', where some distance is kept so that
one can strongly disagree with yet still respect the other (Arendt 1982; Voet
1988a, 1988b).

Within the feminist discussion, another type of argument is that of Mary
Dietz. In 'Citizenship with a Feminist Face: The Problem with Maternal
Thinking' (1985: 20), Dietz argues that feminists like Elshtain and Ruddick
give a stereotypical view of women as creatures of the family and identified
by maternal thinking, and that the mother is a particularly inappropriate
model for political subjectivity in democratic citizenship. According to
Dietz (p. 30), maternal virtues refer to particularity, exclusiveness, inequality, love and intimacy, whereas democratic citizenship requires collectivity,
inclusiveness, generality and distance. She concludes (p. 34) that 'what
feminist political consciousness must draw upon is the potentiality of
women-as-citizens and their historical reality as a collective and democratic
power, not upon the "robust" demands of motherhood' (cf. Young 1995a).

In another article, 'Context is All: Feminism and Theories of Citizenship'
(1987: 17–19), Dietz goes a step further by attacking feminism for its
'womanism' – the notion that women have a superior democratic nature or
a more mature political voice. The answer, according to Dietz, is to avoid
womanism while remaining attentive to women.

While I would agree that a distinction needs to be made between a public
identity and a private identity, I disagree with Dietz's conclusion that a
public identity as a woman or a mother should always be vetoed by feminists. It may still be necessary at times for feminists to present themselves as
women in politics in order to have women's needs addressed, or as mothers
and fathers to have children's needs addressed. In my opinion, what is
crucial here is the acknowledgement that it is a public role that is played on
purpose – in contrast to a natural capacity – and that feminists must not play
the same role continuously.

An obvious advantage of making a distinction between public and private
selves is that feminists can start creating more positive public identities for
women. In this way, one does not simply always appear 'as a woman', but
in one of many complex and diverse public roles, as noted by Carry
Brachvogel in her book *Eva in der Politik* (Eva in Politics 1920). After all,
men do not always simply appear 'as men' in the public sphere either.

Reconstructing agency

We do not need to choose between a universalist individualistic social
liberalism that overlooks all differences between social groups and an identity politics that makes women's difference the foundation for politics.
Political practice offers many more complicated and, for particular situations, appropriate answers than can be imagined.

I can easily accept the postmodern argument that historical struggles have not only constituted interests (Pringle and Watson 1992: 70), but have constituted political subjectivities as well (Mouffe 1993: 77), such as the worker, the woman, the lesbian and the black woman. This does not mean that we do not have to take them seriously. On the contrary, it is even more reason to accept them as references in political dialogue.

Yet if women are not natural, but are constructions – or in other words, if women are not born, but made – does this mean that feminism has lost its major political *agency*: 'woman'? Or, as Ruth Lister puts it (1995b: 10): 'there is a danger that, if "woman" is simply deconstructed and left in fragments, there is no woman left to be a citizen'. It seems to me that it is not necessary to base political subjectivity on one kind of human nature: general, male or female (cf. Lister 1995a: 5). Indeed, I am quite convinced by the deconstructionist argument that this will easily lead to group closure and to restrictive political argumentation and action.

Politically, we already accept the fact that people have different roles at different times. People in politics jump from one capacity to another, depending on which topic they are discussing, for instance from concerned citizens who want to protect the environment to economic experts. Some restrictions exist when one is a party member, in that the party has given itself some kind of identity through a name and a history. But even here, the large variety of arguments within one party is surprising.

The jumping image is useful in reminding ourselves that people also jump between positions of subjection and agency. I believe this is a better perspective than the assumption (Mouffe 1993: 77) that people (always) take a position somewhere between complete subjects and complete free agents. Creating this middle position ignores important distinctions in the degree of freedom between people. Besides, it diverts our attention from those specific moments in which people turn themselves into agents. Although many women may be subjected to sexism, only a few of them may identify themselves politically as feminists and only a few of them turn themselves into political actors.

Finally, the fact that it is possible to articulate a position as a woman does not mean that we have to do this always and everywhere, nor that every woman or man has to agree with its underlying assumptions or with the appropriateness of articulating such a position at a particular point.

Yet Lister suggests there may be another difficulty in deconstructionism with regard to political subjectivity: deconstructionism is likely to *fragment* the category of 'women' into many groups of women, and this may make a unified feminist struggle difficult, if not impossible. I think that it is not at all necessary to go along this route of radical deconstructionism. Feminists can accept a moderate deconstructionism, in the sense that they need to accept the fact that the category of 'women' is constructed, but they should not hesitate to use this as a political subjectivity if and when that appears sensible.

A third potential problem with deconstructionism is that it might also fragment or dissolve the political category of 'feminists'. Yet this category can also be seen as an historically contingent construction, which is variable and open to change. Types of feminists may be differentiated, but this need not hinder people coming forward in politics as 'feminists in general' when this is advantageous.

*   *   *

I have argued in this chapter that feminists should continue to challenge the monopoly of male subjectivity as a foundation for political theory. It is tremendously important that we change our concepts of citizenship, of politics, of participation and of the public sphere, in order that they are also appropriate for female citizens and in order that sex differences can be articulated in our theories and practices of citizenship.

We should continue to create positive political identities for women and to make a distinction between a private self and a public self. Before women are able to choose between types of political subjectivity, they need to have a political identification. They need to see themselves as political subjects. In the process of creating positive political identities, feminists should be wary of a female identity politics that obliges women always to present themselves as women in politics. They should be encouraged to jump between many political roles such as woman, citizen, feminist, and so forth.

Rejecting a female identity politics that is based upon the idea that women are fundamentally different from men raises the question of whether one can still plead for more women in politics. After all, if women are not different, why ask for them? Why should it matter what percentage of men and women are present in politics? This complex topic will be the focus of the next chapter.

8

Political Representation

If feminism is to use a multiplicity of political roles rather than falling back on the political subjectivity of 'woman' only, can feminists still demand more women in decision-making bodies? In order to answer this question the focus of this chapter will be on evaluating existing feminist arguments for getting more female representation in decision-making bodies.

We can find most of these arguments in a pamphlet by an expert group working for the European Commission, *Women in Decision-Making. Facts and Figures on Women in Political and Public Decision-Making in Europe* (European Network 1994). According to this (pp. 7–9), there are five reasons why the European Union and its member states need policies to create a gender balance in public decision-making: it will lead to a better politics and society; it will make effective use of all talents; it is necessary to achieve equality between men and women; only 'parity democracy', in which the representatives are 50 per cent men and 50 per cent women, will realize genuine democracy; and, finally, women will better represent women's interests.

I will discuss and evaluate these arguments in critical dialogue with Anne Phillips's book *The Politics of Presence* (1995), as it is the text most closely related to my argument. I will also examine whether or not my position supports the notion of 'descriptive representation' or 'mirror representation', which is often used by feminists in their demand for a gender balance in politics. This is the idea that a representative body ought to mirror the people in society at large.

Furthermore, I will examine the value of women's representation for the representatives themselves and this means talking about the other side of political representation, namely political participation. While both refer to the same phenomenon of political action which is useful for society as a whole, talking about representation predominantly signifies its use for other people (Birch 1971; Leibholz 1960; Pitkin 1967), whereas talking about participation predominantly refers to its use for the individual actors (Barber 1984; Pateman 1970). Drawing upon some recent feminist literature, I will discuss the inherent value of political participation and whether or not this implies endorsing participatory democracy.

I will start however by describing social-liberal and existing feminist positions on representation, their arguments regarding the demand for more female representation and the inherent value of participation.

Social liberals: one person – one vote

For a long time within classical liberalism 'women and political representation' was not an issue, because it was felt that women did not need political representation of their own, and did not therefore need suffrage. For instance, in his 1820 'Article on Government', James Mill stated that suffrage for women or separate female representation was not necessary because women's interests were already 'virtually represented' in those of their fathers or husbands.

Five years later, however, William Thompson and Anna Wheeler (1983) made an issue of 'women and political representation'. They wrote a pamphlet against James Mill's statement, called *Appeal of One Half the Human Race, Women, Against the Pretensions of the Other Half, Men, to Retain them in Political and Thence in Civil and Domestic Slavery*. Their type of classical liberalism – utilitarianism – supposed that what needed to be represented in politics were interests. They pointed out that the interests of men and women were not identical, and that women needed to be given a chance to defend their own interests. Thompson and Wheeler demanded women's suffrage. They were followed by James Mill's son, John Stuart Mill, who even pleaded for this as an MP in parliament in 1866 and 1867 and whose argument in *Liberty* (1859) and *The Subjection of Women* (1869) was mainly for the effective use of all talents in society.

Since women, after a long struggle, obtained suffrage in liberal democracies, the belief among classical and social liberals has been that 'women and political representation' is no longer an issue; they believe it is already resolved. Social liberals see political representation mainly as a matter of equal political rights: one person, one vote. As women have the same political rights as men, there is, according to social liberals, no specific gender problem left as far as representation is concerned. If fewer women than men happen to be elected as representatives it is because voters have considered them less able. Apparently, even women voters have voted for men overall.

Women also have the freedom to form a women's party but, to date, these have not been very successful. This, according to social liberals, is no wonder because women are too divided amongst themselves on 'general issues'. As most people vote for someone who represents a view on 'the general interests of the country', women's parties hardly stand a chance.

According to social liberals, what ought to be represented in political bodies are opinions, or interests in the case of utilitarianism, but not particular social groups. We choose those representatives who we feel are the most competent. Social liberals hope that parliamentary discussion amongst competent representatives and elaboration by experts on some topics will lead to an agreement as to what best suits the general interest of the country. If disagreements remain (and social liberals see disagreements as unfortunate phenomena in politics), decisions will have to be made by majority rule.

Recently, however, some social liberals such as Will Kymlicka (1989, 1995) have argued that liberal democracy has to give indigenous people special political representation rights, because otherwise these groups will be outvoted continuously by a majority and traditional life for future generations in these indigenous communities will no longer be an option. However, not even Kymlicka argues (1995: 131–151) for 'mirror representation' but rather for 'threshold representation': some representatives of a group are needed in politics but not exactly the same proportion as that group forms in society.

Social liberals emphasize that, due to the size of modern states, we must have representatives and cannot enjoy direct democracy. Moreover, political issues have become so complicated in modern societies that ordinary citizens cannot be expected to have sound judgement on all issues. Political participation does not form an essential part of the social-liberal concept of citizenship because social liberals perceive it as too demanding. Yet some social liberals do feel that there is a value in political participation (Rawls 1971: 424–433; Walzer 1970) and in political debate (Ackerman 1989) for individual political actors.

The feminist debate

How have feminists criticized this social-liberal idea of representation? The differences between the liberal-feminist pamphlet of Thompson and Wheeler and the feminist pamphlet of the European Commission illustrate, in my opinion, several major changes within feminism. To begin with, the latter indicates a move away from claiming a liberal right to equal opportunities, towards a right to equal representation.

Furthermore, in claiming the right to equal representation many feminists have become less reluctant to use coercive methods in politics. Over the last hundred years the problem of women and representation, and feminist attitudes to it, have changed dramatically in western democracies. Women are no longer demanding a vote, but now demand a voice. As Iris Young (1990b: 184) puts it:

> [A] democratic public should provide mechanisms for the effective recognition and representation of the distinct voices and perspectives of those of its constituent groups that are oppressed or disadvantaged.

There also seems to be a broadening of the feminist scope. For a long time feminists focused exclusively on a gender balance in representative political bodies only, that is in parliaments, councils, political parties and sometimes also in governments. Recently however, as the later pamphlet shows, some feminists demand a gender balance in all public decision-making bodies.

Finally, given the reference to parity democracy, feminists have also turned, in the terms of Hanna Pitkin in *The Concept of Representation* (1967), from a concept of representation as accountability to a concept of descriptive representation. Thus, instead of proclaiming that women should have a right to hold representatives to account by choosing whether or not to elect them again, many contemporary feminists argue that representative bodies should reflect differences in society by being composed of its different segments. This general picture of the feminist debate needs to be qualified in terms of the three main feminist positions.

Humanist feminism: representation as citizens

Most humanist feminists think that there is nothing wrong in principle with the political representative system of liberal democracy, but rather with the social structure that underpins it. According to them, 'representation of all individuals' is guaranteed by a one person, one vote system. They think that the difficulties women have are of a more general character and not specifically linked to representation. If women are not represented to the same degree as men, humanist feminists attribute it to a fault or discrimination in education or to the fact that there is an insufficient number of public childcare facilities.

According to Iris Young, in her essay 'Humanism, Gynocentrism, and Feminist Politics' (1990a: 74), 'humanist feminism defines femininity as the primary vehicle of women's oppression and calls upon male dominated institutions to allow women the opportunity to participate fully in the public world-making activities of industry, politics, art, and science'. Humanist feminists thus feel that women should be participating in the public sphere on a level equal to that of men. This would happen if women were really emancipated, as are men. However, many humanist feminists only pay attention to social participation (Firestone 1970; Friedan 1963).

Other humanist feminists do pay attention to women's representation in politics. They are likely to use the argument that equal representation of men and women is necessary in order to achieve real equality between the sexes. They also use the old argument of John Stuart Mill that all talents in a state should be used. Nonetheless, humanist feminists – particularly liberal feminists – are inhibited by their view that it is ultimately a matter of women's personal choice as to whether or not they want to be active in politics. Recently within humanist feminism more emphasis on the inherent value of political participation can be noted (Phillips 1991a, 1995).

The main instruments therefore proposed by humanist feminists to get more women in politics – if they pay attention to political representation – are gender-neutral education and socialization, more public childcare, giving women courses in public speaking and encouraging women to put themselves forward as candidates.

Woman-centred feminism: representation as female citizens

Woman-centred feminists expect female representatives to represent women and the difference they signify in politics, rather than just opinions in general (Pateman 1988: 231; Sapiro 1981). They support a rough version of mirror representation, in which political bodies have equal or proportional representation of the sexes only and not of other oppressed groups. All women in the representative assembly stand for all women in society, simply because of their womanhood. If the most important fact about them was not that they represented women, then women could just as easily be represented by men or by a representative assembly which consisted of a majority of men.

Many woman-centred feminists want more women in decision-making bodies. They sometimes use the argument that all talents in a state must be effectively used, but believe that women have different talents from men. They argue further that if more women are public officeholders, it will make some difference to the responsiveness of government to women's interests (Sapiro 1981). Moreover, they say that if it is accepted that the democratic ideal of participation in governance is valuable, one cannot accept the systematic exclusion of one half of the human species that is so different from the other half. Parity democracy is required (cf. Outshoorn 1993). Finally, woman-centred feminists claim that women would provide a better politics and society by offering different and better values in politics (Hirschmann 1992).

Woman-centred feminists come up with several proposals for getting more women (who will respond as women) involved in politics: women's or feminist parties, ministries for women's affairs, quotas, and a change in the political culture and the working conditions of politics so that it will attract more women.

Other woman-centred feminists believe that women should have their own group politics, such as consciousness-raising collectives and women's groups outside the official decision-making bodies. Political participation by women therefore has an inherent value for them apart from the potential achievement of getting woman-friendly laws through parliament. They believe that participatory democracy is an alternative to representative democracy (cf. Mansbridge 1980). I will come back to this issue in the last section of this chapter.

Deconstructionist feminism: plurality represented

Deconstructionists emphasize that political representation takes place not only in parliament and in political parties, but in any discourse. Everywhere subjects are represented in a particular way, and this power game affects their status in society. Linguistic and other interventions are therefore necessary to undermine the current ways in which some social groups are represented. Most deconstructionists have looked at texts only, although recently some attention can be noted to the professional and institutional mechanisms through which the politics of exclusion operates (Butler and Scott 1992; Yeatman 1990, 1994a).

According to deconstructionist feminists, it is wrong to assume that no link exists between the background of representatives and their opinions. To ignore which groups representatives come from may mean ignoring the evidence of patriarchy and, in several countries, colonization. However, deconstructionist feminists are also critical of the idea that women in politics would represent the interests of all women or would make a better society or politics for all women. Therefore they usually restrict themselves to the argument that true democracy does not allow the exclusion of some groups, without saying that inclusion will guarantee a better representation of women's interests or a better society.

Deconstructionist feminism aims for more plurality in politics. Not only women, but also other oppressed groups, will be given special opportunity to have a voice in public affairs. It has come up with two proposals for this. The first is for special political representation of all kinds of oppressed groups in the process of policy-making. Iris Young's article 'Polity and Group Difference. A Critique of the Ideal of Universal Citizenship' (1989) is an example of the postmodern tendency in her work. She even speaks (p. 258) about 'differentiated citizenship as group representation'. Here, in a second version of descriptive or mirror representation, the aim is to secure a very accurate portrait of the nation. The policy-making assembly should not only reflect different sexes, but also different classes, races, sexualities, religions and languages (Voet 1993).

In later articles however Young pleads for a second, looser form of plurality in the form of a communicative democracy in which dialogues take place between the members of political bodies and minority groups. She is supported in this by other deconstructionists, such as Anna Yeatman. In *Postmodern Revisionings of the Political* (1994a: 89, 90), Yeatman argues that the multiple, potentially conflicting identities of each individual should lead to 'dialogical rights' and various context-responsive processes of consultation, decentralization, organic styles of decision-making, and resourcing of self-identified cultures.

In an earlier article, 'Voice and Representation in the Politics of Difference', Yeatman (1993) suggests that change is possible only if politicians are able to operate within an inclusive politics that listens to the voices of groups for whom policy-making is intended. In their emphasis on consultation, dialogue and voice for minorities, Yeatman and other deconstructionist feminists also seem to plead for at least some elements of a participatory democracy. Yet they do not seem to plead for special group representation in parliament.

Arguments for more women in decision-making

Now I would like to return to the arguments for greater female representation in decision-making put forward in the pamphlet by the expert group of the European Commission (and mostly used by woman-centred feminists), and discuss them in critical dialogue with Anne Phillips's comments in *The Politics of Presence* (1995: esp. Ch. 3).

The first argument which the expert group uses (European Network 1994: 8) is that women will provide a *better politics and government*:

> Because of their history as a group, women have their own and unique perspective. They have different values and ideas and behave differently. Increased participation of women in decision-making will create a new political culture and shed new light on how power should be exercised. Women attach great importance to the needs and views of contemporaries.

Even though the argument is not based on women's essential nature, it still stereotypes women far more than reality seems to warrant. So far, we do not have reliable evidence that women in decision-making would really have another approach, because there have not been enough of them around (Kanter 1977; Schlozman et al. 1995; Skjeie 1991; Welch 1977). I also suspect that Phillips is right when she speculates (1995: 75) that on the point of political culture 'politics is more formative than sex, and that the contrast between those who get involved in politics and those who do not is deeper than any gender difference between those who are elected'.

Moreover, it puts unfair pressure on women to expect them to live up to higher moral standards than male politicians and to listen better to other citizens than male politicians need to. Respecting women as citizens should not require female representatives to appear as angels but as able decision-makers. Indeed, as Mary Dietz (1987: 17–18; also quoted in Phillips 1995) has suggested, assuming that one group of citizens is generally better means that citizenship would lose its special name.

Secondly, the pamphlet pleads for the *effective use of all talents* because (p. 8) it 'is hard to grasp the loss that non-participation of women in decision-making represents to society when it comes to ideas, values and style'. This formulation allows the possibility that women would have different ideas, values and style to men but it could also mean that we should simply enlarge the pool of candidates so that there is a better chance of getting the best-qualified decision-makers. I have no difficulty with either formulation of this argument as long as it is acknowledged that the content of those talents will remain a matter of debate and that the argument does not provide a *right* to equal representation for both sexes, since talents are unlikely to be always absolutely equally divided between the sexes.

The third argument used in the pamphlet is that of *parity democracy*. It says (p. 7) that:

> When women make up 51.3% of the European population but represent only 12% of the political mandates, only one conclusion can be drawn: there is something fundamentally wrong with our democracy.

In its extreme form parity democracy assumes that democracy should reflect the existence of two very different types of human being. The logic of this, according to Joyce Outshoorn discussing proposals for this in the European Council (1993: 24), would lead to separate voting lists for women and for men. In the pamphlet of the European Union, however, a proposal is made for equal or proportional representation of the sexes rather than separate voting lists.

There is, however, nothing in the definition of democracy itself that requires this (nor, however, does it prohibit it; Schmitt 1985), neither in Rousseau's sense of representation of the people by the people nor in Schumpeter's sense of the competitive struggle for citizens' votes. It may only require equal representation of the sexes if we could really say that men and women are two distinct peoples, which I reject. I also want to avoid obliging representatives to represent their sex only. Furthermore, the democracy argument also restricts demands for more women in democratic decision-making bodies. No other elite can be reached by this argument, since none of them even pretend to be democratic. Socio-economic, bureaucratic and military decision-making bodies will not be persuaded to incorporate women in their top ranks by the argument that democracy requires it. In order to plead for more female representation in *all* decision-making bodies another type of justification is needed.

The fourth argument in the pamphlet says: '[b]ased on the human rights principles, an equal participation of men and women in decision-making bodies is a *pre-condition to achieve equality* between men and women' (p. 7, my italics). Phillips points out in the context of a justice argument which resembles this fourth argument (1995: 64–65) that it reduces political office to yet another favourable and privileged position and that there is no *right* to an interesting job. I agree, but it seems sufficient here to claim that following the ideal of political equality, it is important that, seen over a longer period, both sexes participate equally in decision-making and that policies should be developed which encourage this. I will return to this issue in my final chapter.

Even so, Phillips seems doubtful about this kind of justification. She argues (Ch. 2) that the meaning of equality and political equality is too controversial to provide such a justification on its own and that it does not explain why political equality should exist between women and men and not for instance between blue-eyed and brown-eyed people. However, political equality need not be posited as an uncontroversial justification, but merely as a worthwhile aim. One cannot reject an aim simply by saying that not everyone agrees with it. Phillips's own argument for a politics of presence and for gender parity in the elites even seems to confirm the value of this ideal. But indeed, in order to argue in favour of equality for the sexes and not for other categories it needs to be combined with another justification: interests.

I agree with Phillips that one cannot avoid using the argument that women may represent women's *interests* and needs better than men do. This is the fifth argument used in the pamphlet. As Phillips argues (p. 82), it is crucial here that the emphasis is on 'may', because we are talking at the level of probabilities rather than guarantees. We cannot and should not 'require' the representation of women's interests from female decision-makers because it would put too much of a burden on them. Also, as Phillips emphasizes (p. 158), female representatives are not formally accountable to women. If they were, it would support the undesirable idea that every group in politics need only represent its own interests and not those of other people and the general interests.

Still, although we cannot require it of female representatives, it is likely that they will represent women's interests better than men do anyway. Here I fall back on the political-realist and elitist argument that it is unavoidable that groups in power will not only serve the general interests but also their own individual and group interests. Different groups of women may have different interests. Still, as Phillips argues (pp. 67–68), women have some interests in common: those in relation to childbearing, those arising 'from their exposure to sexual harassment and violence, their unequal position in the division of paid and unpaid labour, and their exclusion from most arenas of economic and political power'.

Descriptive representation

I want to pause for a moment to ponder the question of whether or not my argument for more female representation in decision-making presupposes the notion of descriptive representation or mirror representation. The idea of 'descriptive representation' is explained by Hanna Pitkin in *The Concept of Representation* (1967) in terms of parliament being a mirror of society. She quotes (p. 60) the words of John Adams in the American revolutionary period. 'A representative legislature,' he said, 'should be an exact portrait, in miniature, of the people at large, as it should think, feel, reason and act like them.' This way all possible views and criticisms will come to light.

Pitkin distinguishes the concept of descriptive representation from other meanings of representation. She points out that, unlike these other concepts, descriptive representation does not suggest that in order to be a representative it is necessary to have authority over others (as is the case of somebody who represents a child in court, such as a parent, trustee or guardian). Neither does descriptive representation suggest that the legitimacy of the representatives lies in the fact that they can be held to account. Furthermore, it does not mean that, to be really representative, one should have voters who believe in the fact that they are represented. It only indicates how many people of group x are present in a parliament or in another political body.

When I ask for a gender balance in decision-making bodies without making requirements of those representatives I seem indeed to be using the notion of descriptive representation. Yet there are some important differences. First, I only refer to a gender balance, whereas descriptive representation demands in principle a proportional representation of all social categories. Secondly, I do not argue for a gender balance in representative bodies only but in all decision-making bodies and thus in all elites. Thirdly, although mirror representation seems to be the outcome, it is not the intention. The gender balance I am aiming for is not a function of the notion of representation, but stems from the desire for power-sharing and full and equal citizenship for both sexes. I do not require that female decision-makers will always stand for women and also call upon them to represent the general interests. Fourthly, I do not plead for exactly 50 per cent men and 50 per cent women in decision-making bodies all the time. I would prefer to talk about a gender balance in decision-making bodies *over time*. This allows for more flexibility and more liveliness in political struggles (Voet 1992c).

Participation

Apart from the value of representation for others, there is also the value of representation for the representatives themselves – the value of political participation. This follows the suggestion of Thompson and Wheeler in 1825 (1983: 196–197) that political participation by women is necessary in order to obtain respect for women in society:

> To obtain equal rights, the basis of equal happiness with men, you must be *respected* by them; not merely desired like rare meats, to pamper their sexual appetites. To be respected by them, you must be respectable in your own eyes; you must exert more power, you must be more useful. You must regard yourselves as having equal capabilities of contributing to the general happiness with men, and as therefore equally entitled with them to every enjoyment. You must exercise these capabilities, nor cease to remonstrate till no more than equal duties are exacted from you, till no more than equal punishments are inflicted upon you, till equal enjoyments and equal means of seeking happiness are permitted to you as to men.

Despite the participation of feminist activists in the second wave, feminist theorists in that period hardly discussed the inherent value of political participation. They concentrated more on the arbitrariness of the distinction between public and private sphere (Pateman 1989: Ch. 6; Siltanen and Stanworth 1984), on explaining the factors influencing women's participation (Rule 1987), and on criticizing the political culture (Evans, S. 1980) and the oppressive character of the state (McIntosh 1978). Participation of women in the existing political institutions was met with suspicion and was derogatorily called 'liberal feminism', which was seen as the wrong kind of feminism.

There are some exceptions – for instance Josephine Milburn. She suggested in 1976 (p. 38) that *full* citizenship encompasses various aspects of economic and political participation:

> If women are to become full citizens in this sense, they must of necessity become fully active participants in society. Indeed they will have achieved full citizenship . . . only when their participation in decision-making positions has increased well above the current levels of from three to twelve percent.

The aim, according to Milburn (p. 37), both for individuals and for the state, is to achieve women's 'full citizenship and full representation in the professions and in administrative and decision-making positions' (another exception is Ackelsberg 1984, 1989).

Recently, however, important changes have taken place. Contrary to feminist theory of the second wave we now see a lot more discussion about the inherent value of political participation. This is a relatively new phenomenon, and has cropped up in various debates. For example, Maria Helga Hernes (1987), Birthe Siim (1988) and others have argued that the state can also be 'woman-friendly', and thus the march of 'femocrats' (feminist bureaucrats) through the official institutions (Leech 1994; McBride and Mazur 1995) and women's inclusion in existing elites (Epstein and Coser 1981; Skjeie 1991) has become acceptable. Moreover, it became fashionable to criticize 'victim feminism' and plead for a 'macha feminism' that endorses women's urge for power (Wolf 1993).

Feminists have also started to use the framework of Jürgen Habermas to show the importance of public debate. Seyla Benhabib, Nancy Fraser, Iris Marion Young and Joan Landes are critical of Habermas's unified idea of 'the public' and the ways it excludes heterogeneity and issues of 'the good life' and 'private life'. Yet they also emphasize that a modified version of his proposal would allow a discussion of so-called private issues in political life (Fraser 1989: 122–129). It would also help to develop female 'publics' (Fraser 1990; Landes 1992) and to form an alternative type of democracy: communicative democracy (Young 1995b). However, in this framework participation refers to participation in debate and the acts that take place are almost exclusively acts of speech (e.g. Benhabib 1992a, 1992b).

Furthermore, with the growing popularity of civic republicanism within feminism more attention to the inherent value of political participation can be noted (Voet 1991). This becomes clear for instance in feminist publications on Hannah Arendt (Dietz 1991; Honig 1995; Jones 1993; Komter 1990; Voet 1988a). The most important feminist writer on civic republicanism in general is Mary Dietz who pleads for women's participation as citizens in general. Dietz argues (1987: 16):

> The key idea here is that citizenship must be conceived of as a continuous activity and a good in itself, not as a momentary engagement . . . with an eye to a final goal or a societal arrangement. . . . [D]iscussions of civic peers will necessarily centre on issues of social, political and economic concern to the community. But at the same time . . . feminist citizenship must be . . . more than this. Perhaps it is best to say that this is a vision fixed not on an end but rather inspired by a principle – freedom – and by a political activity – positive liberty. That activity is a demanding process that never ends, for it means engaging in public debate and sharing responsibility for self-government. What I am pressing for, in both theory and practice, is a feminist revitalization of this activity.

She considers (p. 18) the feminist activity in the 1970s as an inspiring example of this participatory citizenship.

While Dietz and others emphasize the value for women of increased participation, others have taken a different angle. These theorists (Hirschmann 1992; Jones 1990) argue that the incorporation of women in decision-making has an inherent value for participation in general, because women bring different approaches and interests. For example Jane Mansbridge (1993: 375) states:

> The main task of feminist theory must be to clarify and help redress gender inequality. In doing so, however, it contributes to a more general understanding of democratic community in ways not available to a liberalism restricted to individuals sprung into adulthood fully grown and a politics that excludes the private.

Finally, some feminists go beyond participation in representative democracy, and discuss the pros and cons of participatory democracy for women. Participatory democracy was pleaded for early on by Carole Pateman in her book *Participation and Democratic Theory* (1970), but her feminist arguments remained separate from the argument on participatory democracy for a long time. When she dealt with both it was to emphasize that participatory democrats did not discuss the issue of women (1989: Ch. 9). A similar voice was raised by Iris Young (1990b: Ch. 4) who criticized the forced unified voice of civic republicanism.

On the same topic, Anne Phillips in *Engendering Democracy* (1991a: 142) points out that '[b]ecause women have so often internalized their subordination, they need active participation and discussion if they are to be able to transform and recreate themselves'. The other attraction of participatory democracy for women is, in her view (p. 143), that it opposes 'women's seclusion inside the home', since a view of politics as 'engaging with other people and other concerns' helps to protest against this seclusion. However she also notes that participatory democracy would cost women even more time and they would run a stronger risk of conflict being sent underground than would be the case within representative democracy (for these and other disadvantages see pp. 126–142).

I accept these pleas for the inherent value of women's political participation, but add that political participation should not only entail participation in debate, but also participation in decision-making and in sharing responsibility. In the final chapter of this book I will elaborate on its importance for citizenship. Here I will only state that although my argument hinges upon a notion of many decision-making bodies in society, and the importance for citizenship of women being active in them at all levels, it does not require participatory democracy.

It does not require that all decision-making bodies become democratic or that decision-making should not be in the hands of a few; it does not imply that all the secret back-door decision-making should now take place in the open and be controllable by all citizens; it does not require that the members of these bodies need to be elected; and finally, it does not require that those substantially affected by decisions made by the social and political institutions must be involved in the making of these decisions.

My argument against participatory democracy is a common one.

Full-scale participatory democracy demands too much voluntary work of every ordinary citizen (Hirschman 1982; Walzer 1970) and cannot allow for efficient and quick decision-making. Moreover, not all ordinary citizens possess competent judgement in all areas. I do believe however that *where feasible*, decision-makers should consult the people for whom policies are intended. My argument can thus be considered as one for a moderately participatory decision-making system, rather than for a full-scale participatory democracy.

* * *

Thus, despite the constructed character of 'woman' and the multiplicity of political subjectivities that feminists can and should use, feminists can still demand more female representation in decision-making. These demands can be justified by a combination of the following arguments: that women's interests may be defended better, that it is necessary in order to achieve full and equal citizenship between the sexes, and that it will make a more effective use of all talents.

This should not mean descriptive representation in the sense of precisely mirroring the population everywhere and in all decision-making bodies, but rather that there should be a regular change in the group or groups that rule over time. The inherent element of political participation is indispensable, although it need not and should not be combined with a participatory democracy.

The next chapter focuses on political judgement, and asks: what kind of political judgement is required for a woman-friendly citizenship?

9

Political Judgement

What is political judgement? Judgement is intuitively associated with decision, analysis and discrimination (Arendt 1964). According to Ronald Beiner in *Political Judgment* (1983: 6), we have to distinguish three types of judgement: logical judgement, cognitive judgement and judgement as 'a quality of mind, in the sense in which we predicate of someone that they possess good or sound judgment, or when we say that we trust their judgment'. It is into this last category that political judgement falls. It occupies this category together with moral judgement, instrumental judgement and aesthetic judgement. All these types of judgement are approximately independent of rules and methods. They are based on persuasion, rather than on truth. They presuppose plurality because only plurality enables citizens to think, to see alternatives and to make choices. According to Beiner, although political judgement incorporates parts of logical and cognitive types of judgement, it should be separated from them.

In Beiner's view (pp. 138–143), a typical characteristic of political judgement is that it is not completely detached from existing opinions; it presupposes an existing political community. Political judgement needs to take into account all the opinions in the community, if it intends to make the most responsible judgement for the community and its future. When one makes a political judgement, it is a judgement about an object (politics) that is public and shared by all. Other citizens will therefore call you to account, challenge your judgement and ask you for reasons that are shared by other citizens or by which they can be persuaded. Finally, Beiner argues (pp. 155–157) that in political judgement, only the particular is given and the universal has to be found. One has to begin the process of judging from a concrete case and decide the general experience or category into which it falls – does it remind us of cases that we have recently dealt with, or is it in important respects unlike those cases? In particular, political judgement requires the faculties of identification and discrimination.

According to Beiner, political judgement is not only possessed by political leaders. On the contrary, he claims that all citizens have a capacity for it. He considers his study of political judgement to be a redefinition of citizenship, because it tears down the special privileges of 'experts' in political judgement and reclaims it as a possession of all citizens. He argues (p. 3):

The purpose of inquiring into the nature of judgment is to disclose a mental faculty by which we situate ourselves in the political world without relying upon explicit rules and methods, and thus to open up a space of deliberation that is being closed ever more tightly in technocratic societies. Concerning this faculty, the dignity of the common citizen suffers no derogation. Here the expert can claim no special privileges. If the faculty of judging is a general aptitude that is shared by all citizens, and if the exercise of this faculty is a sufficient qualification for active participation in political life, we have a basis for reclaiming the privilege of responsibility that has been prized from us on grounds of specialized competence. Ultimately, what is sought in this study is a redefinition of citizenship.

Nevertheless, Beiner believes (pp. 160–161) there are two different types of political judgement. The first is the retrospective judgement of Kant's *Critique of Judgement* (cf. Beiner 1982). This is the judgement of the spectator, based on imagination and taste, to some degree critically detached from the existing political opinions in a community. The second is the progressive judgement of Aristotle. This is the judgement of the political actor, based on prudence and civic friendship; it sees political events 'from the inside', applying the kind of concrete understanding that is only possible from this position. Beiner does not choose between the two types of judgement, but considers both of them to be necessary in the political process.

What is political judgement according to social liberals and the three positions of feminism? Is what they propose a reasonable and promising type of political judgement? Does it help us in this research and does it help us in the search for an alternative, feminist concept of citizenship?

I will focus here on some of the meanings of the feminist slogan 'the personal is political', because it is through this statement that feminist revisions of political judgement and of politics have been expressed most explicitly. As Jean Bethke Elshtain remarked in *Public Man, Private Woman* (1981: 202):

> Feminist analysts . . . share at least one overriding imperative: they would redefine the boundaries of the public and the private, the personal and the political, in a manner that opens up certain questions for inquiry.

Social liberalism

Let me start with the social-liberal account. Social liberals have several approaches to the way in which judgement is formed. In Rawls's *Theory of Justice* (1971), it means applying basic principles of justice which are found via the so-called 'veil of ignorance', imagining away all one's particular characteristics. In the rational choice models, one attempts to choose what would be most rational for oneself, given a few private preferences. In Jürgen Habermas's construction of power-free discourse (1990), argumentation rules are only considered to be valid if they can be approved by all participants in a practical discourse and if all affected can freely accept the consequences and side effects of these norms (Benhabib 1992a: 89–120; Fraser 1990, 1989: 113–143). In his article 'Why Dialogue?' Bruce Ackerman (1989) also prefers political participants to talk under conversational restraints – always giving reasons for disagreements, not using violence and not continuing a discussion in the case of a fundamental disagreement.

Despite the important differences among social liberals, there are some interesting parallels. In the first place, social liberals search for rational judgement. Secondly, the debates and deliberations they talk about are usually of a predominantly fictional nature. They are set in some sort of space shuttle, behind a veil of ignorance, in a prison with no information for the prisoners, within the mind of a rational philosopher or in a situation without power or violence. Thirdly, the debates or deliberations are set up predominantly with the same aim – to discover the principles by which society ought to be organized and by which goods ought to be distributed, in a way that is both just and rational. Fourthly, they all have agreement as their aim. A fifth common characteristic follows by implication, but it is nevertheless of great importance – the judgement that social liberals seek is not the political judgement of the ordinary citizen, nor even of the ordinary political actor. Social liberals have nothing at all to say about this sort of judgement. In this respect Benjamin Barber in *Strong Democracy* (1984: 104) remarks:

> What liberalism lacks is precisely what could facilitate the miracle – namely a theory of citizenship. What is missing is politics, the only legitimate form that our natural dependency can take. In practice politics is of course unavoidable even for the liberal, but in theory, it seems too messy, too cumbersome, and too susceptible to passion and opinion, to be a safe repository for the rights and liberties of individuals. Better to rely on benevolent legislators, on good laws, and on sound principles.

How is it possible that social liberals, for whom freedom of opinion is one of the most fundamental citizenship rights, have so little to say about the political judgement of ordinary citizens? One explanation is that it is precisely because they believe that judgement ought to be free. Therefore, they ought not to say anything about it. Yet this cannot be correct, bearing in mind their rigid argumentation rules. It is more plausible that the sort of judgement which social liberals are after does not take place in public at all; it is a thought experiment which can in principle be accomplished by one expert, the experiment being to find the principles of justice with which to organize society. Ordinary citizens do not need to judge or discuss things at all.

In the social-liberal perspective, issues that do not belong to the sphere of justice in which goods are redistributed belong to the 'life-world' or the private sphere (in which people can have their own dominant conceptions of the good life and their own overriding ideologies). If we have fundamental disagreements about certain issues, we ought to remove them from the sphere of politics, so that they can keep their own value. The example often presented is that every family ought to worship according to their own religion (because this is a fundamental citizenship right) and we should therefore keep religion out of the sphere of politics.

Humanist feminism: transcendental truth as a goal for experts

Humanist feminists (Siltanen and Stanworth 1984) raise a series of disconcerting questions for social liberals: why should family issues not fall within the sphere of justice? Who decides where the sphere of 'the right' stops and the sphere of 'the good' begins? Is it not politics itself that decides this? Is the exact location of the border between the private sphere and the public sphere not an outcome of the political process, and thus an effect of political judgement?

It is the lack of a satisfactory social-liberal answer to these questions that enables humanist feminists to gain so much ground. By using the slogan 'the personal is political', they question each so-called personal issue and ask whether it should not fall into the realm of political rather than personal judgement.

Humanist feminists (e.g. Millett 1970) attempt to let women uncover the power, oppression and politics which have made them what they have become and which have put them in a lower social position than men. The message is also: it is not your own fault, but that of patriarchy; it is not a fight against your male partner personally, but against the effects that patriarchy has on all of us. This does not mean that women are not asked to do something themselves. They are asked to think for themselves as free individuals, not as women. They are asked to make independent judgements.

Nevertheless, the main demand is made of politics. Politics ought to set the conditions in which women can live and think freely. Politics ought to bring the family within the sphere of justice (Okin 1989). It should have an eye for gender inequality and alter it. There is hope that society and politics can strip off their patriarchal character and be just and rational environments for all individuals.

Humanist feminists are not opposed to general principles of justice or to thinking in abstract and gender-neutral terms (Johnson 1994; Richards 1982). However, they see this as being an end goal more than a starting point. First one needs to become aware of gender biases in order to be able to remove them.

Here too the thought process is in the hands of experts only. Each tries to make the other aware of gender biases, with the resulting aim being a gender-neutral theory. Ordinary citizens do not appear to need political judgement here. They simply rely on the experts. However, the judgement of experts hardly appears to be political judgement. These experts do not look at actual political cases and judge what the issue is. Rather, they apply their general theory of what a good and just society should look like – or the principles belonging to it – to whatever case they focus on. Their meta-theory is far removed from actual political praxis.

Woman-centred feminism: group experience as the basis for political truth

Woman-centred feminists (Elshtain 1981; Noddings 1984) do not believe that the best political judgement will be obtained by attempting to transcend our gender. For a start, they do not believe it possible to overcome one's particularity, as social liberals and humanist feminists suppose (cf. Grimshaw 1986). Nor do they think that it is desirable to do so. They assume that there is something positive in the way in which women think and that this would alter and improve politics in an important way. For them, the slogan 'the personal is political' means that politics and citizenship would flourish if women's personal experience was taken seriously as a source of inspiration for political judgement, and if the values of the private sphere were taken as an inspiration for the public sphere.

Whereas for humanist feminists the consciousness-raising groups of the women's movement only indicated the 'talking-phase' of the movement, for woman-centred feminists consciousness-raising is a permanent revolution. By exploring women's experience, a new way of political thinking and a view of woman-friendly citizenship will develop. This is the explicit project of Kathleen Jones (1990). She claims and argues very persuasively that our concept of political action and participation will alter if we take the female citizen as our starting point for reflection. In this woman-friendly citizenship the state will serve other kinds of needs than is currently the case and the body politic will take the needs of bodies seriously.

Many other woman-centred feminists have presented a similar sort of argument, but again we need to make a distinction between woman-centred feminists of the women's forum mould and those of the women's morality mould. The women's forum feminists concentrate on the idea that we cannot have universal, gender-neutral political judgement, at least not in the short term. Even if we were to attempt to integrate women's views and needs into a theory, they would too easily be usurped by the so-called general view. This is because we are forced to forget our particularity as soon as we attempt to come to this abstract, general view. Further, by ignoring our particularity we dismiss what is special and valuable about ourselves: our personality, our identity.

The task for women's forum feminists is rather to safeguard women's own identity, to take pride in women's own judgement, to let it ripen before it disappears in transcendental judgement. Women's forum feminists claim that it is important to let this different political judgement grow, to see what it is and in what way it is different from men's. After all, women have not yet had a chance to discover what they are really thinking politically, while men have had this chance for a very long time. This is why women's forum feminists consider it necessary to have separate public spheres and political groups for women. Sometimes, they also present a practical argument – in mixed discussion groups men will always dominate women, men will talk and women will be silent, men will give opinions and women will pose questions (Fraser 1990). Mixed groups will be developed eventually, but first women have to gain strength and find out what they really want. As long as there is a structural oppression of women by men, women's political judgement needs space, not transcendence.

The aim of women's morality feminists (Hanen and Nielsen 1987; Held 1993; Hirschmann 1992; Walker 1989) is an alternative type of political judgement shared by women, and in contrast to the women's forum feminists, they already know what this type of judgement is. The source of inspiration is to be found in women's ways of judging. In response to Carol Gilligan's *In a Different Voice* (1982), women's morality feminists have claimed that, generally speaking, women think less abstractly, judge more contextually and look more at the specific circumstances and needs of the people involved. Women think more concretely and more in terms of care than of rights. Instead of being ashamed of this – as social liberals and humanist feminists suggest we ought to be – women should be proud of it. It leads to a valuable sort of 'ethics' that has a great deal to offer to women and men: e.g. an 'ethics of care' (Noddings 1984), an 'ethics of compassion' (Elshtain 1981) or 'maternal thinking' (Ruddick 1989).

Women's morality feminists, who propose a special ethics which is derived from and designed for women, differ from feminists who propose an ethics of care as a type of judgement for both men and women (Sevenhuijsen 1991; Tronto 1987a, 1987b, 1993). For instance, Sevenhuijsen argues (1992) that situated moralities of care are a useful supplement to an ethics of justice in politics, because the strong universal criteria in this ethics of justice are not satisfactory on their own. According to her (p. 143), the reason for this is to be found in the specific character of politics:

> After all, politics has to do with developing arguments in specific situations, directed at the solution of specific needs and problems: open forms of situational and consequential forms of moral reasoning constitute the indispensable elements of a 'good' and responsible politics.

Equality and reciprocity, the values defended in an ethics of justice, are not sufficient, according to Sevenhuijsen. Situated moralities of care would supplement this moral life and language with values of trust, respect for differences, the promotion of self-respect and the acknowledgement of vulnerability (cf. Sevenhuijsen 1996).

Both women's forum feminism and women's morality feminism therefore emphasize the judgement of ordinary woman citizens. Women's forum feminism does so because it puts women in separate spheres and groups to develop their judgement; women's morality feminism does so because it suggests that women's judgement is an exemplary kind of judgement.

Deconstructionist feminism: it is all a matter of subjectivity and power

A completely different form of judgement has been developed by deconstructionist feminists. They do not think that a new type of feminist ethics needs to be developed as an answer to social liberals' ethics of justice or rational-choice models. Neither do they think that an alternative authoritative model of political judgement can be found through women's experience.

Deconstructionist feminists try to debunk any argument, try to demystify any opposition by looking for underlying commonalities or issues which have been excluded from debate. This is a political activity, and in this way deconstructionism broadens the meaning of politics – showing how one can undermine existing dominant ideologies and even political praxis without being in parliament, in a political party or a member of some organization.

Some may argue that if this is the only tool deconstructionist politics has, then it will be a very poor politics. Deconstructionism is more a method to be applied to politics than a political programme. Its power is in refutation, not in the construction of a theory of liberation or equality. Consequentially, deconstructionists do not concern themselves with the problem of what feminists should do and what should be done. This may explain why deconstructionism cannot provide answers to the questions of what freedom should be, what political equality should be, what idea of rights we should have, and so on. As Seyla Benhabib says (in this case discussing postmodernism in general) in her article 'Feminism and Postmodernism: An Uneasy Alliance' (1991), it has no utopia, and this is wrong in her view because we need some kind of normative thought in politics (cf. Benhabib 1992a).

A response to this has come from Kirstie McClure in her article 'The Issue of Foundations: Scientized Politics, Political Science, and Feminist Critical Practice' (1992b). McClure does not defend herself against this accusation, but turns the tables by saying that it is an accusation of the wrong kind. The accusation presumes that one will only be able to have normative judgement if one sets up one big political theory which can be applied in practice. McClure has strong objections to this idea. Why? First, it assumes that science should be the primary guide to political action. Secondly, McClure does not want such a unitary theory, because it will restrict our actions. Thirdly, she wants to see theorizing as a political practice which should be valued as highly as any other political practice. After all, we take into account that feminists have enlarged the terrain of the 'political', so, according to McClure, we cannot return to the distinction between theory on the one hand and political action on the other. We can no longer assume one 'correct theory' to be applied in practice.

If the slogan 'the personal is political' has any value for deconstructionst feminists, it is that no sphere of life is exempt from language power games and interventions. There is no freedom from power. All so-called personal life is influenced by the disciplining power of discourses and institutions and is therefore part of the sphere of politics. Furthermore, there is no authority and no meta-language that we can use as neutral mediators. We can only, and must, take part in this use of power.

The feminist debate

One might wonder whether the feminist contributions are really about
political judgement. All too often, the judgement which feminists are aiming
for is ethical rather than political. The feminist ethics debate sometimes
appears to dominate feminist discussion. For the most part, the debate is
about whether we need a female ethics, a feminist ethics or a general ethics
like the ethics of justice. The question of whether feminists should talk
about ethics at all when discussing politics is never raised. In that ethics is
a typical contemporary feminist theme, the suspicion is raised that feminists still believe that women or feminists ought to have a higher morality
than men.

In my view, political judgement should be a reflection upon two questions
in particular: (1) are the consequences of a particular action positive or
negative? and (2) what, if anything, could or should politics or the state do
to improve the situation, without creating negative side effects? Neither of
these questions can be ignored.

Deconstructionist feminism seems to deal only with what is going on and
does not ask what should happen or whether the consequences of an action
are beneficial. It is cognitive judgement rather than normative judgement.
Woman-centred feminism has a normative perspective but it is only that of
the outsider. It does not put itself in the position of the decision-maker, nor
does it ask how we should act in a particular situation. The women's forum
strand only creates a procedure through which we can start a discussion. The
women's morality strand assumes that women have a higher morality and
does not examine whether this superior morality would have beneficial
effects in a particular case. Humanist feminism appears satisfied with some
principles of justice and fairness, but does not take a close look at particular situations. It does not ask whether its deontological ethics would have
beneficial effects. It automatically assumes that its principles are good and
therefore only need to be implemented as practical politics.

Moreover, feminists hardly ever pose questions about the political-institutional conditions for political judgement. For instance, they seldom ask
who the people are with whom one must try to come to an agreement and
who the people are who are going to decide what is to be done after the
process of judgement. Nor do they ask where the processes of judgement
and decision-making are located and how they can be promoted.

Other politically relevant questions which are hardly ever addressed by
feminists are those that refer to the political consequences of applying a particular sort of reasoning to a particular case. The defenders of women's
morality would like judgement to be more concrete and contextual, but they
do not ask themselves whether application of their ideal kind of ethics
would have a satisfactory political result. They do not question the respects
in which political judgement is different from ethics. After all, politics is, for
an important part, about harm and conflict and all kinds of things that are
usually 'not very nice'. If feminists use as 'political judgement' an ethics

which excludes enmity, conflict and harm, they will not develop the skills that would make them better able to deal with these phenomena.

The elites at all levels are predominantly male and this means that women as a group do not practise the political judgement of the 'decision-maker'. This implies a great poverty in the political judgement of women. Women have not had to imagine themselves in positions of responsible judgement, and can therefore afford to make nice and kind judgements. When it is predominantly men who are exercising the political judgement of the 'citizen in function', it also means that the perspectives, needs and interests of women will be taken into account relatively less often than those of men.

It does make a difference as to which positions we occupy in the power-language game. It matters not only for the influence we have, but also for the type of judgement we pass. This is why it is no use telling women that they have to pass judgements which are more socially and politically responsible, without giving them more socially and politically responsible positions. Imagination can achieve a lot but it is likely to take the easiest route rather than the hardest.

Political judgement: imagination and prudence

By making a distinction between the political judgement of the actor and the spectator, Beiner (1982, 1983) risks contradicting himself: the more emphasis he puts on the judgement of the political actor, the more easily he will return the privilege of 'real political judgement' to the experts.

There are good reasons to make a distinction between the judgement of the spectator and that of the political actor. We need the critical judgement of the spectator to keep distance from the norms of our own community and to be able to disapprove of what is politically advantageous in the short term. On the other hand, political actors need a different type of political judgement because they need to think about the consequences of a particular action for society as a whole and cannot allow themselves to let a deontological morality or aesthetics guide their judgements.

We also need to make a distinction between the judgement of the spectator and that of the political actor in another sense. Here we enter the field of elitist theories. Joseph Schumpeter, for instance, in *Capitalism, Socialism and Democracy* (1987: 256–268) explained that it is ridiculous to expect as good a judgement from ordinary citizens as from rulers. Ordinary citizens do not feel the need to inform themselves before they judge. Is Schumpeter not right in his analysis of how the masses easily err and are misled in politics, and of how human nature leads to the fact that people will judge much more simplistically and ignorantly in politics than at the bridge table? They talk about politics as if there are no clear-set aims, no rules, and no direct responsibility to bear if an ordinary citizen makes a silly judgement. By contrast, according to Schumpeter and other elitists, political judgement implies the competence to judge. It is important to acknowledge that not

everyone possesses this competence, although Schumpeter is far too opti-
mistic in his belief that the political elite cannot be misled and err in their
judgements.

It seems to me that Schumpeter presents a more plausible view of the type
of judgement that is needed by the actor than does Beiner in his interpretation of Aristotle. In Schumpeter's view, political judgement is connected
more with decision-making than with civic friendship. It is indeed judging
things 'from within' and with a concrete understanding of what is going on.
It is the judgement of citizens who have political or public functions (*de jure*
and *de facto*) and who bear some responsibility for the consequences of
their decisions. It is the judgement of citizens who will not only have to think
'what is morally right?', but also 'what kind of consequences will this
decision have for the *res publica* in the short and long term?' It seems to me
that this is indeed a different sort of political judgement than that of ordinary citizens, who do not have to bear responsibility, who will hardly ever
be questioned on their judgement and who are consequently able to let aesthetic or normative judgements prevail.

We now have two types of political judgement: Kantian taste or imagination and Schumpeter's prudence; the first belonging more to the spectator
or the ordinary citizen; the second belonging more to the decision-maker or
the citizen in a public position. However, as soon as this distinction leads to
giving the expert in an official decision-making position the privilege and
absolute power to judge, we devalue the status of citizenship. At such a
stage, citizens are turned into uncritical subjects who have handed over all
power to judge to their 'representatives'. By not using the faculty of judgement, they will even lose the capacity to judge which representative is the
most capable.

Participation and political-institutional conditions for judgement

However, we do not need to give the experts the privilege and the absolute
power to judge. First of all, they should be checked by public opinion. Citizens, male and female, need to obtain more information about political
affairs and need to be given a chance to acquire some experience in
decision-making. In this way, 'public opinion' will become informed and
critical.

Secondly, citizens can be encouraged to take part in the process of
decision-making and thereby obtain prudent judgement. This leads me to
the issue of the political-institutional conditions for political judgement by
ordinary citizens. One proposal for the kind of institutions we need is
offered by Ernst Vollrath in his book *Die Rekonstruktion der politische
Urteilskraft* (The Reconstruction of Political Judgement 1977).

According to Vollrath (p. 74) the kind of 'phronesis' or practical wisdom
that citizens need is neither knowledge about the universal, nor knowledge
about the particular, but rather that knowledge which will mediate between

them. What is interesting is that Vollrath gives a precise idea (p. 93) of the kinds of institution which will encourage the development of political judgement for ordinary citizens:

> Institutions, in which political judgment will be unfolded, can only be created in the reality, which are the actions of people themselves: these institutions are the acting communities of people, de Tocqueville's *associations politiques*. . . . The point is therefore not to demand an institutional council of the intelligent, but to create institutions in which intelligent judgment can unfold itself. These institutions can only be the associations of free acting people. In these is the reality present, which judgment needs and on which it depends.

The political judgement of decision-makers will be developed not only in official political jobs, but also in countless jobs and offices at all levels of social participation in which elements of this type of political judgement are acquired. Needing to negotiate with others, bearing responsibility, learning to judge the effect of an action on others, are skills that can be learned in many professions and fields. What is required is that people are given responsibility to do this in their jobs and that they do not simply follow instructions. On the one hand this implies, in the terms of Max Weber (1964), a *Verantwortungsethik* (an ethic of responsibility), where citizens first look at the consequences of certain actions and then decide for or against them, instead of a *Gesinnungsethik* (an ethic of ultimate ends). On the other hand, as Weber rightly indicated himself (p. 127), one cannot do this without having some values, criteria and interests.

Because of the limitations of each job and sector, and because of the restricted information one receives in each, it would be desirable that decision-makers who are competent are given new challenges and rewards. In this way, one acknowledges the special talent someone has and tries to improve it so that society will benefit from it.

We need institutions that will encourage and develop the political judgement of the ordinary citizen or the spectator, a type of judgement that will hopefully always remain accessible and expressible by citizens in their political and social participation. Many different institutions can play an important role here: educational institutions and families; and institutions connected to the expression and formation of public opinion, such as newspapers, television, magazines, social movements like the feminist movement and, to some degree, universities. It is crucial that not only men's voices are expressed and that a critical public opinion is formed. The aims of this public opinion are to discuss publicly what is going on, to ask the decision-makers to give reasons for their judgements, to challenge them and to confront them with new ideas. One should not only challenge the decision-makers, but also question the frameworks within which they are working and the male bias in political institutions and theories, and even the way in which reason and rationality are portrayed. After all, as Phyllis Rooney points out in 'A Different Different Voice: On the Feminist Challenge in Moral Theory' (1991: 77):

Reason has regularly been portrayed and understood in terms of images and metaphors that involve the exclusion or denigration of some element – body, passion, nature, instinct – that is cast as 'feminine'. . . . The politics of 'rational' discourse has been set up in ways that still subtly but powerfully inhibit the voice and agency of women.

* * *

Equal citizenship means an alternation of 'to rule' and 'to be ruled'. Applying this to the sexes means that women and men should take equal parts in ruling. It thus also implies that women should not always use the judgement of the spectator, but also practise the judgement of the political actor. This can be done if women imagine themselves in the position of rulers, but even better by creating the institutional conditions for women really to share the responsibility of decision-making and being political actors in the widest sense.

We will always maintain the two different types of political judgement: the critical imagination of the spectator and the prudence of the political actor. Yet we should avoid letting moral and aesthetic judgement be the female prerogative and prudence the male one. Equal citizenship for men and women requires that both sexes can unfold both types of judgement, and that we get more of a dialogical relationship between the two types of judgement in the sense that more people of both sexes obtain experience in both types of judging.

In order for women to shift from second-class citizens to equal full citizens they must acquire the political judgement of the political actor. Women should be encouraged to think in terms of the consequences of certain decisions in public affairs and be prepared to take responsibility for them. Yet this means that the institutional preconditions have to be created in which women can share this responsibility in practice.

PART III

EVALUATION

10

Evaluating Feminist and Other Citizenship Concepts

I began this book with the question: 'To what degree has feminism offered satisfactory criticisms of and alternatives to the social-liberal concept of citizenship?' Now the time has come to answer this question. In this chapter I will summarize the social-liberal conception of citizenship and the humanist, woman-centred, and deconstructionist feminist critiques of and alternatives to it. I will then evaluate whether or not they provide satisfactory alternative concepts of citizenship for feminism. Finally, I will examine the communitarian, the civic-republican and neo-liberal concepts of citizenship, which I discussed briefly in Chapter 1. After all, these are other sources from which a woman-friendly concept of citizenship could in principle be derived.

Social liberalism and feminist critiques

A social-liberal concept of citizenship takes rights as its central focus. It offers a rather passive account of citizenship. It aims to guarantee each mature citizen equal civil, political and social rights and does not consider the degree to which citizens exercise these rights. Political participation is therefore not important to this concept of citizenship. It is up to citizens themselves as to how they exercise their rights and whether or not they want to exercise them at all.

Social liberals feel that citizens have the right to live the life of a civilized human being and they do not want the socially weak to fall below the poverty line. In this context, some social liberals develop policies for the private sphere; here though, policies focus on households and families, whereas the focus in the public sphere is on individuals. Moreover, social and private differences do not affect the rights citizens have. These are the same for all citizens. Social liberals argue that social and private differences ought to matter as little as possible for someone's status as a citizen. They prefer to talk about citizens in an abstract way. They are on the whole anti-discriminatory and individualistic and make a strict distinction between the public sphere and the private sphere. The public sphere is the sphere of political decision-making regarding justice and the private sphere is the sphere of private decision-making regarding the good life.

Three feminist critiques of the concept of social-liberal citizenship have been offered: humanist feminism, woman-centred feminism and deconstructionist feminism. *Humanist feminism* radicalizes the social-liberal concept of citizenship, wanting to remove any 'gender', 'familialism' or 'patriarchy' from it and thereby attempting to make it truly individualistic. It also broadens its notion of justice to encompass the private sphere and adds more preconditions to equal (individualistic) citizenship. According to humanist feminists, social liberalism is not adequately individualistic and sex-neutral and does not offer a view of real equality of the sexes.

By contrast, *woman-centred feminism* tries to challenge social-liberal citizenship by taking women's experience, values and activities as the authoritative basis of what good citizenship looks like. Women's practices are seen as a basis for change. Woman-centred feminism points out that social liberalism's goal of equality is one of assimilation in which women's difference cannot be heard or seen. A generality has been created in social liberalism that does not take women's difference into account. It is therefore just patriarchal. This patriarchal character can be attacked only by drawing upon an idea of woman's citizenship, based on women's experiences and values.

Deconstructionist feminism tries to deconstruct the equality–difference dichotomy. Equality is not sameness and therefore much more room for manoeuvre is available than most feminists assume. Deconstructionist feminism offers a particular method of examining citizenship concepts and theories. It is able to show where groups of people are excluded from (full) citizenship or assimilated into a particular type of citizenship. Its main goal is to create more plurality than is allowed for in social-liberal citizenship without giving up the idea of equal citizenship.

Feminist alternatives

Feminists have not offered a new concept or model of citizenship as such. What they have done is present alternatives to the answers that social liberals give to sub-thematic questions: how to consider freedom, political subjectivity, political representation, rights, social equality and political judgement. By combining the answers of each type of feminism, one might detect the foundations of alternative concepts of citizenship.

Humanist feminists do not imply in their responses a radically new conception of citizenship. They accept the main social-liberal ideas and apply them to women and the private sphere. According to them, women are not yet free and should be emancipated. Women should have equal rights where welfare benefits are concerned. They should, as equal citizens, claim the same rights and treatment that men receive. It is up to them whether or not they want to stand for parliament or enter the public sphere in other ways, but until they do so to the same degree as men, the ultimate aim of emancipation will not be reached. Redistribution of income should take place between individuals and not between households. For humanist feminists political judgement is a matter of finding out what justice is according to experts. Moreover, justice should not only occur between classes but also between the sexes.

Woman-centred feminist responses to sub-themes of citizenship indeed indicate the beginning of a new alternative concept of citizenship or rather, two new concepts of citizenship: that of women's forum feminism and that of women's morality feminism. Their responses to the sub-themes of freedom, political judgement and social equality are shared. Within both of these concepts, freedom for women implies feminization instead of assimilation. For both, political judgement means revising male standards in politics based on women's experience. Both also argue that women should not try to emulate men in the private and public sphere, but should be equally respected in their difference.

Yet on the other three sub-themes of rights, political subjectivity and representation, they take different stands. The *women's forum* side of woman-centred feminism suggests special collective rights and special treatment for women. It argues that women should present themselves in politics as women and not as gender-neutral citizens and it pleads for special group representation for women in politics.

The *women's morality* side argues for special rights for carers, and suggests a different morality in political thought – an ethics of care, an ethics of compassion or maternal thinking. We need to feminize public life, not necessarily by the presence of women, but by the endorsement of 'female' values by both sexes.

The *deconstructionist feminist* position challenges many of the assumptions of the above-mentioned feminists and social liberals. It doubts whether liberty really exists and challenges the dichotomy of equal versus special rights. Deconstructionist feminism perceives any identity as constructed and therefore raises doubts about both human nature and female nature as foundations for politics and citizenship. Political representation is, for deconstructionist feminists, a contingent outcome of a power game. For them, civil and social equality is not sameness, but women are not and should not be different to men either. Political judgement is a process of debunking assumptions, questioning the existence of oppositions and revealing how language and definitions are a result of power relations. Deconstructionist feminism appears to be more a method for examining a concept of citizenship than an exploration of any coherent alternative concept.

Are the feminist responses satisfactory?

My main criterion in deciding whether or not the feminist alternatives to social-liberal citizenship are satisfactory is that they should increase women's participation in social and political decision-making. The current difficulties with women's citizenship are not so much related to the issue of rights as to that of participation. Women are still socialized as non-political human beings. They are not encouraged to the same degree as men to be involved in paid social participation at higher levels in the public sphere. Women take little part in social and political decision-making, and therefore determine the future of society to a lesser degree than men. The most important improvement in women's citizenship would be for women to take part in social and political decision-making to the same extent and at the same level as men.

To address this low participation, citizenship theories must address women's needs. That is not easily achieved within the dominant framework of social-liberal citizenship. This philosophy assumes that equal respect will follow automatically from equal formal citizenship status, thereby undermining the ability to address women's marginalization in public life and the low regard for female citizens which follows from this. Furthermore, the social-liberal focus on rights implies a passive citizenship. Because participation in public life is not important to the philosophy, social liberalism ignores gender inequality in participation and the second-rate citizenship position of female citizens generally.

Humanist feminism

Humanist feminism offers a normative concept of citizenship. It has a programme for the political relations between citizens and the state, but does not even seem to imply political relationships between citizens. It is about rights, but not about activities, opinions and virtues connected to citizenship. Humanist feminism identifies as few obligations as possible for citizens. It recognizes only the duty to obey the laws of the state and to pay taxes. It does provide some guidelines for citizens who rule: namely, that they should implement some concept of justice in their institutions and policy. It does not, however, provide guidelines for citizens who do not rule. It hardly pays attention to differences within groups in actual life, because it talks only about the ideal situation, although it does not preclude differences either. It is able to demand temporary affirmative action to reach real equality, but has difficulties in allowing for plurality in the public sphere.

In other words, like social liberals, humanist feminists invoke only a passive notion of citizenship. As Iris Young (1990a: 74) points out, humanist feminism may originally have called 'upon male-dominated institutions to allow women the opportunity to participate fully in the public world-making activities of industry, politics, art, and science'. However, this was basically only a plea for the removal of barriers. Humanist feminism –

excluding the more recent publications which emphasize participation – does not have a strong enough political rhetoric to be able to call upon women to participate fully in these spheres or to ask public institutions to encourage women in this task. Humanist feminists have sunk into the more comfortable position of possessing equal rights without feeling the need to exercise them.

By focusing predominantly on the relationship between the state and the individual citizen, and on rights, humanist feminism has evoked a legalistic vocabulary. However, this vocabulary has its limits. One can say that feminism has been engaged in this legalist project for a long time. Feminists have demanded political rights, civil rights and social rights. They have always been engaged in the debate over whether women should simply get equal rights or special rights as well. Although this debate will continue, it is not likely that the main feminist battle will be on a legalistic front in the future. The formal, legal position that women occupy in modern western liberal democracies is not bad at all. It is the actual, material position of women that is worrying, and a legalist discourse has nothing to say about this. The majority of humanist-feminist publications therefore cannot improve the situation of the low participation of women in social and political bodies and does not have the means by which to increase it.

Humanist feminism has been useful in claiming social-liberal citizenship for women, in making it more consistently individualistic and in applying many citizenship rights to the private sphere. In this way, it has improved the situation and status of women's citizenship somewhat. However, although humanist feminism offers a perspective on citizenship, it is a rudimentary one and differs too little from the social-liberal perspective to be an interesting alternative.

Woman-centred feminism

Woman-centred feminism asks much more of its female citizens. Like social liberalism and humanist feminism, it provides a normative concept of citizenship. Yet it has a programme not only for the political relations between citizens and the state but also for relations amongst citizens: namely, that of care and that of identity politics. Woman-centred feminism is not only about rights, but also about the obligations, activities, opinions and virtues of citizenship. The women's morality position provides guidelines for citizens who rule and who are being ruled. The women's forum position, however, focuses only on groups which are oppressed and how they should organize themselves.

Again, the major problem appears at the point of participation. Woman-centred feminism only considers the way in which women ought to participate. It does not address the discrepancy in the amounts of female and male participation, and so does not increase women's social and political participation. If woman-centred norms are endorsed, only the value of women's participation will be altered, as it will be more respected.

Would woman-centred feminism in its implications improve the situation and status of women's citizenship? Partly it would, by taking women's experiences and opinions as a new foundation for politics, but it accepts these in such an uncritical way that the value of citizenship and politics themselves would be at stake. Citizenship and politics would no longer be based on judgement, on disagreement about opinions. My answer therefore is: it would improve women's status, but not as citizens.

The woman-centred critique of social liberalism, that it offers too little scope for difference, does not seem justified. For a start, social liberalism's consideration of difference is much more complex than woman-centred feminism assumes. Social liberalism does not simply overlook all (group) differences, or declare all of them to be politically irrelevant. True, one has to present demands for special rights or special provisions for groups in a particular form within social liberalism. One has to use the language of compensation for past injustice or for unfair discrimination in the present. Nevertheless, the social-liberal language is enormously flexible and one can use it to express almost any claim.

Thus far, then, humanist feminism does not sound innovative, and woman-centred feminism could exacerbate the problem, in that whilst it offers an alternative concept of citizenship, it has little room for critical judgement of what women do or say. Should we therefore advocate deconstructionist feminism?

Deconstructionist feminism

Deconstructionist feminism does not have a normative concept of citizenship. It does not have a programme for political relations between the state and citizens and amongst citizens. It does not offer a substantial account of the rights necessary in citizenship, nor does it indicate the duties, activities, opinions and virtues that would be desirable within citizenship. It provides only one guideline for all citizens: deconstruct and unravel all so-called truths, unities and oppositions. All it says is that we should not create an opposition between equality and difference. It does not address the issue of low female participation in social and political decision-making, as it sees power-language games at all levels. Women are just as much engaged in these games as men are.

Deconstructionist feminism cannot improve the situation and status of women's citizenship because it takes us more and more down the familiar side-track of pluralism in the feminist debate on citizenship. Even more strongly than the other two forms of feminism, deconstructionism focuses on equality and difference. It breaks down these categories, reveals underlying assumptions, shows how each category assumes the other, and highlights the many different forms of equality and difference. Deconstructionism is against equality as sameness, but it cannot tell us exactly what kind of equality it wants in its place. Similarly, deconstructionism favours plurality and a multiplicity of differences, but it cannot say what kind of differences it wants.

It is unable to do this because it is only a method to be used; it is not a substantial political theory in itself. It has, above all, no special attachment to citizenship or politics. Deconstructionism is critical, but it may be applied as a method just as well to literary theory as to political theory. We can use a deconstructionist method to examine existing vocabularies on citizenship, but in order to come closer to a better idea of citizenship for current liberal democracies (which is different from one grand theory of citizenship), we need something else.

Deconstructionist feminism attacks social liberalism because of its emphasis on equality and because it affirms the equality–difference dichotomy. However, this is too simplistic a critique. It does not see that social liberalism accepts certain differences and rejects others. Neither can deconstructionism say what is wrong with this, since it lacks a substantial account of what equality, difference and citizenship ought to be.

Deconstructionist feminism does not appear to have an alternative concept of citizenship. It often lacks a position on particular sub-themes of citizenship and it cannot offer a substantive view, because it has no normative perspective.

The equality–difference debate

The feminist critiques of and alternatives to social-liberal citizenship derive from the equality–difference debate within feminism. Humanist feminism emphasizes equality with men, women-centred feminism emphasizes women's difference, and deconstructionist feminism emphasizes plurality in general. This 25-year-old feminist debate on equality and difference has some value. It has shown how modern concepts of citizenship still take the male citizen as their model. It has led to a debate over what differences social liberalism can accept and the sort of differences it should accept. It has raised questions about the type of equality, the type of plurality, the type of equal rights, and the type of treatment that social liberals want. However, whilst all of this is of great importance, it is not enough.

The equality–difference debate amongst feminists has taken the criticism of social-liberal citizenship along the wrong track – that social liberalism offers women passive rather than active citizenship has been overlooked. Feminists have been so absorbed in the question of whether women should be equal or different that they have disregarded the fact that, before we can know whether or not women will make a difference in politics, women will have to have a presence there.

It can be concluded that the feminist critiques of social-liberal citizenship are unsatisfactory. They focus on the amount of equality and difference that citizenship requires, but this issue is too abstract and distracts attention from the real difficulty of women's citizenship: the low level of female participation in social and political decision-making. This issue is over-looked by all three main alternatives within contemporary feminism.

In sum, so far feminists have not offered an alternative concept of citizenship and have even failed to phrase their proposals explicitly in terms of citizenship. The existing feminist philosophies – some recent publications excluded – cannot improve women's participation in decision-making because they do not support the ideal of active citizenship in the sense of being active in decision-making.

Back to social-liberal citizenship?

Social liberalism does offer women protection against many types of inequality, discrimination and oppression, particularly formal ones. Despite some inconsistencies and often imperfect practices, it offers women a vocabulary of justice and fairness, of equal treatment despite irrelevant differences. Its roots in seventeenth- and eighteenth-century social-contract theory promise women enlightenment and reason, instead of patriarchy and prejudice. It offers them an escape from custom, habits, and century-long ideas about what women should and should not do. Social liberalism encourages them to trust their own reason. In principle, it offers women – just like other autonomous individuals – the equal capacity for rationality and, therefore, equal rights. The political vocabulary that social-contract theory offered to certain men could be taken up easily by other groups and this is exactly what has happened. Humanist feminists are correct in their criticism that social liberalism is not always consistent in its individualism, but this is no reason to reject social liberalism as a whole.

Nonetheless, some other problematic aspects of social-liberal citizenship are often overlooked by feminists. Social liberalism does not pay any attention to participation, and in particular to political participation. Social liberals are, as Iris Young has pointed out (1990b: Ch. 1), for the most part interested in formal laws and the distribution of goods, and seldom consider the processes of oppression and power that cause unequal distribution of goods in the first place. Social liberals have nothing to say about public duties, responsibility, beliefs and behaviour. Instead of encouraging citizens to judge politically for themselves, social liberalism has already explored the anatomy of justice for them. Social liberals already know how justice should be created and maintained and what the correct priority of values is. As a result, this theory can be turned into policy by specialists without judgement.

At a time in which 'the law' no longer appears to be a major obstacle for women's 'liberation', the lack of attention to participation in social-liberal citizenship is very unsatisfactory. Legalism is not the answer at a time in which there are no legal hindrances for women.

Social-liberal citizenship makes it impossible for women to complain about the fact that only a very small percentage of women belong to political, financial, industrial, academic, cultural and religious elites. Social liberals do not see this as a problem but rather see women's present low level of participation as emanating from their personal choices. Because social liberalism does not encourage people to partake in active citizenship, it cannot question passiveness or group differences in participation.

All of this leads us to the conclusion that the narrow concept of citizenship offered by social liberalism needs to be extended in two directions. First, instead of looking only at the relationship between the state and individual citizens, we should also look at relationships among citizens themselves. Secondly, instead of just concentrating on rights, we should also look at obligations, actions and virtues. We cannot rely on the social-liberal concept of citizenship if we want to address the issue of low female participation in decision-making.

Oppositional concepts: communitarianism, civic republicanism, neo-liberalism

In this book, I have only examined the social-liberal concept of citizenship and the feminist responses to it (feminists have not yet developed their own concept or model of citizenship). None of them is satisfactory. However, there are also other important concepts of citizenship, such as the communitarian, the civic-republican, and perhaps even the neo-liberal one, from which a woman-friendly citizenship concept might also be derived. Perhaps I do not need to develop a woman-friendly concept out of the blue, but can fall back on another existing concept of citizenship. Due to the scope of this project, I can only be very brief here. References to authors and books can be found in Chapter 1.

The *communitarian* concept of citizenship emphasizes the importance of the underlying community, culture and ethics that citizens share. The strength of communitarianism is that it stresses the responsibility that we ought to feel for our co-citizens and it acknowledges that we have commitments because of the relationships and communities into which we are born. However, it does not offer a substantial view on all sub-themes of citizenship. Communitarianism has little to say about liberty, political representation and political (autonomous) judgement. Communitarianism does not pay attention to differences between social groups and does not attempt to combine equality with difference. Although it pays attention to the *res publica*, it does so in such a way that plurality is assumed to be negative, and therefore has to be assimilated into the common culture. It does not lead to an increase in women's participation, as it only looks at social participation. Besides, it does not pay specific attention to women and usually has a very traditional view of the family.

The *civic-republican* concept of citizenship emphasizes the importance of political participation, public debate, civic friendship, political judgement, autonomy and the *res publica*. It is concrete and normative enough, and the modern versions consider democracy and individual rights to be important. In these respects, civic-republican citizenship meets some of my criteria. However, there is often a position within civic republicanism which says that people who are not autonomous cannot be citizens, because they are still engaged in the material struggle for life and because they are financially dependent on others. This would make many primary carers non-citizens. Civic republicanism has, in fact, nothing to say about social equality. Apart from this, the core requirements of a citizenship theory are met. Does it also offer a satisfactory citizenship theory? In some senses it does. It has a great deal to say about the obligations, activities, opinions and duties of citizenship. It also focuses on the political relationship amongst citizens. However, it seems that civic republicanism perceives plurality in terms of the opinions of individuals and often overlooks the plurality of group opinions and interests.

Moreover, it does not seem to see an increase in women's participation as important. Civic republicanism also has a long tradition of understanding the citizen as a male citizen and connecting *virtù* (public virtues) to manliness. Furthermore, civic republicanism interprets public affairs in a way which suggests that affairs in the private sphere ought not to be politicized. This too causes a severe difficulty for feminism, if one accepts that 'the personal is political'.

Recently the term *libertarian* citizenship has been introduced. I am not sure whether the term 'citizenship' is justified here, because it focuses more on the individual than on the political relationships that an individual has with the state or with co-citizens. The libertarian or neo-liberal concept of 'citizenship' perceives the individual as a bundle of preferences. The state is merely a rational necessity for meeting some of these preferences. There will have to be a minimal state in order to offer the individual a maximum amount of freedom. For this reason, the libertarian citizenship theory has little to say about sub-themes of citizenship, other than that of liberty and political judgement. The libertarian concept of 'citizenship' is able to consider women as independent and as actors, but it does not encourage them to become active in a political way. The public sphere does not have a higher value than the private sphere. Moreover, neo-liberalism denies that the state should have the task of creating the preconditions for equal citizenship and the equal exercise of citizenship. By way of the free market, full citizens and half citizens will be created. Neo-liberalism thinks only in terms of equal opportunities, not equal outcomes. So, although it invokes an active spirit, it is the spirit of the egoistic bourgeois, rather than that of the citizen.

None of these oppositional philosophies of citizenship leads to more participation of women in decision-making either. Although some of them invoke an active ideal of citizenship, it is not sex-equal.

*   *   *

Recent feminisms have criticized social liberalism too much from the perspective of the equality–difference debate, too implicitly on its concept of citizenship and too little from the perspective of the lack of female participation in decision-making. With regard to feminist alternatives to the social-liberal conception of citizenship, one can conclude that humanist feminism barely offers an alternative, that deconstructionist feminism does not offer a substantial concept of citizenship, and that woman-centred feminism offers two embryonic alternative concepts, neither of which is convincing. In these respects we can conclude that the existing feminist critiques of, and alternatives to, the concept of social-liberal citizenship are not satisfactory.

The existing feminist philosophies cannot lead to more female participation in decision-making because they do not support the ideal of active citizenship. Nor does social liberalism support this ideal. The oppositional philosophies of citizenship that do support this ideal of active citizenship cannot lead to more female participation in decision-making either because their ideal of citizenship is not sex-equal. Only the ideal of *active* citizenship can address the problem of low participation and only the ideal of *sex-equal* active citizenship can address the fact that this low participation concerns women. In the next chapter I will show what such a concept of active and sex-equal citizenship should look like.

11

Active and Sex-equal Citizenship

Only an active and sex-equal concept of citizenship can address the issue of low female participation in decision-making. In this chapter I will explore such a concept. I will start with the definition of the citizen developed by political theorist Aristotle in the fourth century BC and examine what active citizenship should mean. I will then describe what I mean by a sex-equal version of this. Accordingly, I will suggest that Aristotle's idea of citizenship as alternation between ruling and being ruled can be combined with the idea of a necessary circulation of elites, and that these ideas provide a good foundation for the demand for a gender balance in decision-making bodies.

A satisfactory conception of citizenship for feminists must not only include the ideas of active citizenship, sex-equal citizenship and circulation of elites, but also the idea of woman-friendly citizenship. In spelling out the consequences of my proposal for the sub-themes of citizenship, and indicating its conditions and side-effects, I will conclude by arguing that the proposal will abolish women's second-class citizenship status and will increase respect for women.

Active citizenship

According to Aristotle in *Politics* ([1959] Book III: State and Citizen, 1275a), the special characteristic of a citizen 'is that he has a share both in the administration of justice and the holding of office'. Aristotle also regards a citizen as someone who has the right to share in deliberative and judicial offices, but it becomes clear in the text that the *good* citizen actually sometimes takes part in the conduct of public affairs. For instance, Aristotle points out that a good citizen need not possess the virtue which makes a good man (1276a), but he must possess civic virtue. This means, in the first place, that he must have as his purpose a secure association of citizens and thus a secure constitution. In the second place, however, it means (1277b) that he 'ought to be capable of both' ruling and obeying; 'civic virtue consists in knowing how to govern like a freeman and how to obey like a freeman'. The underlying reason is that political rule is different from master-slave rule in that it is a rulership 'which men exercise over those who are their equals by birth and free'. Finally, Aristotle points out (1283b and 1284a; my italics):

> Citizens, in the ordinary sense of the word, are all those *who take their turn of ruling and being ruled*. . . . They vary from one constitution to another, and in an ideal state they are those who are able and willing to rule and to obey with the virtuous life as their aim.

Aristotle assumes here that all citizens have to realize their potential as political animals. I do not share this strong assumption, yet I want to accept his definition of the citizen as that of the full citizen. Thus, in my view, the citizen is he or she who has the right to share public offices; the *full* citizen, on the other hand, is he or she who actually takes part in legislation or decision-making in public affairs.

This last description is probably somewhat wider than Aristotle's. He talks about public offices, particularly legislative and judiciary offices, but I think that his idea of rulership in public affairs can go further than these. In my opinion, it should refer to all decision-making bodies in which the content of the existing and future society is determined. The old Aristotelian citizenship ideal of to rule and to be ruled is revitalized, but not as Aristotle intended it to be; it means decision-making not just in politics in the narrow sense, but also in other areas such as the economy.

A full citizen in its most complete sense is someone who participates in legislation or decision-making in public affairs. It concerns participation through which one reflects upon the desirable new character of society and through which one rejuvenates society by cooperating with other people. It is participation whereby one discusses common affairs with others, reflects upon the common good, learns to bear responsibility, to judge and to decide.

It becomes clear that in these activities the borderline between social and political participation evaporates. After all, decision-making on the issues facing society does not exclusively take place within the narrow arena of parliament and government. Moreover, decision-making in other areas is a good preparation for governing in the strict sense of the term. Participation in decision-making therefore refers not only to parliaments, governments, local councils and administrations, and the judiciary, but also to socio-economic boards, the top echelons of the military and police, ministries, university councils and senates, unions, and boards of media organizations.

Instead of a distinction between political and social participation, it makes more sense from this perspective to make a distinction between participation in decision-making bodies and participation in other (paid) work. The former is the more highly regarded, but the latter is also needed for material welfare, autonomy, respect, status and influence (Marx). It may also be helpful as a learning process for decision-making in public affairs since citizens learn active citizenship skills and through their work bear responsibility for enacting them (Tocqueville).

Full citizenship does not only consist of participation in decision-making, but also of having a political subjectivity, knowing how to play political roles, and being capable of political judgement. It means showing in your actions that you are not a subject, but a citizen; that you are not an obedient slave, but someone who is capable of determining, together with others, the future of public affairs. These are the characteristics of full citizenship, but in order to reach it the following preconditions need to be met: freedom, rights and a certain level of material welfare. We have to be autonomous citizens, free from utter poverty and protected by and against the state before we can play the part of the active citizen.

In sum, active citizenship implies participation in decision-making and in paid labour. Citizens prepare themselves and improve their skills for their task of rulership. Citizenship is therefore like a craft (van Gunsteren 1994). It is not a fixed status, but something one can develop and exercise. A strong republic needs responsible and active citizens. Not all citizens have to participate in decision-making, only those who are interested. Active citizenship presumes that the virtues, activities, opinions and obligations which promote the 'common good' are positive. It also presupposes a public debate about the content of the 'common good'.

Following this ideal of active citizenship, we should not only aim for everyone becoming a citizen, but also for everyone being able to be a full or active citizen. Although it neither requires participation of everyone, nor that all full citizens participate simultaneously, the ideal does call upon people to be full citizens.

Sex-equal citizenship

My next step is a major revision of Aristotle's theory. Instead of aspiring only to male active citizenship, which he does, my plea is for sex-equal active citizenship. This means that I do not restrict myself to an individualist citizenship perspective, but also take a group perspective: that of the two sexes. Within this gender view, it is important that both sexes spend an equal amount of time over a longer period ruling and being ruled. It would be wrong if one sex were to be permanently excluded from participation in decision-making and if the other sex were to have a monopoly on rulership (cf. Dietz 1985, 1987; Mouffe 1993; Phillips 1991b). The sex-equal aspect of this ideal refers, as Iris Marion Young (1989) suggests, to the idea of equality in participation (by groups). It does not refer to equality in treatment, nor to the generality of all citizens, but to equal outcomes.

This ideal of active and sex-equal citizenship takes two possible forms. The first is equal participation in decision-making in all areas by men and women and concerns only a small percentage of male and female citizens (Milburn 1976). Citizens cannot just leave the task of the design of their society exclusively to their governments. They must prepare themselves for the possibility of taking part in decision-making in some area. The second form is that of sex-equal socio-economic participation, and concerns the majority of male and female citizens (cf. Lister 1989, 1990, 1995a). This form of participation has predominantly an instrumental value, because female citizens will become more autonomous and powerful through their improved financial situation. However, it may also have an inherent value. Like participation in decision-making, it has the potential to familiarize citizens with bearing responsibility, thinking about the common good and acting together with other citizens in a common task.

Equal participation in jobs does not lead automatically to equal participation in decision-making bodies, but may promote it through the skills and talents that are developed. Similarly, equal participation in decision-making bodies does not lead automatically to equal participation in jobs, but again women in these bodies may promote programmes that encourage or impose this.

Alternation and circulation

I would not argue, however, that all men and all women need to be full or active citizens all the time. My argument is that among those who are full citizens there should be sex equality *over time* (Voet 1992c). My argument for a gender balance in decision-making seen over a longer period does not fall back on the ideal of descriptive representation or mirror representation. Instead, it uses the Aristotelian ideal of citizenship as alternation between ruling and being ruled. My proposal is that we look at this ideal not only from an individualist perspective, but also from a gendered group perspective. Women have seldom been among the rulers throughout history, and it is now time for them to be included in the process of alternating between ruling and being ruled.

This leads me to seek further support in the elitist argument that there be a necessary circulation of elites (Burnham 1949). By this, elitist theorists mean that existing elites should incorporate members of other social groups in order to prevent abuse of power, inertia, a weakening of the qualities of rulers, revolution or neglect of resources and talents. I believe that we should use the maxim of a necessary circulation of elites with regard not only to social classes, but also to the sexes. It is high time that women are incorporated into the elites (Voet 1995).

This argument would apply to many more decision-making bodies than just the democratic ones and does not ask that a 50:50 division of men and women in all decision-making bodies all the time be guaranteed. Nor does the argument require that women stand for women, that they represent women's interests, or that female decision-makers have a higher morality than male ones.

In order that the alternation and circulation argument also apply at the level of individuals (and not just at the collective level of the sexes), limited incumbency periods for decision-making positions are required. It seems likely that the processes of alternation of 'to rule and to be ruled' for the sexes and for individuals will strengthen each other.

Circulation of the sexes in decision-making positions touches precisely on the point where the problem of women and citizenship lies. After all, it is within the sphere of public participation that the inequality of men and women appears, not in the legal sphere. We cannot on the one hand complain about women's lack of participation in politics and society, and on the other hand confine ourselves strictly to a passive notion of citizenship based on legal status. The first position indicates that women are currently second-class citizens, while the second accepts that women are already full citizens and in this sense equal to men. These positions are incompatible. If we were to accept the second position, nothing would need to change. If we accept the first position, we need to and can discuss the means and policies by which women can be turned into full citizens.

In sum, we need better participation of women in decision-making. However, this is not because it is guaranteed that women will do something different or better than men if they are in decision-making positions. Rather, the argument follows from the definition of full citizenship. If we want this to be equal citizenship, and therefore also sex-equal citizenship, we need to have a circulation of elites so that, seen over a longer period, an equal number of men and women are amongst the decision-makers.

Woman-friendly citizenship

In order to get more female active citizens it requires more than merely establishing procedures of circulation. These procedures might create the positions, but we would still need women who are willing to fill these positions. For this to happen, several things need to change in the concept and practice of citizenship. It is a two-pronged process: we can neither do without establishing decision-making positions for women, nor without changing the content of citizenship itself. If these processes are chosen simultaneously, they may reinforce each other. Woman-friendly citizenship implies a citizenship with which women can empathize, and one to which they can and want to be committed (Jones 1990). It implies a citizenship for which they can make time and in which they want to be active.

To begin with, we have to take into account the fact that politics and political thought have been dominated by men for a long period. Such a male bias needs to be corrected by rethinking the idea of citizenship from the perspective of the female and the feminist citizen. Among other things this implies challenging the masculine founding myths of states, the idea of fraternity, the assumed necessary detachment of political actors from their bodies, backgrounds, group interests and group identities (Benton 1988, 1991; Jones 1990; Phillips 1993, 1995). The images of the citizen and the metaphors of citizenship need to be changed so that women feel included.

Based on the feminist slogan 'the personal is political' a woman-friendly concept of citizenship would also imply a recasting of the borderline between public and private (cf. Lister 1995a: 10–11). Nevertheless, both within the public–private divide and within the slogan many different issues are hidden and it seems unwise to take the same position on each of these issues. It is indeed important to politicize so-called private affairs, to demand state intervention in the family, to acknowledge group interests and a heterogeneity of 'publics', to broaden the meaning of politics and of political participation so that women's local or 'parochial' political activity is acknowledged (Jones 1988, 1990). Yet this does not mean that any divide between the private and the public sphere needs to be rejected (Phillips 1991a: Ch. 4). It is within the public sphere that people come together in greater numbers, discuss public affairs, are more likely to be called to account for what they are saying and doing, and may bear responsibility in decision-making for society as a whole. It is essential to call upon women to enter this sphere.

Changing the concepts of citizenship and politics also requires changing their practices. Decision-making positions must be arranged in such a way that they are attractive for men and women who want to keep in contact with their family and friends. Spare time for political actors is important for the psycho-hygiene of politics, as Joke Kool-Smit (1984: 104–111) has pointed out. Being an active citizen need no longer be an 80-hour-a-week profession for a few during their whole working life, but a capacity in which many more people are involved at some stage in their life: in public office or other decision-making bodies, paid or voluntarily, elected or nominated.

Kool-Smit has made another point that is relevant for the establishment of woman-friendly citizenship. She has argued (p. 106) that politics should not just welcome women on the condition that they ignore their femaleness. On the contrary, citizenship would, in the words of Kool-Smit again, also mean that feminism should no longer be relegated to women's spare time. Instead politics should accept into its ranks the fighters of political minority groups and thus provide psychic and material space for feminists and others. According to Kool-Smit psychic space is needed in the sense that the macho-culture in politics with its sexual jokes needs to go and feminists ought to be welcomed to undertake initiatives for women. Material space is needed in the sense of giving feminists in politics the time and the means to develop policies for women (cf. Yeatman 1990; Young 1989).

A further aspect of woman-friendly citizenship is that all decision-makers would have to look at the position of women in practice. The desired result of equal participation for both sexes does not necessarily imply that the procedure used to reach this result must be sex-neutral or sex-blind. On the contrary, in a situation of unequal participation of men and women, equal treatment can perpetuate this inequality (Young 1990b: 165). We therefore need special women-addressing and even women-promoting measures.

Being an active citizen can still be a calling, but it does not have to imply that all other aspects of one's life, other interests, needs and activities must be subsumed by the aim of serving the common good. On the contrary, the common good is served by allowing more plurality in politics. Woman-friendly citizenship would finally require material conditions under which women (and men) would be happy to be involved in decision-making positions in terms of leave, childcare facilities and safety.

Consequences for the sub-themes of citizenship

In order to abolish women's second-class citizenship status and achieve the same number of female full citizens as male full citizens we need to address women's needs and difficulties in the sub-themes of citizenship (cf. Jones 1990; Lister 1989; Pateman 1989, 1992).

With regard to the sub-theme of liberty, active and sex-equal citizenship implies that liberty in participation is the most important type of liberty. Liberty in participation means exercising freedom in the public sphere. It is visible and may, therefore, appeal to others. Citizens' liberty is empty if it is not shown in action. As soon as it is collectively exercised by a group of citizens, it acquires an extra value over and above individual liberties. Together, citizens can make a new beginning and contribute something extra to the existing republic, if they have the will to do so. Liberty as enacted in participation forces citizens to be realistic in their aims. Citizens will gain strength and power in participating and will increase their skills. As this type of liberty is exercised by a group of citizens in the public realm, it will have further-reaching consequences for other citizens' lives than will liberty exercised mainly in the private sphere. Liberty in participation is a crucial part of exercising citizenship. As long as women are not free to act in the public sphere, they will not be free citizens. Furthermore, as long as women's participation in decision-making is perceived to be in contrast to their femininity, women are not free and full citizens, but oppressed, second-class citizens.

With regard to the sub-theme of political subjectivity, the proposal of active and sex-equal citizenship implies that women need a political identity. If they do not identify themselves as political beings, women will not become politically active, nor will they feel the urge to participate in decision-making. This would mean leaving decision-making to men, while women reduce themselves to second-class citizens. The future of society would be determined in a one-dimensional way and many talents would not be used. Possessing political subjectivity is a necessary condition to valuing, beginning and continuing participation in decision-making. This does not mean that political subjectivity needs to be the same for all women. Different political subjectivities and roles can be used in different contexts. In order to acquire equal citizenship for the sexes, we need equally positive images of male and female political actors. Citizenship theorists need to take the issue of political identity seriously, without pleading for an identity politics.

This leads us to the issue of political representation. In order to guarantee an alternation between 'to rule' and 'to be ruled' for men and women, a gender balance in decision-making bodies seen over a longer period is needed. Skilled citizens of both sexes need to be available to take over positions. This idea forces us to look at more decision-making bodies than democratic ones only. It does not require of women that they represent women's interests or be morally superior to men. It merely states that as long as a vast distinction exists in the degree to and level at which the sexes are represented in decision-making, equal citizenship has not yet been reached.

Rights are a condition for citizenship, but women have already acquired these. It is the exercise of rights that is more important and more problematic in modern liberal democracies. Women do not exercise their legal rights to the same degree and to the same effect as men do, because of existing oppression, gender roles and lack of material conditions. It is in the exercise of rights that the inequality between the sexes becomes apparent. By exercising rights, women will become stronger citizens with more opportunity to determine the course of their own lives. They can even affect the content of formal rights themselves (for instance, by creating 'relational rights' that improve women's lives). By exercising their rights, women can also determine the direction of our society. Exercising rights is therefore a crucial part of exercising citizenship. As long as women do not exercise their formal rights to the same degree as men do, they are not yet equal citizens.

Social equality is usually understood as material welfare. This is indeed an important condition for equal citizenship, although we have to consider it for individuals, not families, and we have to redistribute more than incomes. More material welfare for women will lead to more respect and greater means for participation. However, we should not forget the more significant second meaning of social equality, which is equal social participation. This gives citizens paid jobs and, with them, money, respect, skills and an attitude of responsibility. It can be combined with plurality in behaviour, opinions and policies. One particular form of social participation is even more desirable for citizenship – political participation or participation in decision-making. Other forms of social participation may be useful in the preparation for participation in decision-making. As long as men and women are socially unequal – in material welfare and in the form and level of social participation – they are not yet equal citizens.

Political judgement, finally, will become extremely important as a consequence of the proposal for active and sex-equal citizenship. In order to prepare for the task of ruling, citizens have to inform themselves and imagine themselves in the positions of decision-makers. Women, in particular, will then train themselves not only in the judgement of the critical spectator, but also in that of the responsible decision-maker. Political judgement is not the same as deontological ethics. It looks more like Weber's *Verantwortungsethik*, in which we force ourselves to think about the consequences of a particular action. In order that women be encouraged to judge as a decision-maker, they must be put in decision-making positions. A close link thus exists between political judgement and political participation. Women could scrutinize existing political judgement for a sexist male bias and use judgement to change society into a more woman-friendly polity. As long as it is predominantly men who are forming political opinions, men and women are not equal citizens.

Active and sex-equal citizenship as a means of increasing respect for women

My proposal for active and sex-equal citizenship would lead to increased female participation in decision-making. I argue that this will further lead to equal respect for female and male citizens. As stated, a political philosophy can only indirectly affect political practice. An active philosophy of citizenship will affect practice by simply no longer ignoring the needs of female citizens, as is the case in the social-liberal citizenship model. Women's needs will no longer be regarded as irrelevant, but as very relevant. Female citizens currently appear to lead exactly the opposite life to the ideal advocated by active and sex-equal citizenship. In other words, women's current needs and interests appear to be effects of the idea of passive and sex-unequal citizenship.

My alternative citizenship philosophy will encourage political programmes and citizens' actions to meet these needs of female citizens, because current practice in liberal democracies cannot be reconciled with its values. Isolation of women in the private sphere cannot be reconciled with the aim of public liberty for both sexes. Economic marginalization of women is in contrast to the ideal of socio-economic equality. Discrimination and injustice to female citizens can be counteracted by providing women with more and different rights. The lack of political socialization of women and the absence of women in political philosophies and programmes cannot be combined with the ideal of political identity for male and female citizens. Political powerlessness and women's relative absence from elites cannot exist in the ideal of sex-equal participation in decision-making. Finally, seeing oneself and being seen by others as a powerless outsider cannot be reconciled with the aim of political judgement as potential decision-makers.

Social and political participation and the exercise of political judgement are necessary if female citizens are to gain equal respect. Through social or political participation one can acquire independence, social status, money, power and influence. All these matters appear to be necessary in practice if people are to command respect. So far men have succeeded in this better than women, even though men often pretend to have a different, if equitable, respect for women than for other men. In public life there is little respect for women, and public life is seen almost exclusively as a male domain. 'Public women' is still a derogatory term. Even where women are respected, it is because they stand for values of the private sphere. In other words, women in general have to remain in the private sphere to allow respect for just a few women in the public sphere. If women as a large group wish to gain respect in the public sphere, they will need to break the male monopoly of power in this sphere and participate to the same degree as men.

The ideal of active sex-equal citizenship will also lead to equal respect for male and female citizens because participation in public decision-making can be regarded as the highest form of human activity. I refer here to

Hannah Arendt's (1958) threefold distinction between labour, making and acting. People can do various things. Some, however, demand more from us than others. In the process of labour we do not add anything to society, but only recreate what already exists. In the process of production, we add something through our menial skills and our instrumental rationality. In action, however, we genuinely create something new and at the same time create a new society. In this the highest creativity and the greatest freedom is required. This is the highest state of human capacity.

Action has this surplus value partly because it involves people working, talking and deciding together. The highest form of human capacity is to build a community and to change it. To bear responsibility in this is the highest aim. Those who are able to forget their private interest and mould the general interest, who can use their talents for the well-being of every-one deserve the highest respect. If we want the sexes to be equally respected as citizens, they must also equally devote their best talents to public action. Decision-making with regard to the content of our society is such an impor-tant matter that if women want to be respected, and if they want to respect themselves, they must take part in it.

Emphasizing the importance of women's participation in decision-making in order to be respected may seem self-evident in a concept of citizenship, but it is not. In the spirit of several Christians and conservatives, and of many woman-centred and deconstructionist feminists, women should simply be respected on the basis of what they are already doing or saying and nothing needs to change apart from the amount of respect for women.

We should not forget that there is also a link between participation and respect in the reverse order: namely in order to be eager to participate one must respect oneself. Although feminist citizenship does not require that women must always mobilize themselves on the basis of their gender con-sciousness, it does require that femininity in a society is not disrespected, that positive images of female citizens and politicians exist and that female or feminist identity can be a source of pride. After all, people who look down on themselves cannot be confident political actors.

Active and sex-equal citizenship: the proposal

My proposal of active and sex-equal citizenship comprises a number of key ingredients. A new emphasis on the need for women's participation in decision-making bodies is essential, combined with the principle of the necessary alternation between ruling and being ruled. Responsibility must be taken and shared, especially with regard to public affairs. Public virtues need to be developed and practised; in particular doing the best one can for the public good, promoting political justice for women and men, and developing and using the skills of speaking, acting and judgement. Public duties are required, such as the duty to encourage others to use their talents and to participate in decision-making bodies, and the duty to share in less appreciated jobs in order to make the former possible. Women need to exercise political judgement, both as ordinary citizens and as decision-makers. Plurality is a further essential ingredient, taking two forms.

First, the idea of equal participation in decision-making needs to be combined with special provisions for people in disadvantaged or vulnerable positions. Secondly, a plurality in styles, aims and opinions (within the constraints of a woman-friendly citizenship) needs to be fostered and sustained. The final ingredient of my feminist participatory concept of citizenship is a materialist approach, in the sense that good intentions are not enough if women are to become equal participating citizens in practice.

Ideas are extremely important in changing the practice of citizenship. Without alternative ideas we would not feel the urge to change anything or to be active in the practices of citizenship. Nonetheless, ideas are not sufficient. This is why we must have a materialist approach. Good intentions are not enough. In order to change existing citizenship they need to be combined with social conditions and psychological demands.

Three social conditions seem essential for the goal of feminist participatory citizenship. The first is an equal division of labour between the sexes. Men and women ought to have paid jobs to the same degree and at the same levels. The second condition is vertical mobilization. Talented people who have experience of decision-making at lower levels must be able to use their talents at higher levels. The third and final essential social condition is an equal division of household tasks and care tasks between the sexes. If this condition is not met because of biology, history and gender socialization, there is a great danger that women will still be assigned these tasks, resulting in reduced opportunities to participate in decision-making.

Active and sex-equal citizenship can only be reached if women wish to participate in decision-making and manage to do so. Some psychological demands therefore have to be met. First, mental preparation for the task of decision-making is demanded. This means that women have to acquire a political identity. They must see themselves as political beings with a potential contribution to and responsibility for their state and society. Women should further practise judgement as responsible decision-makers, and in their education and career plans they should focus on decision-making posts to the same degree as men do. Secondly, once in possession of these posts women must have the desire to assert themselves. Women have to take responsibility as often as possible. They must defend their own interests and take control. They must be willing to speak with the voice of authority and perceive themselves as insiders rather than outsiders. Women must develop their skills and be eager to use them at higher levels of decision-making. It is important that they affirm that they are responsible citizens and leaders who are willing to determine with others the content and future of our society.

The proposal of active and sex-equal citizenship also assumes the existence of some general preconditions. It assumes the provision of accessible and thorough information on current affairs to all interested citizens. It further presupposes public debate about these current affairs. Finally, it requires that care and education arrangements are directed towards the idea that both men and women are involved in paid labour.

*   *   *

Existing concepts of citizenship are not satisfactory for feminists. I have suggested that a more satisfactory concept of citizenship is conceivable. In this chapter I have discussed four ideas that must underpin such a concept: active citizenship, sex-equal citizenship, a necessary circulation of elites, and woman-friendly citizenship.

By offering this vision of citizenship, and discussing its advantages and consequences for the sub-themes of social-liberal citizenship, I have not answered all questions readers may have. I have not said exactly how group differences should be dealt with. I have not extensively dealt with the political-institutional conditions that would favour women's participation in decision-making. I have not explained in detail how this notion of citizenship, if acted upon, would change our actual lives. What I have attempted to do is to persuade readers that this notion of citizenship is more attractive for feminists than its alternatives; that it is worth trying to imagine how our world might look if we took it as our ideal.

References

Abbott, Grace (1920) After Suffrage–Citizenship. *The Survey*, 44(19), 655–657.

Abbott, Elizabeth and Bompas, Katherine (1943) *The Woman Citizen and Social Security: A Criticism of the Proposals Made in the Beveridge Report as They Affect Woman*. London: s.n.

Ackelsberg, Martha A. (1983) 'Sisters' or 'Comrades'? The Politics of Friends and Families. In Irene Diamond (ed.), *Families, Politics, and Public Policy: A Feminist Dialogue on Women and the State*. New York: Longman, 339–356.

—— (1984) Women's Collaborative Activities and City Life: Politics and Policy. In Janet A. Flamming (ed.), *Political Women: Current Roles in State and Local Government*. Beverley Hills: Sage, 242–259.

—— (1989) Communities, Resistance, and Women's Activism: Some Implications for a Democratic Polity. In Ann Bookman and Sandra Morgan (eds), *Women and the Politics of Empowerment*. Philadelphia: Temple University Press, 297–313.

Ackerman, Bruce (1980) *Social Justice in a Liberal State*. New Haven: Yale University Press.

—— (1989) Why Dialogue? *The Journal of Philosophy*, 86(1), 5–22.

Adams, Mary Louise (1989) There's No Place Like Home: On the Place of Identity in Feminist Politics. *Feminist Review*, 31, 22–33.

Aerts, Mieke (1986) Het persoonlijke is politiek. Een poging tot herdenken. *Ter Elfder Ure*, 29(39), 78–108.

Akkerman, Tjitske (1992) *Women's Vices, Public Benefits: Women and Commerce in the French Enlightenment*. Amsterdam: Het Spinhuis.

Alberti, Johanna (1989) *Beyond Suffrage. Feminists in War and Peace, 1914–1928*. Basingstoke: Macmillan.

Alcoff, Linda (1988) Cultural Feminism versus Poststructuralism: The Identity Crisis in Feminist Theory. *Signs*, 13(3), 405–436.

Allen, B.A. (1981) Democracy in America Revisited: An Application of Tocqueville's Political Theory to Feminist Theory and Action. PhD. Indiana University.

Amstel-van Löben Sels, J.C. van (1945) *De Vrouw als Gemeenschapsmensch*. Bussum: F.G. Koonder.

Andrews, Geoff (ed.) (1991) *Citizenship*. London: Lawrence & Wishart.

Arendt, Hannah (1958) *The Human Condition*. Chicago: University of Chicago Press.

—— (1961) *Between Past and Future. Six Exercises in Political Thought*. London: Faber & Faber.

—— (1963) *On Revolution*. London: Faber & Faber.

—— (1964) *Eichmann in Jerusalem: a Report on the Banality of Evil*. New York: Viking Press.

—— (1979) [1948] *The Origins of Totalitarianism*. Orlando: Harcourt Brace Jovanovich.

—— (1982) *Lectures on Kant's Political Philosophy*. Edited by Ronald Beiner. Chicago: University of Chicago Press.

Aristotle (1959) *Politics*. London: Everyman's Library.

Astell, Mary (1706) [1700] *Some Reflections on Marriage*, 3rd edn. London.

Bacchi, Carol (1990) *Same Difference. Feminism and Sexual Difference*. Sydney and London: Allen & Unwin.

Barbalet, J.M. (1988) *Citizenship: Rights, Struggle and Class Inequality*. In the series 'Concepts in the Social Sciences'. Milton Keynes: Open University Press.

Barber, Benjamin (1984) *Strong Democracy: Participatory Democracy for a New Age*. Berkeley: University of California Press.

Barrett, Michèle (1980) *Women's Oppression Today: Problems in Marxist Feminist Analysis*. London: NLB.

Barrett, Michèle and Phillips, Anne (eds) (1992) *Destabilizing Theory: Contemporary Feminist Essays*. Cambridge: Polity Press.

Beauvoir, Simone de (1953) [1949] *The Second Sex*. London: Jonathan Cape.

Bebel, August (1910) [1879] *Woman in the Past, Present and Future* (Die Frau und der Sozialismus), 4th edn. London: Reeves.

Beiner, Ronald (1982) Interpretive Essay. In Ronald Beiner (ed.), *Hannah Arendt: Lectures on Kant's Political Philosophy*. Chicago: University of Chicago Press, 89–156.

—— (1983) *Political Judgment*. London: Methuen.

Bell, Susan Groag and Offen, Karen M. (eds) (1983) *Women, the Family and Freedom. The Debate in Documents*. Vol. 1, 1750–1880. Stanford, CA: Stanford University Press.

Benhabib, Seyla (1991) Feminism and Postmodernism: An Uneasy Alliance. *Praxis International*, 11(2): 137–149.

—— (1992a) *Situating the Self. Gender, Community and Postmodernism in Contemporary Ethics*. Cambridge: Polity Press.

—— (1992b) Models of Public Space: Hannah Arendt, the Liberal Tradition and Jürgen Habermas. In Craig Calhoun (ed.), *Habermas and the Public Sphere*. Cambridge, MA: MIT Press, 73–98.

Benhabib, Seyla and Cornell, Drucilla (eds) (1987) *Feminism as Critique. On the Politics of Gender*. Cambridge: Polity Press.

Benton, Sarah (1988) Citizen Cain's Silenced Sisters. *New Statesman & Society*, 2 December, 18–19.

—— (1991) Gender, Sexuality and Citizenship. In Geoff Andrews (ed.), *Citizenship*. London: Lawrence & Wishart, 151–163.

Berlin, Isaiah (1969) *Four Essays on Liberty*. London: Oxford University Press.

Bhabba, Jacqueline, Klug, Francesca and Shutter, Sue (eds) (1985) *Worlds Apart: Women under Immigration and Nationality Laws*. London: Pluto.

Birch, Anthony H. (1971) *Representation*. London: Pall Mall Press.

Bock, Gisela and James, Susan (eds) (1992) *Beyond Equality and Difference. Citizenship, Feminist Politics and Female Subjectivity*. London and New York: Routledge.

Borchost, Anette and Siim, Birte (1987) Women and the Advanced Welfare State: The Transition from Private to Public Dependency. In Anne Showstack Sassoon (ed.), *Women and the State. The Shifting Boundaries of Public and Private*. London: Hutchinson, 128–158.

Boyd, Mary Brown Summer (1918) *The Woman Citizen; a General Handbook of Civics, with Special Consideration of Women's Citizenship*. New York: Frederick A. Stokes.

Brachvogel, Carry (1920) *Eva in der Politik. Ein Buch über die politische Tätigkeit der Frau*. Leipzig-Gaschwitz: Dürr & Weber.

Braidotti, Rosi (1991) *Patterns of Dissonance*. Cambridge: Polity Press.

Brünott, Loes (1991) Mensenrechten als Vrouwenrechten. *Nemesis*, 7(2), 27–30.

Bryson, Valerie (1992) *Feminist Political Theory: An Introduction*. New York: Paragon House.

Burnham, James (1949) *Die Machiavellisten. Verteidiger der Freiheit*. Zurich: Pan Verlag.

Burton, Elizabeth (1942) *And Your Verdict? The Accusation is That Women of Britain Have not Been Allowed to Take Their Full Share as Citizens in This War. Council for the Prosecution: The Women of the UK; Council for the Defence: The Government*. London: Frederick Müller.

Bussemaker, Jet and Voet, Rian (eds) (1998) *Gender, Participation and Citizenship in the Netherlands*. Aldershot: Ashgate.

Butler, Judith (1990a) *Gender Trouble. Feminism and the Subversion of Identity*. London and New York: Routledge.

—— (1990b) Gender Trouble, Feminist Theory, and Psychoanalytic Discourse. In Linda J. Nicholson (ed.), *Feminism/Postmodernism*. London: Routledge, 324–340.

—— (1991) Contingent Foundations: Feminism and the Question of 'Postmodernism'. *Praxis International*, 11(2), 150–165.

Butler, Judith and Scott, Joan W. (eds) (1992) *Feminists Theorize the Political*. New York: Routledge.

Carter, April (1988) *The Politics of Women's Rights*. London: Longman.

—— (1996) Women, Military Service and Citizenship. In Barbara Sullivan and Gilian Whitehouse (eds), *Gender, Politics and Citizenship in the 1990s*. Sydney: University of New South Wales Press, 100–119.

Cass, Bettina (1990) Gender and Social Citizenship. Women's Pursuit of Citizenship in the 1990s, with Particular Reference to Australia. Paper presented at the Annual SPA Conference, Bath. 10–12 July.

—— (1994) Citizenship, Work and Welfare. The Dilemma for Australian Women. *Social Politics, International Studies in Gender, State and Society*, 1(1), 106–125.

Chodorow, Nancy (1978) *The Reproduction of Mothering: Psychoanalysis and the Sociology of Gender*. Berkeley: University of California Press.

Clark, Lorenna M.G. and Lange, Lynda (eds) (1979) *The Sexism of Social and Political Theory*. Toronto: University of Toronto Press.

Code, Lorraine (1986) Simple Equality is not Enough. *Australasian Journal of Philosophy*, 64 Supplement (June), 48–65.

Coole, Diana (1988) *Women in Political Theory. From Ancient Misogyny to Contemporary Feminism*. Brighton: Wheatsheaf.

—— (1993) Constructing and Deconstructing Liberty: A Feminist and Post-structuralist Analysis. *Political Studies*, 41(1), 83–95.

Cornell, Drucilla L. (1992) Gender, Sex and Equivalent Rights. In Judith Butler and Joan W. Scott (eds), *Feminists Theorize the Political*. New York: Routledge, 280–296.

Crawhall, Phyllis Challoner and Laughton, Vera Matthews (1928) *Towards Citizenship: A Handbook of Women's Emancipation*. London: King.

Dahl, Robert A. (1970) *After the Revolution? Authority in a Good Society*. New Haven and London: Yale University Press.

Dahlerup, Drude (ed.) (1986) *The New Women's Movement. Feminism and Political Power in Europe and the USA*. London: Sage.

Diamond, Irene and Hartsock, Nancy (1981) Beyond Interests in Politics: A Comment on Virginia Sapiro's 'When Are Interests Interesting? The Problem of Political Representation of Women'. *American Political Science Review*, 75, 717–721.

Dietz, Mary G. (1985) Citizenship with a Feminist Face: The Problem with Maternal Thinking. *Political Theory*, 13(1), 19–39.

—— (1987) Context is All: Feminism and Theories of Citizenship. *Daedalus*, 116(4), 1–25.

—— (1991) Hannah Arendt and Feminist Politics. In Mary Shanley and Carole Pateman (eds), *Feminist Interpretations and Political Theory*. Cambridge: Polity Press, 232–253.

Diquinzio, Patricia (1995) Feminist Theory and the Question of Citizenship – A Response to Dietz' Critique of Maternalism. *Women & Politics*, 15(3), 23–42.

Dworkin, Ronald (1985) *A Matter of Principle*. Cambridge, MA: Harvard University Press.

—— (1987a) [1977] *Taking Rights Seriously*. London: Duckworth.

—— (1987b) What is Equality? Part 3: The Place of Liberty. *Iowa Law Review*, 73, 1–54.

Einhorn, Barbara (1993) *Cinderella Goes to Market: Citizenship, Gender, and Women's Movements in East Central Europe*. London: Verso.

Eisenstein, Zillah (1981) *The Radical Future of Liberal Feminism*. New York: Longman.

Ellis, Caroline (1991) Sisters and Citizens. In Geoff Andrews (ed.), *Citizenship*. London: Lawrence & Wishart, 235–243.

Elshtain, Jean Bethke (1981) *Public Man, Private Woman. Women in Social and Political Thought*. Princeton, NJ: Princeton University Press.

—— (1983) Antigone's Daughters: Reflection on Female Identity and the State. In Irene Diamond (ed.), *Families, Politics and Public Policy: A Feminist Dialogue on Women and the State*. New York: Longman, 300–356.

—— (1986) *Meditations on Modern Political Thought: Masculine/Feminine Themes from Luther to Arendt*. New York: Praeger.

—— (1987) *Women and War*. New York: Basic Books.

—— (1990) *Power Trips and Other Journeys. Essays in Feminism as Civic Discourse*. Madison, WI: University of Wisconsin Press.

—— (1992) The Power and Powerlessness of Women. In Gisela Bock and Susan James (eds), *Beyond Equality and Difference. Citizenship, Feminist Politics and Female Subjectivity*. London and New York: Routledge, 110–126.

Epstein, Cynthia Fuchs and Coser, Rose Laub (eds) (1981) *Access to Power: Cross-national Studies of Women and Elites*. London and Boston: Allen & Unwin.

European Network of Experts 'Women in Decision-Making' Created in the Framework of the Third Medium-Term Community Action Programme on Equal Opportunities for Women and Men (For the European Commission) (1994) *Women in Decision-Making. Facts and Figures on Women in Political and Public Decision-Making in Europe. Coordinated by Sabine de Bethune*. 2nd edn. Brussels.

Evans, Judith (1986) Feminist Theory and Political Analysis. In Judith Evans et al., *Feminism and Political Theory*. London: Sage, 103-119.

Evans, Sara (1980) *Personal Politics: The Roots of Women's Liberation in the Civil Rights Movement and the New Left*. New York: Vintage Books.

Feder Kittay, Eva and Meyers, Diana (eds) (1987) *Women and Moral Theory*. Totowa, NJ: Rowman & Littlefield.

Firestone, Shulamith (1970) *The Dialectic of Sex*. New York: Morrow.

Flax, Jane (1990a) *Thinking Fragments. Psychoanalysis, Feminism & Postmodernism in the Contemporary West*. Berkeley: University of California Press.

—— (1990b) Postmodernism and Gender Relations. In Linda J. Nicholson (ed.), *Feminism/Postmodernism*. London: Routledge, 19–38.

Foucault, Michel (1970) *The Order of Things: An Archaeology of the Human Sciences*. London: Tavistock.

Frankena, William K. (1973) *Ethics*. Englewood Cliffs, NJ: Prentice-Hall.

Franzway, Suzanne, Court, Diana and Connell, R.W. (1988) *Staking a Claim. Feminism, Bureaucracy and the State*. Cambridge: Polity Press.

Fraser, Nancy (1989) *Unruly Practices. Power, Discourse and Gender in Contemporary Social Theory*. Cambridge: Polity Press.

—— (1990) Gender, Citizenship and the Public Sphere: Toward a Feminist Reconstruction of Habermas. In Selma Sevenhuijsen and Kathy Davis (eds), *Feminism, Citizenship and Care*. Utrecht: Anna Maria van Schuurman Centrum, 76–121.

—— (1994) After the Family Wage: Gender Equity and the Welfare State. *Political Theory*, 22(4), 591–618.

Fraser, Nancy and Gordon, Linda (1994) Civil Citizenship against Social Citizenship? In Bart van Steenbergen (ed.), *The Condition of Citizenship*. London: Sage, 90–107.

Frazer, Elizabeth and Lacey, Nicola (1993) *The Politics of Community: A Feminist Critique of the Liberal-Communitarian Debate*. Brighton: Harvester Wheatsheaf.

Friedan, Betty (1963) *The Feminine Mystique*. New York: Dell.

Frye, Marilyn (1983) *The Politics of Reality: Essays in Feminist Theory*. Trumansburg, NY: Crossing Press.

Gerhard, Ute (1990) *Gleichheit ohne Angleichung. Frauen im Recht*. Munich: Beck.

Gilligan, Carol (1982) *In a Different Voice: Psychological Theory and Women's Development*. Cambridge, MA: Harvard University Press.

Gilman, Charlotte Perkins (1979) [1915] *Herland*. New York: Pantheon.

Girvetz, Harry K. (1963) *The Evolution of Liberalism*. New York: Collier Books.

Grimshaw, Jean (1986) *Feminist Philosophers. Women's Perspectives on Philosophical Traditions*. Brighton: Wheatsheaf.

Gundersen, Joan R. (1987) Independence, Citizenship and the American Revolution. *Signs*, 13(1), 59–77.

Gunew, Sneja and Yeatman, Anna (eds) (1993) *Feminism and the Politics of Difference*. St Leonards, New South Wales: Allen & Unwin.

Gunsteren, Herman R. van (1994) Four Conceptions of Citizenship. In Bart van Steenbergen (ed.), *The Condition of Citizenship*. London: Sage, 36–48.

Habermas, Jürgen (1990) *Moral Consciousness and Communicative Action*. Cambridge: Polity Press.

—— (1992) Citizenship and National Identity. Some Reflections on the Future of Europe. *Praxis International*, 12(1), 1–19.

Hall, Stuart and Held, David (1989) Left and Rights. *Marxism Today*, June, 16–23.

Hampshire, Stuart (ed.) (1980) [1978] *Public and Private Morality*. Cambridge: Cambridge University Press.

Hanen, Marsha and Nielsen, Kai (eds) (1987) *Science, Morality & Feminist Theory. Supplementary Volume 13, Canadian Journal of Philosophy*. Calgary: University of Calgary Press.

Hanish, Carol (1970) The Personal is Political. In *Notes from the Second Year. Major Writings of the Radical Feminists*. New York: Radical Feminists, 76–78.

Haraway, Donna (1990) A Manifesto for Cyborgs: Science, Technology, and

Socialist Feminism in the 1980s. In Linda J. Nicholson (ed.), *Feminism/ Postmodernism*. New York and London: Routledge, 190–233.

—— (1992) Ecce Homo, Ain't I a Woman, and Inappropriate/d Others: The Human in a Post-Humanist Landscape. In Judith Butler and Joan W. Scott (eds), *Feminists Theorize the Political*. New York: Routledge, 86–100.

Hardie, Keir James (1906) *The Citizenship of Women. A Plea for Woman's Suffrage*. In the series, Coming Men on Coming Questions. 4th edn. London: n.p.

Hart, Herbert L.A. (1963) *Law, Liberty and Morality*. London: Oxford University Press.

Hayek, Friedrich A. von (1944) *The Road to Serfdom*. Sydney: Dymock's Book Arcade.

Heater, Derek (1990) *Citizenship. The Civic Ideal in World History, Politics and Education*. London and New York: Longman.

Heitland, Margaret (1919) Women Citizens' Associations. Their Work and Possibilities. *The Common Cause*, 15 August, 226–227.

Hekman, Susan (1991) Reconstructing the Subject: Feminism, Modernism and Postmodernism. *Hypatia*, 6(2), 44–63.

Held, Virginia (1993) *Feminist Morality: Transforming Culture, Society, and Politics*. Chicago: University of Chicago Press.

Hermsen, Joke J. and Lenning, Alkeline van (eds) (1991) *Sharing the Difference. Feminist Debates in Holland*. London and New York: Routledge.

Hernes, Helga Maria (1984) Women and the Welfare State: The Transition from Private to Public Dependency. In *Patriarchy and the Welfare Society*. Oslo: Universitetsforlaget.

—— (1987) *Welfare State and Woman Power: Essays in State Feminism*. Oslo: Norwegian University Press.

—— (1988) The Welfare State Citizenship of Scandinavian Women. In Kathleen B. Jones and Anna G. Jónasdóttir (eds), *The Political Interests of Gender: Developing Theory and Research with a Feminist Face*. London: Sage, 187–214.

Hirschman, Albert O. (1982) *Shifting Involvements. Private Interests and Public Action*. Oxford: Basil Blackwell.

Hirschmann, Nancy J. (1992) *Rethinking Obligation: A Feminist Method for Political Theory*. Ithaca, NY: Cornell University Press.

Hollister, Horace A. (1918) *The Woman Citizen: A Problem in Education*. New York: Appleton.

Holmes, Helen Bequaert (1984) A Feminist Analysis of the Universal Declaration of Human Rights. In Carol G. Gould (ed.), *Beyond Domination. New Perspectives on Women and Philosophy*. Totowa, NJ: Rowman & Allanheld, 250–264.

Holtmaat, Riki (1988a) Naar Een Ander Recht I. *Nemesis*, 4(1), 3–14.

—— (1988b) Naar Een Ander Recht II. *Nemesis*, 4(2), 60–67.

Honig, Bonnie (ed.) (1995) *Feminist Interpretations of Hannah Arendt*. Pennsylvania: Pennsylvania University Press.

Humm, Maggie (ed.) (1992) *Feminisms. A Reader*. Hemel Hempstead: Wheatsheaf.

Jaggar, Alison (1983a) *Feminist Politics and Human Nature*. New York: Rowman & Allanheld.

—— (1983b) Political Philosophies of Women's Liberation. In Braggin M. Vetterling, Frederick A. Elliston and Jane English (eds), *Feminism and Philosophy*. New York: Rowman & Littlefield, 5–21.

James, Susan (1992) The Good-Enough Citizen: Citizenship and Independence. In Gisela Bock and Susan James (eds), *Beyond Equality and Difference. Citizenship, Feminist Politics and Female Subjectivity*. London and New York: Routledge, 48–68.

Johnson, Pauline (1994) *Feminism as Radical Humanism*. St Leonards, New South Wales: Allen & Unwin.

Jones, Kathleen B. (1984) Dividing the Ranks: Women and the Draft. *Women and Politics*, 4(4), 75–87.

—— (1988) Towards the Revision of Politics. In Kathleen B. Jones and Anna G. Jónasdóttir (eds), *The Political Interests of Gender: Developing Theory and Research with a Feminist Face*. London: Sage, 11–33.

—— (1990) Citizenship in a Woman-friendly Polity. *Signs*, 15(4), 781–812.

—— (1993) *Compassionate Authority: Democracy and the Representation of Women*. New York: Routledge.

Jordan, Bill (1989) *The Common Good. Citizenship, Morality and Self-Interest*. Oxford: Basil Blackwell.

Kant, Immanuel (1990) [1792] On the Common Saying: This May Be True in Theory, but It Does Not Apply in Practice. In *Kant Political Writings*. Cambridge: Cambridge University Press, 62–92.

Kanter, Rosabeth Moss (1977) *Men and Women of the Corporation*. New York: Basic Books.

Kelly, Rita Mae and Boutelier, Mary A. (1978) *The Making of Political Women: A Study of Socialization and Role Conflict*. New York: Nelson-Hall.

Kennedy, Ellen and Mendus, Susan (eds) (1988) *Women in Western Political Philosophy. Kant to Nietzsche*. New York: St Martin's Press.

Kerber, Linda K. (1980) *Women of the Republic. Intellect and Ideology in Revolutionary America*. Chapel Hill: University of North Carolina Press.

—— (1992) The Paradox of Women's Citizenship in the Early Republic – The Case of Martin vs. Massachusetts, 1805. *American Historical Review*, 97(2), 349–378.

Komter, Aafke (1990) Feministische visies op het werk van Hannah Arendt: 'Creative Misreading'? *Socialisties-Feministiese Teksten*, 11, 8–27.

Kool-Smit, Joke (1984) *Er is een land waar vrouwen willen wonen. Teksten 1967–1981*. Amsterdam: Sara.

Krosenbrink-Gelisen, Liliane Ernestine (1991) *Sexual Equality as an Aboriginal Right. The Native Women's Association of Canada and the Constitutional Process on Aboriginal Matters, 1982–1987*. Saarbrücken: Breitenbach.

Kukathas, Chandran (1992a) Are There Any Cultural Rights? *Political Theory*, 20(1), 105–146.

—— (1992b) Cultural Rights Again: A Rejoinder to Kymlicka. *Political Theory*, 20(4), 674–680.

—— (ed.) (1993) *Multicultural Citizens: The Philosophy and Politics of Identity* (CIS Readings, 9). St Leonards, NSW: Centre for Independent Studies.

Kymlicka, Will (1989) *Liberalism, Community and Culture*. Oxford: Clarendon Press.

—— (1995) *Multicultural Citizenship: A Liberal Theory of Minority Rights*. New York: Clarendon Press.

Lake, Marilyn (1994) Personality, Individuality, Nationality: Feminist Conceptions of Citizenship 1902–1940. *Australian Feminist Studies*, 19 (Special Issue: Women and Citizenship), 25–38.

Landes, Joan B. (1984a) *Women and the Public Sphere in the Age of the French Revolution*. Ithaca, NY: Cornell University Press.

—— (1984b) Women and the Public Sphere. A Modern Perspective. *Social Analysis*, 15, 20–31.

—— (1992) Rethinking Habermas's Public Sphere. *Political Theory Newsletter*, 4(1), 51–69.

Langley, Winston E. (ed.) (1991) *Women's Rights in International Documents: A Source Book with Commentary*. Jefferson, NC: McFarland.

Laski, Harold Joseph (1936) *The Rise of European Liberalism: An Essay in Interpretation*. London: Allen & Unwin.

Leech, Marie (1994) Women, the State and Citizenship: Are Women in the Building or in a Separate Annex? *Australian Feminist Studies*, 19 (Special Issue: Women and Citizenship), 79–91.

Leibholz, Gerhard (1960) *Das Wesen der Repräsentation und der Gestaltwandel der Demokratie in 20 Jahrhundert*. Berlin: Walter de Gruyter.

Leira, Arnlaug (1989) *Models of Motherhood. Welfare State Policies and Everyday Practices: The Scandinavian Experience*. Oslo: Institut for Samfunns Forskning.

Lister, Ruth (1989) *The Female Citizen*. Liverpool: Liverpool University Press.

—— (1990) Women, Economic Dependency and Citizenship. *Journal for Social Policy*, 19(4), 445–467.

—— (1991) Citizenship Engendered. *Critical Social Policy*, 32 (Autumn), 65–71.

—— (1992) *Women: Economic Dependency and Social Security*. Manchester: Equal Opportunities Commission.

—— (1993) Tracing the Contours of Women's Citizenship. *Policy and Politics*, 21(1), 3–16.

—— (1994) 'She Has Other Duties' – Women, Citizenship and Social Security. In Sally Baldwin and Jane Falkingham (eds), *Social Security and Social Change. New Challenges to the Beveridge Model*. New York: Harvester/Wheatsheaf, 31–44.

—— (1995a) Dilemmas in Engendering Citizenship. *Economy and Society*, 24(1), 1–40.

—— (1995b) Whose Citizenship? The Gendering of Social Rights and Obligations. Paper presented at the European Sociological Association, Budapest. 30 August–2 Sept.

Littleton, Christine (1987) Reconstructing Sexual Equality. *California Law Review*, 75, 1279–1337.

Lloyd, Genevieve (1986) Selfhood, War and Masculinity. In Carole Pateman and Elizabeth Gross (eds), *Feminist Challenges: Social and Political Theory*. Boston: Northeastern University Press, 63–76.

—— (1989) *The Man of Reason. 'Male' and 'Female' in Western Philosophy*. London: Methuen.

Lyotard, Jean François (1984) *The Postmodern Condition: A Report on Knowledge*. Manchester: Manchester University Press.

Macadam, Elizabeth (1919a) Education of the Woman Citizen I. *The Common Cause*, 28 June, 129–130.

—— (1919b) Education of the Woman Citizen II. *The Common Cause*, 18 July, 173–174.

MacIntyre, Alasdair (1985) [1981] *After Virtue. A Study in Moral Theory*. London: Duckworth.

MacKinnon, Catharine A. (1987) *Feminism Unmodified. Discourses on Life and Law*. Cambridge, MA: Harvard University Press.

—— (1989) *Toward a Feminist Theory of the State*. Cambridge, MA: Harvard University Press.

MacPherson, Crawford Brough (1962) *The Political Theory of Possessive Individualism: Hobbes to Locke*. London: Oxford University Press.

—— (1977) *The Life and Times of Liberal Democracy*. New York: Oxford University Press.

Maihofer, Andrea (1988) Ansätze zur Kritik des moralischen Universalismus. Zur moraltheoretischen Diskussion um Gilligans Theses zu einer 'Weiblichen' Moralauffassung. *Feministischen Studien*, 6(1), 32–52.

Mansbridge, Jane (1980) *Beyond Adversary Democracy*. New York: Basic Books.

—— (1993) Feminism and Democratic Community. In John W. Chapman and Ian Shapiro (eds), *Democratic Community, NOMOS XXXV*. New York: New York University Press, 339–395.

Marcil-Lacoste, Louise (1992) The Paradoxes of Pluralism. In Chantal Mouffe (ed.), *Dimensions of Radical Democracy. Pluralism, Citizenship, Community*. London and New York: Verso, 128–144.

Marquand, David (1989) Subversive Language of Citizenship. *The Guardian*, 2 January.

Marshall, Thomas Humphrey (1967) [1950] Citizenship and Social Class. In T.H. Marshall, *Citizenship and Social Development*. New York: Anchor, 71–134.

McBride, Dorothy Stetson and Mazur, Amy G. (eds) (1995) *Comparative State Feminism*. London and Thousand Oaks, CA: Sage.

McClure, Kirstie (1992a) On the Subject of Rights: Pluralism, Plurality and Political Identity. In Chantal Mouffe (ed.), *Dimensions of Radical Democracy. Pluralism, Citizenship, Community*. London and New York: Verso, 108–127.

—— (1992b) The Issue of Foundations: Scientized Politics, Political Science, and Feminist Critical Practice. In Judith Butler and Joan W. Scott (eds), *Feminists Theorize the Political*. New York: Routledge, 341–368.

McIntosh, Mary (1978) The State and the Oppression of Women. In A. Kuhn and A. Wolpe (eds), *Feminism and Materialism*. London: Routledge & Kegan Paul, 254–289.

—— (1984) The Family, Regulation and the Public Sphere. In Gregor McLennan, David Held and Stuart Hall (eds), *State and Society in Contemporary Britain. A Critical Introduction*. Cambridge, MA: Harvard University Press, 204–240.

Mead, Lawrence (1986) *Beyond Entitlement: The Social Obligation of Citizenship*. New York: Free Press.

Meehan, Elizabeth and Sevenhuijsen, Selma (1991) Problems in Principles and Policies. In Elizabeth Meehan and Selma Sevenhuijsen (eds), *Equality, Politics and Gender*. London: Sage, 1–16.

Metcalfe, Agnes Edith (1917) *Woman's Effort. A Chronicle of British Women's Fifty Years' Struggle for Citizenship (1865–1914)*. Oxford: Basil Blackwell.

Milburn, Josephine F. (1976) *Women as Citizens: A Comparative Review*. London: Sage.

Miller, David (1994) Citizenship and Pluralism. *Political Studies*, 43 (6), 432–450.

Millett, Kate (1970) *Sexual Politics*. New York: Ballantine Books.

Minow, Martha (1990) *Making All the Difference. Inclusion, Exclusion and American Law*. Ithaca, NY: Cornell University Press.

Mitchell, Juliette (1971) *Woman's Estate*. New York: Vintage Books.

Mitchell, Juliette and Oakley, Ann (eds) (1986) *What is Feminism?* Oxford: Basil Blackwell.

Molloy, Maureen (1992) Citizenship, Property and Bodies: Discourses on Gender and the Inter-War Labour Government in New Zealand. *Gender & History*, 4(3), 293–304.

Mouffe, Chantal (1993) Feminism, Citizenship and Radical Democratic Politics. In Chantal Mouffe, *The Return of the Political*. London and New York: Verso, 74–89.

Nelson, Barbara (1984) Women's Poverty and Women's Citizenship: Some Political Consequences of Economic Marginality. *Signs*, 10(2), 209–231.

Neville-Rolfe, Dorothy (1961) *Nothing Venture. The Story of the House of Citizenship*. Aylesbury: Hazell, Watson & Vincy.

Nicholson, Linda J. (ed.) (1990) *Feminism/Postmodernism*. New York: Routledge.

Noddings, Nel (1984) *Caring. A Feminine Approach to Ethics & Moral Education*. Berkeley: University of California Press.

Nozick, Robert (1975) *Anarchy, State and Utopia*. Oxford: Basil Blackwell.

NWCA (1933) *The Citizenship of Women*. Reprint of Report of NWCA Inaugural Meeting 31 May 1918. In *NCWA Leaflet No. 6*, National Women Citizens' Association (Fawcett library).

—— (1936) [1918] *The Constitution of the National Women Citizens' Associations: As Finally Passed at a General Meeting of Representatives of Local Women Citizens' Associations on 8 November 1918*. London: National Women's Citizenship Association (Fawcett library).

Oakley, Ann (1972) *Sex, Gender and Society*. London: Maurice Temple Smith.

O'Connor, Julia (1993) Gender, Class and Citizenship in the Comparative Analysis of Welfare States: Theoretical and Methodological Issues. *British Journal of Sociology*, 44, 501–518.

Offen, Karen (1988) Defining Feminism: A Comparative Historical Approach. *Signs*, 14(1), 119–157.

Okin, Susan Moller (1979) *Women in Western Political Thought*. Princeton, NJ: Princeton University Press.

—— (1989) *Justice, Gender and the Family*. New York: Basic Books.

Orloff, Ann S. (1993) Gender and the Social Rights of Citizenship: The Comparative Analysis of State Policies and Gender Relations. *American Sociological Review*, 58(3), 303–328.

Outshoorn, Joyce (1993) Parity Democracy: A Critical Look at a New Strategy. Paper presented at the Annual ECPR Conference, Leyden. 2–5 April.

Parker, Hermione (1993) *Citizens' Income and Women*. London: Citizens' Income.

Pascall, Gillian (1986) *Social Policy: A Feminist Analysis*. London: Tavistock.

—— (1993) Citizenship. A Feminist Analysis. In G. Drover and P. Kerans (eds), *New Approaches to Welfare Theory*. Aldershot: Edward Elgar, 113–126.

Pateman, Carole (1970) *Participation and Democratic Theory*. Cambridge: Cambridge University Press.

—— (1985) Women and Democratic Citizenship (The Jefferson Memorial Lecture). Berkeley.

—— (1988) *The Sexual Contract*. Cambridge: Polity Press.

—— (1989) *The Disorder of Women. Democracy, Feminism and Political Theory*. Cambridge: Polity Press.

—— (1992) Equality, Difference, Subordination: The Politics of Motherhood and Women's Citizenship. In Gisela Bock and Susan James (eds), *Beyond Equality & Difference. Citizenship, Feminist Politics and Female Subjectivity*. London and New York: Routledge, 17–31.

Pateman, Carole and Brennan, Teresa (1979) Mere Auxiliaries to the Commonwealth: Women and the Origins of Liberalism. *Political Studies*, 27(2), 183–200.

Pateman, Carole and Gross, Elizabeth (eds) (1986) *Feminist Challenges. Social and Political Theory*. Sydney: Allen & Unwin.

Pedersen, Susan (1990) Gender, Welfare, and Citizenship in Britain during the Great War. *American Historical Review*, 95(4), 983–1006.

Phillips, Anne (1991a) *Engendering Democracy*. Cambridge: Polity Press.

—— (1991b) Citizenship and Feminist Theory. In Geoff Andrews (ed.), *Citizenship*. London: Lawrence & Wishart, 76–91.

—— (1993) *Democracy and Difference*. Cambridge: Polity Press.

—— (1995) *The Politics of Presence*. Oxford: Clarendon Press.

Pitkin, Hanna Fenichel (1967) *The Concept of Representation*. Berkeley: University of California Press.

—— (1984) *Fortune is a Woman. Gender and Politics in the Thought of Niccolò Machiavelli*. Berkeley: University of California Press.

Pringle, Rosemary and Watson, Sophie (1992) Women's 'Interests' and the Post-Structuralist State. In Michèle Barrett and Anne Phillips (eds), *Destabilizing Theory. Contemporary Feminist Debates*. Cambridge: Polity Press, 53–74.

Ramazanoglu, Caroline (1989) *Feminism and the Contradictions of Oppression*. London: Routledge.

Rathbone, Eleanor (1929) *Milestones 1920–1929. Presidential Addresses at the Annual Council Meetings of the National Union of Societies for Equal Citizenship*. Liverpool: Lee & Nightingale.

—— (1936) Changes in Public Life. In Ray Strachey (ed.), *Our Freedom and Its Results*. London: Hogarth Press, 57–61.

—— (1940) *The Case for Family Allowances*. Harmondsworth: Penguin.

—— (1945) Speech. *House of Commons Hansard*, cols 1418–1420 (11 June).

Rawls, John (1971) *A Theory of Justice*. Cambridge, MA: Harvard University Press.

—— (1985) Justice as Fairness: Political not Metaphysical. *Philosophy and Public Affairs*, 14(3), 223–251.

—— (1987) The Idea of an Overlapping Consensus. *Oxford Journal of Legal Studies*, 7(1), 1–25.

—— (1989) The Domain of the Political and Overlapping Consensus. *New York University Law Review*, 64(2), 233–255.

—— (1993) *Political Liberalism*. New York: Columbia University Press.

Raymond, Janice (1986) *A Passion for Friends: Towards a Philosophy of Female Affection*. London: The Women's Press.

Rendall, Jane (1985) *The Origins of Modern Feminism: Women in Britain, France and the United States 1780–1860*. London: Macmillan.

—— (ed.) (1987) *Equal or Different. Women's Politics 1800–1914*. Oxford: Basil Blackwell.

—— (1994) Citizenship, Culture and Civilization: The Languages of British Suffragists, 1866–1874. In Caroline Daley and Melanie Nolan (eds), *Suffrage and Beyond*. Auckland: Auckland University Press, 127–150.

Rhode, Deborah L. (1986) Feminist Perspectives on Legal Ideology. In Juliette Mitchell and Ann Oakley (eds), *What is Feminism?* Oxford: Basil Blackwell, 151–160.

Rich, Ruby B. (1986) Feminism and Sexuality in the 1980s. *Feminist Studies*, 12(3), 525–561.

Richards, Janet Radcliffe (1982) [1980] *The Sceptical Feminist. A Philosophical Enquiry*. Harmondsworth: Penguin.

Riley, Denise (1988) *'Am I That Name?': Feminism and the Category of 'Women' in History*. Basingstoke: Macmillan.

—— (1992) Citizenship and the Welfare State. In John Allen, Peter Braham and Paul Lewis (eds), *Political and Economical Forms of Modernity*. Cambridge: Polity Press/The Open University, 179–228.

Roche, Maurice (1992) *Rethinking Citizenship. Welfare, Ideology and Change in Modern Society*. Cambridge: Polity Press.

Rooney, Phyllis (1991) A Different Different Voice: On the Feminist Challenge in Moral Theory. *The Philosophical Forum*, 12(4), 335–361.

Rorty, Richard (1989) *Contingency, Irony, and Solidarity*. New York: Cambridge University Press.

Rosenblum, Nancy L. (ed.) (1989) *Liberalism and the Moral Life*. Cambridge, MA: Harvard University Press.

Rubery, Jill and Fagan, Colette [for the European Commission] (1995) *Social Europe. Wage Determination and Sex Segregation in Employment in the European Community*. Luxembourg: Office for Official Publications of the European Communities.

Ruddick, Sarah (1980) Maternal Thinking. *Feminist Studies*, 6(2), 342–367.

—— (1983a) Pacifying the Forces: Women in the Interests of Peace. *Signs*, 8(3), 471–489.

—— (1983b) *Mothering: Essays on Feminist Theory*. Totowa, NJ: Littlefield Adams.

—— (1989) *Maternal Thinking. Towards a Politics of Peace*. New York: Ballantine Books.

Rule, Wilma (1987) Electoral Systems, Contextual Factors and Women's Opportunity for Election to Parliament in Twenty-three Democracies. *Western Political Quarterly*, 40(3), 154–177.

Russo, Ann (1987) Conflicts and Contradictions among Feminists over Issues of Pornography and Sexual Freedom. *Women's Studies International Forum*, 10(2), 103–112.

Sabine, George H. (1964) *A History of Political Theory*, 3rd edn. London: George G. Harrap.

Sandel, Michael (1982) *Liberalism and the Limits of Justice*. Cambridge: Polity Press.

Sapiro, Virginia (1981) When Are Interests Interesting? The Problem of Political Representation of Women. *American Political Science Review*, 75, 701–716.

—— (1983) *The Political Integration of Women: Roles, Socialization, and Politics*. Urbana: University of Illinois Press.

—— (1984) Women's Citizenship and Nationality: Immigration and Naturalization Policies in the United States. *Politics and Society*, 13(1), 1–26.

Sarvasy, Wendy (1992) Beyond the Difference versus Equality Policy

Debate: Postsuffrage Feminism, Citizenship, and the Quest for a Feminist Welfare State. *Signs*, 17(2), 329–362.

—— (1994) From Man and Philanthropic Service to Feminist Social Citizenship. *Social Politics. International Studies in Gender, State and Society*, 1(3), 306–325.

Saxonhouse, Arlene W. (1985) *Women in the History of Political Thought. From Ancient Greece to Machiavelli*. New York: Praeger.

Schlozman, Kay Lehman, Burns, Nancy and Donahue, Jesse (1995) Gender and Citizenship Participation – Is There a Different Voice? *American Journal of Political Science*, 39(2), 267–293.

Schmitt, Carl (1976) [1927] *The Concept of the Political* [Der Begriff des Politischen]. Edited by G. Schwab. New Brunswick, NJ: Rutgers University Press.

—— (1985) [1923] *The Crisis of Parliamentary Democracy* [Die geistes-geschichtliche Lage des heutigen Parlementarismus]. Edited by Ellen Kennedy. Cambridge, MA: MIT Press.

Schochet, Gordon J. (1975) *Patriarchalism in Political Thought*. New York: Basic Books.

Schuler, Margaret A. (ed.) (1990) *Women, Law, and Development: Action for Change*. Washington, DC: OEF International.

Schumpeter, Joseph A. (1987) [1943] *Capitalism, Socialism and Democracy*. London and Boston: Counterpoint.

Scott, Joan Wallach (1988) Deconstructing Equality-versus-Difference. On the Uses of Poststructuralist Theory for Feminism. *Feminist Studies*, 14(1), 33–50.

Sennett, Richard (1977) [1976] *The Fall of Public Man*. New York: Knopf.

Sevenhuijsen, Selma Louise (1991) The Morality of Feminism. *Hypatia*, 6(2), 173–192.

—— (1992) Paradoxes of Gender. Ethical and Epistemological Perspectives on Care in Feminist Political Theory. *Acta Politica*, 28, 131–151.

—— (1996) *Oordelen met zorg. Feministische beschouwingen over recht, moraal en politiek*. Amsterdam and Meppel: Boom.

Shanley, Mary Lyndon and Pateman, Carole (eds) (1991) *Feminist Interpretations and Political Theory*. Cambridge: Polity Press.

Shore, Louise (1874) *The Citizenship of Women Socially Considered*. Westminster: Women's Printing Society.

Siim, Birte (1988) Towards a Feminist Rethinking of the Welfare State. In Kathleen B. Jones and Anna G. Jónasdóttir (eds), *The Political Interests of Gender: Developing Theory and Research with a Feminist Face*. London: Sage, 160–187.

—— (1994) Engendering Democracy: The Interplay between Women's Citizenship and Political Participation in Scandinavia. *Social Politics. International Studies in Gender, State and Society*, 1(3), 286–305.

Siltanen, Janet and Stanworth, Michèlle (eds) (1984) *Women and the Public Sphere. A Critique of Sociology and Politics*. New York: St Martin's Press.

Skjeie, Hege (1991) The Rhetoric of Difference: On Women's Inclusion into Political Elites. *Politics and Society*, 19(2), 233–263.

Soper, Kate (1990) Feminism, Humanism and Postmodernism. *Radical Philosophy*, 55, 11–18.

Spaulding, Christina (1988–89) Anti-Pornography Laws as a Claim for Equal Respect: Feminism, Liberalism & Community. *Berkeley Women's Law Journal*, 4, 128–165.

Spelman, Elizabeth V. (1988) *Inessential Woman: Problems of Exclusion in Feminist Thought*. Boston: Beacon Press.

Spinner, Jef (1995) *The Boundaries of Citizenship. Race, Ethnicity, and Nationality in the Liberal State*. Baltimore: Johns Hopkins University Press.

Stacey, Margaret and Price, Marion (1981) *Women, Power and Politics*. London: Tavistock.

Stanley, J. Lemons (1973) *The Woman Citizen. Social Feminism in the 1920s*. Urbana: University of Illinois Press.

Steenbergen, Bart van (ed.) (1994) *The Condition of Citizenship*. London: Sage.

Stefano, Christine Di (1994) Trouble with Autonomy: Some Feminist Considerations. In Susan Moller Okin and Jane Mansbridge (eds), *Feminism. Volume 1* (Schools of Thought in Politics 6). Aldershot: Edward Elgar, 383–404.

Sullivan, Barbara and Whitehouse, Gillian (eds) (1996) *Gender, Politics and Citizenship in the 1990s*. Sydney: University of New South Wales Press.

Tapper, Marion (1993) *Ressentiment* and Power. Some Reflections of Feminist Practices. In Paul Patton (ed.), *Nietzsche, Feminism and Political Theory*. St Leonards, New York: Allen & Unwin/Routledge, 130–144.

Taylor, Charles (1989) *Sources of the Self. The Making of Modern Identity*. Cambridge, MA: Harvard University Press.

Thompson, William and Wheeler, Anna (1983) [1825] *Appeal of One Half the Human Race, Women, Against the Pretensions of the Other Half, Men, to Retain Them in Political and Thence in Civil and Domestic Slavery*. London: Virago.

Thornton, Merle (1986) Sex Equality is Not Enough for Feminists. In Carole Pateman and Elizabeth Gross (eds), *Feminist Challenges. Social and Political Theory*. Sydney: Allen & Unwin, 77–99.

Tronto, Joan C. (1987a) Beyond Gender Difference to a Theory of Care. *Signs*, 12(4), 644–663.

—— (1987b) Political Science and Caring *or* The Perils of Balkanized Social Science. *Women and Politics*, 7(3), 85–97.

—— (1993) *Moral Boundaries. A Political Argument for an Ethic of Care*. New York and London: Routledge.

Tuck, Richard (1979) *Natural Rights Theories. Their Origin and Development*. Cambridge: Cambridge University Press.

Turner, Bryan S. and Hamilton, Peter (1994) *Citizenship: Critical Concepts*. London and New York: Routledge.

Ungerson, Claire (1993) Caring and Citizenship: A Complex Relationship. In Joanna Bornat (ed.), *Community Care: A Reader*. Basingstoke: Macmillan/Open University, 143–151.

United Nations (1995) *The World's Women 1995. Trends and Statistics*. New York: UN Publications.

Vega, Judith (1989) Feminist Republicanism. Etta Palm-Aelders on Justice, Virtue and Men. *History of European Ideas*, 10(3), 333–351.

Voet, Rian (1988a) Republikeins feminisme. *Krisis*, 31 (Special Issue: Republican Politics), 65–80.

—— (1988b) Zusters of Kenau's. Een debat tussen Hannah Arendt, Jean Bethke Elshtain en Carl Schmitt over esthetisch verantwoord feministisch burgerschap. MA Thesis. University of Amsterdam, Department of Political and Social-Cultural Sciences.

—— (1990) Response to Nancy Fraser's 'Gender, Citizenship and the Public Sphere: Toward a Feminist Reconstruction of Habermas'. In Selma Sevenhuijsen (ed.), *Feminism, Citizenship and Care*. Utrecht: Utrecht University, Anna Maria van Schuurman Centre, 121–126.

—— (1991) Feminism and Republican Citizenship. Paper presented at the Political Theory Workshop. Department of Politics, University of York, York.

—— (1992a) Vrouwen als burgers. In J.B.D. Simonis, Anton C. Hemerijck and Percy B. Lehning (eds), *De staat van de burger. Beschouwingen over hedendaags burgerschap*. Meppel and Amsterdam: Boom, 78–92.

—— (1992b) Social Equality. Paper presented at the Annual Conference of the European Network for Theory and Research on Women, Welfare State and Citizenship, Utrecht. 16–17 October.

—— (1992c) Political Representation and Quotas: Hanna Pitkin's Concept(s) of Representation in the Context of Feminist Politics. *Acta Politica*, 27(4), 389–405.

—— (1993) Citizenship, Plurality and Group Representation. In Selma Sevenhuijsen (ed.), *Feminism and Justice Reconsidered*. Utrecht: Utrecht University, Anna Maria van Schuurman Centre, 49–52.

—— (1994a) Women as Citizens: A Feminist Debate. *Australian Feminist Studies*, 19 (Special Issue: Women and Citizenship), 61–78.

—— (1994b) Groepsidentiteiten en identiteitspolitiek. *Tijdschrift voor Vrouwenstudies*, 15(1), 139–149.

—— (1995) Ongelijkheid blijkt bij de daadwerkelijke participatie. Over een actief burgerschap. In Mieke de Wit (ed.), *Politieke Vernieuwing & Sekse*. Amsterdam: Instituut voor Publiek en Politiek, 194–213.

Vogel, Ursula (1986) Rationalism and Romanticism: Two Strategies for Women's Liberation. In Judith Evans et al. (eds), *Feminism and Political Theory*. London: Sage, 17–46.

—— (1988) Under Permanent Guardianship: Women's Condition under Modern Civil Law. In Kathleen B. Jones and Anna G. Jónasdóttir (eds), *The Political Interests of Gender*. London: Sage, 135–160.

—— (1991) Is Citizenship Gender-Specific? In Ursula Vogel and Michael Moran (eds), *The Frontiers of Citizenship*. Basingstoke: Macmillan, 58–85.

—— (1994) Marriage and the Boundaries of Citizenship. In Bart van Steenbergen (ed.), *The Condition of Citizenship*. London: Sage, 76–89.

Vogel, Ursula and Moran, Michael (eds) (1991) *The Frontiers of Citizenship*. London: Macmillan.

Vollrath, Ernst (1977) *Die Rekonstruktion der politische Urteilskraft*. Stuttgart: Ernst Klett.

Vries, Petra de (1987) Het persoonlijke is politiek en het ontstaan van de tweede golf in Nederland 1968–1973. *Socialistische Feministische Teksten*, 10, 15–35.

Walby, Sylvia (1994) Is Citizenship Gendered? *Sociology – The Journal of the British Sociological Association*, 28(2), 379–395.

Walker, Urban M. (1989) Moral Understandings: Alternative Epistemology for a Feminist Ethics. *Hypatia*, 4(2), 15–28.

Walzer, Michael (1970) Three Kinds of Citizenship. In *Obligations: Essays on Disobedience, War and Citizenship*. Cambridge, MA: Harvard University Press.

—— (1983) *Spheres of Justice. A Defence of Pluralism & Equality*. Oxford: Basil Blackwell.

Weber, Max (1964) [1921] Politics as Vocation [Politik als Beruf]. In H.H. Gerth and C. Wright Mills (eds), *From Max Weber: Essays in Sociology*. London: Routledge & Kegan Paul, 77–128.

Welch, Susan (1977) Women as Political Animals: A Test of Some Explanations for Male–Female Political Participation Differences. *American Journal of Political Science*, 21, 711–730.

Whittick, Arnold (1979) *Woman into Citizen. The World Movement towards the Emancipation of Women in the Twentieth Century with Accounts of the International Alliance of Women, The League of Nations and the Relevant Organizations of United Nations*. London: Athenaeum with Frederick Müller.

Wilson, Margaret and Yeatman, Anna (eds) (1995) *Justice & Identity: Antipodean Practices*. Wellington: Bridget Williams Books.

Wolf, Naomi (1993) *Fire with Fire. The New Female Power and How It Will Change the 21st Century*. London: Chatto & Windus.

Wolgast, Elizabeth (1980) *Equality and the Rights of Women*. Ithaca, NY: Cornell University Press.

—— (1987) Wrong Rights. *Hypatia*, 2(1), 25–43.

Women and Men in the European Union. A Statistical Portrait (1995) Luxembourg: Office for Official Publications of the European Communities.

Yeatman, Anna (1984) Despotism and Civil Society: The Limits of Patriarchal Citizenship. In Judith Stiehm (ed.), *Women's Views of the Political World of Men*. New York: Transnational, 153–176.

—— (1990) *Bureaucrats, Technocrats, Femocrats: Essays on the Contemporary Australian State*. Sydney: Allen & Unwin.

—— (1992) Women's Citizenship's Claims, Labour Market Policy and Globalisation. *Australian Journal of Political Science*, 27(3), 449–461.

—— (1993) Voice and Representation in the Politics of Difference. In Sneja Gunew and Anna Yeatman (eds), *Feminism and the Politics of Difference*. St Leonards: Allen & Unwin, 228–245.

—— (1994a) *Postmodern Revisionings of the Political*. New York: Routledge.

—— (1994b) Feminism and Power. *Women's Studies Journal (NZ)*, 10 (1), 79–100.

Young, Iris Marion (1989) Polity and Group Difference. A Critique of the Ideal of Universal Citizenship. *Ethics*, 99, 250–274.

—— (1990a) *Throwing Like a Girl and Other Essays in Feminist Philosophy and Social Theory*. Bloomington and Indianapolis: Indiana University Press.

—— (1990b) *Justice and the Politics of Difference*. Princeton, NJ: Princeton University Press.

—— (1995a) Mothers, Citizenship, and Independence: A Critique of Pure Family Values. *Ethics*, 105(3), 535–556.

—— (1995b) Communication and the Other: Beyond Deliberative Democracy. In Margaret Wilson and Anna Yeatman (eds), *Justice & Identity. Antipodean Practices*. Wellington: Bridget Williams Books, 134–152.

Yuval-Davis, Nira (1991) The Citizenship Debate: Women, Ethnic Processes and the State. *Feminist Review*, 39, 58–68.

—— (1992) Women and Citizens. In Anna Ward, Jeanne Gregory and Nira Yuval-Davies (eds), *Women and Citizenship in Europe*. Stoke: Trentham Books and AFSF.

Index